Captive Populations

CAPTIVE POPULATIONS

Caring for the Young, the Sick, the Imprisoned, and the Elderly

JENNIE JACOBS KRONENFELD
AND MARCIA LYNN WHICKER

New York
Westport, Connecticut
London

Library of Congress Cataloging-in-Publication Data

Kronenfeld, Jennie Jacobs.
   Captive populations : caring for the young, the sick, the
imprisoned, and the elderly / Jennie Jacobs Kronenfeld and Marcia
Lynn Whicker.
     p.   cm.
   Includes bibliographical references.
   ISBN 0–275–92723–7 (alk. paper)
   1. Human services—United States.   2. Public welfare—United
States.   I. Whicker, Marcia Lynn.   II. Title.
HV91.K75   1990
361.973—dc20   89–72125

Library of Congress Catalog Card Number: 89–72125
ISBN: 0–275–92723–7

First published in 1990

Praeger Publishers, One Madison Avenue, New York, NY 10010
An imprint of Greenwood Publishing Group, Inc.

Printed in the United States of America

The paper used in this book complies with the Permanent
Paper Standard issued by the National Information Standards
Organization (Z39.48—1984).

10 9 8 7 6 5 4 3 2 1

Contents

Preface

During the last ten to fifteen years American policy experts and to an even greater extent, business leaders and politicians have been discussing the role of the public sector in the delivery of various health and human services. Business leaders have questioned the expansion of the public sector, a trend that has been under way in the United States in many service areas since the 1930s. Politicians, especially conservatives associated with the political success of Ronald Reagan in his presidential bid in 1980, have questioned the growth of government and raised the question of whether certain services traditionally provided by government over the past forty years could better be provided by the for-profit, private business sector. Such questioning has been combined with a period of taxpayer revolt and attempts to reduce taxation rates at the federal level and also in many states.

The goal of this book is to contribute to the debate over modes of service delivery in various human service areas. One policy issue in health and human service areas is: What is the best modality for the delivery of services—should these services be delivered as public services, private nonprofit services, or for-profit services? This book contributes to the debate in four specific health and human service delivery areas: education, prisons, health care, and health-related services for the elderly.

Our reason for choosing these service areas (and not such others as transportation or postal services) is a desire to focus on those services people tend to receive personally, as individuals, and generally require because of specific life circumstances or age, rather than at all points in time. These are services for populations increasingly reliant on government, and thus the notion of "captive" populations in the title of this book.

We discuss these issues in six chapters. The first chapter, "The Public versus the Private Sector," focuses on differentiating between the public and private sectors. This includes a discussion of the different functions of each sector, the measurement of output and efficiency, and the translation of preferences in services into action. Included in this chapter, a special section discusses the impact of federalism on service delivery to captivate populations. One initial conclusion is that of the four captive or dependent populations addressed in this book—the young, the criminally incarcerated, the sick, and the elderly—all except the criminally incarcerated, have had the option of receiving services at some point through governmental, nonprofit, and for-profit mechanisms.

Chapter 2, "Schools and Day Care," deals with service delivery to the young via the mechanisms of schools and day care. In this service area, providers are expected to give not only physical care connected with the maintenance of bodily well-being and physical safety but also to educate and teach the young basic skills and, in later years, those skills needed to enter the labor market and become economically productive members of society. We review the historical context of the provision of school services to the young, including battles over the roles of religion and the public schools. Facts on private and public school enrollment are included, and there is a discussion of some of the current federal policies as they apply to the private provision of elementary and secondary education. Proposals to broaden federal funding of private schools are also discussed. In education the dominant deliverer of services is the public sector; it is also the dominant payor for these services, although much funding originates at the state and local levels, rather than at the federal level.

The last portion of Chapter 2 addresses the issue of day-care services for children too young for elementary education. Until recently there was an assumption in American society that this was not a service that government needed to provide; mothers with young children were assumed to be in their homes personally providing such care. This area of service provision is receiving greatly increased discussion currently in American society due to increased labor force participation by women, especially mothers of children six and under.

Chapter 3, "The Incarcerated," deals with those persons who are in prisons. First, the history of the provision of prison services is reviewed. This is followed by a discussion of modern prisons and correctional ideologies. Then we review various economic issues relating to prison services, including a projection of prison growth and a discussion of initial privatization efforts in prison services. Related issues discussed are the role of the prison industry and prison reform. Except in a few specialized situations and at very specific moments in history, the provision of prison services has traditionally been a governmental function in the United States, with services paid for through taxation. The unit of government providing the service has varied, typically depending on the nature and severity of the crime.

Chapter 4, "The Sick and the Health Care System," deals with the provision of both inpatient (hospital) and outpatient (ambulatory or doctors') care to those who are sick or trying to keep from becoming sick. Initially we review the history of for-profit care delivery in the United States and some of the early objections to a major role of for-profit care delivery mechanisms. Hospital care then receives a thorough exploration, including a discussion of current trends in the growth of for-profit provision in this service area. Next the critical issues of financial capital, costs of care, access, and quality are reviewed. Aspects of ambulatory care are also examined, including the provision of managed care services, other specialized types of ambulatory care, such as outpatient surgery, and the impact of for-profit corporations and their effect on traditional physician services. Unlike the previous two areas in which public provision of services has been the dominant mode, nonprofit voluntary provision of service has been the dominant mode of delivery of hospital services, with the public sector providing such care only for those who had no other method of obtaining the services. For outpatient care, the dominant mode of provision was by an individual physician in his (or occasionally her) office. A major change in the area of services to the sick has been an increasing role of government as a payor of services, even if not the direct provider.

Chapter 5 "The Elderly, Long-Term Care, and Home-Based Services," concentrates on health-related services that are mostly custodial and frequently provided to the elderly; they include nursing home care, home health care, and retirement homes. Such services in contrast with those described in the preceding chapter, which are designed to cure diseases. After initially reviewing some basic statistics on the elderly, we present the history of custodial services provision in the United States. Then we discuss the provision of nursing home services, focusing especially on the role of federal funding through the medicare and medicaid programs; growth patterns in this service sector; and issues of access, quality, and cost. Also, we discuss the less extensively developed service areas of home health services and retirement homes. The history of government's role in service provision in these areas is more complicated. One hundred years ago, most services were provided either in the home by family (somewhat akin to day-care services) or by the county government if no family or private means were available. Since 1965, the dominant pattern of provision of nursing home services has been services supplied by for-profit companies, but paid for by public funds. Patterns differ somewhat for other areas of elderly services, home health, and retirement communities.

Chapter 6, "Summary and Conclusions," compares the similarities and differences across the four service and captive population areas and discusses recommendations based on the material covered in the rest of the book. Essentially, we conclude that no one service provider (for-profit, not-for-profit, or public) necessarily does a better job in all service areas. There is great variability by area due to historical circumstances. Competition works best when the client can choose the deliverer of services and has the financial means to act on that choice. In service delivery areas in which such conditions are missing, public sector provision typically works best. Costs have also become an important consideration in all areas.

Captive Populations

1

The Public versus the Private Sector

This chapter introduces the debate that has been going on in the United States for the past decade concerning the appropriate mode of service delivery for populations increasingly reliant on government. Among these populations are the young, the incarcerated, the sick, and the elderly. Each is dependent to some degree on others in society for their daily well-being.

One of the most important services to the young is education, a service traditionally provided in America at the local level, with some aid from the state level. For the incarcerated, criminal justice services are provided at all levels of government—through local jails, state prisons, and federal prisons and detention centers. Health care and care to the elderly were traditionally provided by the private sector or by families. In this area, government has long provided services for populations with no money and no other choices, as indicated by the traditions of public hospitals for the poor and county poor farms (old age homes for the elderly poor). With the expansion of social welfare programs from the 1930s through the 1960s, the role of government as provider of services to the sick and elderly increased.

DIFFERENCES IN THE PUBLIC AND PRIVATE SECTORS

Public finance theorists have identified several ways in which the public sector differs from the private sector: The two sectors typically address different functions, use different measures of output, confront different dependencies on external forces, and employ distinct mechanisms for translating citizens' preferences into action.

Different Functions

The Role of Public Goods. The public and private sectors have traditionally addressed fundamentally different functions. Even though sound-
ing tautological, the primary purpose of the private sector has been to
produce private goods, while the primary purpose of the public sector
has been to provide public goods. Public and private goods are fundamentally different in character. Private goods are divisible into small
units that can be purchased by single individuals and corporations.
Because private goods are divisible, their consumption is mutually exclusive; that is, the consumption of a private good by one person pre-
cludes other persons from consuming the same private good.

The allocation function of government includes the provision of public
goods, those that are nondivisible, and therefore, whose consumption
is not mutually exclusive. Because no one can be excluded from consuming a pure public good once a decision to purchase it has been made,
a free rider problem arises in that no one has an incentive to contribute
to its funding, as long as someone else pays the bill. Mandatory funding
through government taxes, coupled with collective decisions to purchase
public goods by those who will pay and benefit, become the solution to
the free rider problem.

The notions of public and private goods represent theoretical proto-
types, while in reality, most goods and services lie along a continuum
between the two extremes. Most services have some public character
and simultaneously benefit some groups more than others. Often goods
may be heavily used by certain age groups but not by others. Although
public schools have some programs for the adult population, they are
used predominantly by people under twenty. Of course, all adults were
at some point young people and many used public schools, but not
necessarily the public schools where they currently live. Even though
children are the direct users of public education, their parents receive a
direct benefit as well from the free educations provided their offspring.

The total community also receives a benefit from appropriate education of children, especially in the modern economy where a well-trained
labor force is a requisite for economic growth. Communities or states
with inadequate educational facilities may not be able to attract newer
and higher paying industries, causing everyone living there to suffer.
Another community benefit of providing education—less direct but still
important—is the relationship of education to the need for other government services, especially welfare and demands on the criminal justice
system. High school dropouts are far more likely to need welfare services
and to be detained by the criminal justice system—both costly future
drains on the public treasury—than are those who receive their diplo-
mas.

Criminal justice services have both public and private components. Youth services and rehabilitation programs for youths and adults are designed to restore individuals in trouble with the law to productive jobs and life styles the community views as useful. When they achieve their rehabilitation goals and reduce recidivism, these services benefit the individuals concerned. Similarly, criminal justice services also are designed to meet community concerns about protection from violence and crime. Criminal perpetrators locked behind bars are no longer free to inflict further illegal activities on the communities in which they reside.

Publicly funded health care services provide direct relief to a sick individual. Purchasing equivalent services through the private sector would cost the sick person either directly, or indirectly through the maintenance of a private insurance policy. In the best of cases, the sick person's health is restored; in most cases, health is improved or suffering is relieved. These are direct positive benefits to the individual and often to the individual's family that might be called on to help bear the financial burden for the sick member.

Especially in the cases of communicable diseases, the total community benefits from the individual's direct receipt of publicly funded health care services. When persons with a communicable disease do not receive treatment, they spread the disease to many in the community with whom they have relevant contact. Not only the total amount of sickness but also each individual's chances of becoming sick are reduced through publicly funded preventative and curative services. Even if the disease is not communicable, health care services fulfill a community function similar to education and rehabilitative prison services. That is, restoring an individual to a level of health where he or she can be productive benefits the overall community as well as that individual.

With nursing home, retirement home, and home-based services for the elderly, the private dimension of service delivery is more obvious than the community dimension. Plainly, those who receive such services benefit directly. Their lives are considerably improved by having safe, secure residences with adequate medical care in their "golden years." Many middle-aged persons also benefit, although less directly, from publicly funded services for the elderly. These services relieve them of bearing alone the financial costs of caring for their aged parents. Money aside, in some geographic areas, public services are the only services available for the elderly. Supervised gathering places with meals available for senior citizens are not something that any single individual could provide alone. Nor has the private market resulted in the wide dissemination of such services.

Less obviously, the community members benefit from knowing that they and their relatives may receive some services in their old age, given the availability of publicly funded care for the elderly. Most citizens do not feel comfortable or happy living in a society that neglects the old enough to make their lack of services visible. Public services for the elderly mitigates this community discomfort by preventing the sector of senior citizens without homes or care.

Controlling Externalities. Part of the allocation function of the public sector and the provision of public goods is to control externalities, or spillovers. Spillovers occur when there are unintended mismatches between beneficiaries of goods and those who pay for them. Particularly in education, spillovers have been used to justify greater involvement by the public sector. When one community fails to educate its youth, eventually they may migrate to other communities, negatively affecting the crime rate and economy in those areas, and increasing the demand for other public services. Conversely, when a community educates its youth very well, they move to other communities that reap the benefits of the first locality's education expenditures. These spillovers have increased both the nature and level of public involvement in education.

Spillovers also exist in other areas that impact on captive populations. Communities that inadequately incarcerate and service prisoners may produce negative spillovers for other communities. Inadequate facilities may lead to more attempted and actual escapes by prisoners. Even more problematic, in communities where prisons are inadequately staffed and the behavior of prisoners is not monitored and controlled, prisons become breeding grounds for crime and violence inflicted by more powerful and brutal inmates on weaker inmates.

A lawless atmosphere in an inmate-controlled institution may produce greater contempt for the law among inmates, not less. Prisoners in such environments are also likely to acquire new criminal skills that better equip them to perpetuate a life of crime on release, instead of developing skills enabling them to function effectively within the labor force. Concern over these negative spillovers, as well as for protection of the civil rights of prisoners, and enhancement of the general security of the population at large has made privatization of prisons more difficult than privatizing services for some other captive populations.

Spillovers also occur in the health area. Perhaps the most prominent example of negative externalities in this area is the care of indigents or near-indigents lacking either third-party health care coverage or private wealth to finance their own medical care. Poor people in these conditions often delay seeking out health care until a medical problem has worsened substantially and pain or inability to function drives them to seek a physician's services. Often indigents then turn to emergency room services in public hospitals. The poor in geographic areas with no public hospitals, such as certain rural areas and municipalities, may travel to jurisdictions where public hospitals are available.

Care for people who cannot pay, then, becomes a large expenditure in the annual budget of public hospitals, an unreimbursed cost these hospitals attempt to defray by raising room and service charges for paying customers. The failure of various local jurisdictions to provide adequate medical care and facilities for indigents and the tendency of some localities to dump their sick poor on jurisdictions that provide public hospitals have long concerned medical service providers and general taxpayers. These externalities have also increased governmental regulations and federal involvement in health care financing.

Just as the public component of nursing home care for the elderly is less obvious than for other captive populations, so are the externalities associated with service delivery to the elderly. Yet even in this area, externalities exist with the predictable result of increasing pressure for government involvement at higher levels. The dreaded county home to which indigent elderly were assigned when they could not pay for their own living costs or care has largely become a social relic. Further, the most common form of government income support for the elderly— social security—is federally financed and administered, and does not depend on state and local policies that might vary and generate externalities. Yet increasingly, medicaid has become a source of funds for nursing home costs for middle-class elderly who have disposed of their assets and have inadequate income to cover nursing home costs. Medicaid requirements and benefits do vary from state to state, thus creating the potential for the elderly to move to states with more favorable nursing home funding. States with an influx of elderly must then provide services for a group from whom they did not collect taxes during their productive years. This potential for externalities extends to other services for the elderly as well.

Regulating Natural Monopolies. In theory, the private sector is competitive, and by virtue of the nature of public goods, the public sector is not. The private sector presumably does not have monopolies, while government service delivery is monopolistic. When natural monopolies occur—situations where the high degree of initial capital costs make competition neither feasible nor beneficial in lowering unit costs—those services should either be provided within the public sector, or under public regulation. Without public regulations, private corporations providing a monopolistic service would have no incentive to hold down prices to a reasonable margin over costs.

Traditionally, due to the high capital costs of building prisons, their high maintenance costs, and the natural right of the state to exercise sole authority over punishment of crimes—even to the point of death— prisons have been state-run monopolies. In recent years, this monopoly power of the state has been challenged by those who wish to privatize many aspects of prison management.

Even though hospitals also have high capital and maintenance costs, and hold a different power over life and death, most hospital services have been provided through the mechanism of nonprofit but private institutions. In any particular geographic area in the past, especially rural areas, a hospital may have had a monopoly over the delivery of those services, if citizens had few alternatives that were geographically proximate and reasonable. Today, partial monopolies are being created within specific service areas in health care as part of hospital marketing plans. Increasingly, after choosing to specialize in high profit areas, hospitals are developing images with the public for excellence in those areas. At some future point, the development of these private-sector partial monopolies may prompt greater government regulation and coordination.

Regarding payments to hospitals, there is much greater regulation now than thirty years ago. Before the federally funded medicare and medicaid programs, hospitals set their own charges for services and individuals and/or their insurance companies paid them. Initially, medicare and medicaid also operated this way. Now most states play a major role if not wielding total authority over payments for patients in medicaid. The Diagnostic Related Group (DRG) legislation of the early 1980s has resulted in federally regulated rates for medicare patients.

Stabilizing the Economy. The public and private sectors also differ in the expectations placed on each for stabilizing the economy and maintaining economic growth. Long-term experience with capitalistic economies has shown them to vascillate through business cycles of varying duration. During a cycle, the economy first heats up, with inflation becoming a problem, and finally cools down through counteractive recessionary forces. Increasingly, in modern economies, government has been given the function of controlling and mitigating these swings in the economy, as well as stabilizing state and local economies, and promoting stable, long-term growth.

One factor contributing to the economic stability in a particular local area is the size of government spending there. Publicly funded education services and more limited services for the elderly form a core of stable employment in every community. Communities that house prisons and other criminal justice facilities also have a stable source of jobs, albeit, often low-paying. In many rural communities, the county hospital may be the largest single employer. Thus service provision for captive populations, whether through the public or private sector, help achieve the public sector's mission of stabilizing local economies and providing a steady source of jobs and income.

Redistribution of Income. A major difference between public and private sectors is the role each plays in redistribution of income. Even though the private sector theoretically distributes assets and income according to contributions to economic productivity measured through profits, the public sector employs other criteria, especially that of ability to pay. Under the ability-to-pay principle, the affluent are proportionately more heavily taxed with a progressive tax system, while the poor receive greater benefits than the affluent when benefits are measured as a portion of total personal income.

Although some government programs have very little redistributive impact, others have greater redistributive effects. Perhaps the greatest short-run redistribution exists in the health care system of the four captive populations considered here. Third-party payments, especially the government-sponsored medicaid and medicare programs, have increased U.S. health care costs as a percent of the gross national product (GNP) to over 11 percent. This percentage exceeds that of Britain, which has a national health care system and where medical costs constitute about 5 percent of GNP, as well as exceeding the proportionate health care costs in most other industrialized nations. Just in sheer dollar volume, then, health care programs and the U.S. health care delivery system shift a substantial amount of dollars from producers and consumers in other areas to medical care.

Third-party health care payment systems also shift income across income classes. The primary beneficiaries of large government spending on health care are at either end of the income distribution. The poor who receive health care services benefit from in-kind transfers to their income and improved health care. At the upper end of the income scale, physicians, anesthesiologists, and other high income service providers, as well as owners of medical laboratories and private hospitals, benefit from government health care programs that redistribute money from other areas to the health care delivery system.

Excluding medicaid nursing home services financed for the middle-class elderly, services for the elderly also redistribute wealth to the poor. The middle class and nursing home owners also benefit from the use of medicaid to cover nursing home costs for the newly indigent elderly. However, in part because nursing home care is less technologically oriented and sophisticated than is hospitalization, nursing homes have tended not to merge into large private corporate chains, unlike hospitals. Nonprofit nursing homes that are church-affiliated or linked to some other nonprofit organization are also prevalent. Thus, the overall redistributive impact of public services for the elderly is more progressive in redistributive impact than that of government-financed services for the sick.

Educational services have the greatest potential for long-run redistributive impact, due to the positive correlation between education level for an individual and lifetime earnings. The considerable earnings variability that exists is often a result of racial and/or sexual discrimination.

For example, controlling for educational levels, female workers earn 70 percent as much as male workers, and blacks earn about two-thirds of the incomes of whites. College-educated women continue to earn less on average than men who did not complete high school. Nonetheless, the level of education does contribute significantly as an explanatory factor in why lifetime earnings vary across individuals. The redistribution that occurs from education often results from the enhanced earning power of individuals, rather than through the immediate receipt of cash payments or selectively provided in-kind services.

Perhaps least redistributive in nature are prison services. In different eras prisons have emphasized rehabilitation and taught skills leading to more productive lives on release through jobs paying wages sufficient to attain lower-middle- or middle-class status. Even so, rehabilitation programs have often failed; recidivism remains high among released inmates. Unlike health care services, providers of prison services—corrections officers, for example—are compensated at much lower levels than physicians. Thus, arguably, prison services redistribute less to service providers or to service recipients than other captive populations providers discussed here.

Different Abilities to Measure Output and Efficiency

Private and public sectors differ in their abilities to measure output, and consequently production efficiency. For any producer of goods or services, efficiency is typically defined as a ratio between outputs and inputs measured in the same unit. The unit preferred is a currency value; in the United States it is dollars. For any single service provider, the higher the ratio of the dollar value of outputs to the dollar value of its inputs, the more efficient the provider is. Efficient producers either maximize output for a given dollar of input or minimize input for a given dollar of output.

For private-sector producers, both outputs and inputs can be measured in dollar value. For a private firm, the dollar value of input is derived by adding up the amounts spent on various factors used in production, such as rent, supplies, and personnel costs. As the input of the firm is sold in markets, the value of the output can be measured in dollar units. The value of the output of a private firm is the price customers are willing to pay for that output. With dollar figures for the value of both output and input, the firm can calculate an output/input ratio, to determine its total efficiency.

The market value of the output of a private firm most likely reflects the true market value of output if the output is sold in competitive markets. Because competitive markets have many producers and many consumers, the action of any single producer or consumer cannot influence the price of the product or service, or the quantity that is produced. Often services provided to captive populations are not sold in competitive markets, even if they are produced by private-sector firms rather than government agencies. More typically, the government purchases the services from the private producer, creating a monopsony—a situation where there is just one buyer. In some instances, there is also just one private service provider; this creates a monopoly, where there is just one producer.

In these situations, the price for which the firm sells the service may differ from its true market value. In monopsonistic situations, the buyer may exert leverage to lower the price. In monopolistic situations, the seller or producer may exert leverage to raise the price. Politics and favoritism may also distort the price for which services for captive populations are sold from their true market value. Nonetheless, private-sector firms producing services for captive populations under conditions that do not approximate competitive markets are still able to measure their output in dollar terms, and to calculate efficiency ratios.

By contrast, public-sector service delivery agencies do not process their output through markets. Public sector output is not sold; rather it is delivered directly to the clients or consumers of the service. In some instances, the collective nature of goods produced and in other instances, the redistributive nature of transfer payments and services prevent public sector agencies' output from being sold in the marketplace in the same manner as private goods.

Thus, public agencies are deprived of acquiring an independent measure of the value of their output. Consequently, calculating efficiency at the agency level is considerably more difficult. Inputs of public agencies can be measured in dollar terms, because public agencies—just like private firms—must buy inputs needed to operate in supply markets. Public agencies must purchase rent, supplies, equipment, personnel, and other items to operate. The total of these purchases is the total dollar value of input. Dollar values for planned purchases or expenditures are found in the line item or object-of-expenditure budgets that nearly all agencies have. The absence of a sales-generated dollar value on output, however, has caused public agencies to take other approaches to measure output value and efficiency.

Equating Outputs to Inputs. Often, politicians and other high-level public officials equate output to input, assuming that whatever is spent in a particular area of governmental activity is the value of what is produced. For example, if X dollars are spent on producing and delivering education to the young, the value of the educational services is assumed to be X dollars. The same logic is sometimes applied to services delivered to other captive populations as well.

Yet, equating outputs to inputs is patently flawed when applied to the private sector because no firm can assume that the cost of production is equal to the value of output. Rarely, in fact, is such the case. For profitable firms, the value of output exceeds the cost of production; while for unprofitable firms, the value of output is less than the cost of production. Although the approach of equating outputs to inputs for public sector agencies may provide information on the priorities of public decisionmakers in allocating monies across different functions and for different client groups, it is considerably less valuable as an analytic approach to calculate efficiency of public-sector service delivery at the agency level.

Counting Units Serviced and Comparing to Total Costs per Time Period. A second approach to calculate efficiency for public agencies in the absence of a market-determined dollar value for their output is to count units of output produced or serviced per time period. This second approach is the most widely used to measure the efficiency of service delivery for captive populations. For education, this would be the pupils serviced per time period; for day care, the children serviced per time period; for prisons, the prisoners incarcerated per time period; for the sick, the patients hospitalized per time period; and for the elderly, the senior citizens receiving nursing home or home health services per time period.

Even finer graduations in types of clients serviced may be used. For educational services, for example, the number of gifted students serviced or students with learning disabilities serviced may be distinguished from the number of mainstream students, because the costs of servicing each type of student may vary. Similarly, for hospital patients, those in intensive care or neonatal units may be distinguished from those on regular nursing floors. For prisoners, those in maximum-security facilities may be distinguished from those in minimum-security or medium-security facilities.

Under this approach for public agencies, efficiency is measured by calculating a ratio of the total costs of servicing those units for that time period to the clients or units serviced per time period to derive the unit cost of service delivery. This approach has many advantages over the first approach. Unlike the first approach, which measures mainly public sector priorities, the unit cost approach attempts to directly measure efficiency at the agency level. The resulting measure facilitates comparisons across agencies producing the same service in similar conditions. Thus, the unit costs of servicing prisoners in maximum security facilities in one region or state may be compared with the unit costs of servicing prisoners in maximum security facilities in another region or state. Similarly, the unit costs of servicing patients in intensive care in one hospital may be compared to the unit costs of servicing patients in intensive care in another hospital. Furthermore, the unit costs of providing service in public agencies may be compared with the unit costs of nonprofit agencies and private firms when those comparisons are relevant.

Despite its advantages over the first approach, however, this method of measuring the efficiency of public agency service delivery has several disadvantages. First, unit costs are only meaningful as long as the units of service delivery are standardized. Exceptional cases do not fit into this approach very well. Exceptional cases are often very costly, and tend to skew the average costs upward, presenting a false impression of how efficiently the average case is handled.

Second, comparing the units serviced to the total costs of service delivery per time period says nothing about the quality of service produced. Lower unit costs may represent a poorer quality of service delivery as easily as they might represent more efficient service production. In some cases, low unit costs may represent underfunding of service delivery, not more efficient production. This approach does not measure the quality of service produced, but implicitly assumes that all units serviced are done so at a comparable and acceptable quality of service.

Given the great potential for variability in quality of services produced for captive populations across public and private agencies, as well as the potential for variability in unit costs, the inability of this approach to grapple with quality variability other than by creating broad categories of clients services is troublesome. Typically, regulation and oversight mechanisms attempt to assure that all captive population clients are serviced at a minimally acceptable level; then, subsequent units of service delivery that meet the minimum standards are assumed to be equivalent.

Estimating the Dollar Value of Outputs for Benefit-Cost Analysis. A third approach often used to measure the efficiency of service delivery by public agencies to captive populations is benefit-cost analysis. This method is similar to the second approach of counting units of output, but goes further by attempting to estimate the dollar value of services delivered. Because analysts who do this do not have the benefit of figures for market-generated sales, unlike accountants who calculate the efficiency and profitability of private firms, the figures generated for benefits are estimates. One way to make estimates on the value of service delivery is to use the price service recipients are willing to pay for the service when it is provided in the private for-profit market without government subsidies.

Yet this approach is flawed: the quality of the service provided in the private market may differ from that provided by public agencies. For example, education in some private schools not only costs more than that in public schools but also is assumed to be of higher quality by parents willing to pay the higher price. To use that market figure to value public school education, independent of the curriculum and the teacher/student ratios provided in each setting, is not realistic. In other service areas for captive populations—incarcerated criminals, for example—there is no private-sector equivalent, nor would clients be willing to pay for it if there were.

For some captive populations, such as the elderly, one major benefit of service delivery is improvement in the quality of life and, potentially, prolongation of life. Placing a dollar value on such output is very difficult. Standard methods of valuing life used by insurance companies, such as using the projected lifetime earnings of individuals based on occupations, do not apply in analyzing the value of service delivery to the elderly.

Even in education where lifetime earnings are affected, ascertaining the degree to which earnings are improved by exposure to a particular curriculum is difficult. Comparing the lifetime earnings of those who attend school with those who do not is not possible, because school attendance is compulsory until age sixteen. Nor do educational systems often track students after graduating or dropping our to evaluate the impact of specific curricula and school programs.

The impact of educational programs on lifetime earnings does not measure other benefits to the individuals receiving the educational services and to society at large. As is the case with the elderly, quality-of-life impacts resulting from services received are difficult to measure. For society, the list of long-term benefits to society from high-quality education is long: reduced crime, reduced welfare expenses, an improved labor force contributing to potentially greater economic growth, greater potential for scientific inventions and innovations, more effective democracy, and for specific locales, higher property values and more desirable neighborhoods. Yet measuring any of these benefits more specifically is difficult.

In benefit-cost analysis, multiyear comparisons are discounted, to account for the time value of money. In general, money received today is more valuable than the same dollar amount received in subsequent years, because in the interim today's money could be invested and earning interest. The further into the future a fixed dollar amount is received, the lower is its value in today's terms, since more interest has been lost by not holding the money earlier. The interest rate as well as the number of years between the present and future years when benefits are received and costs incurred is used to translate future value into present value, and vice versa. Benefit-cost analysis and discounting streams of future benefits and costs are particularly relevant for large capital construction, such as building prisons, hospitals, nursing homes, and schools.

When discounting future benefit and cost streams, analysts must typically assume an interest rate rather arbitrarily since knowledge of interest rates for years into the future is limited and uncertain. A further flaw in benefit-cost analysis, in addition to the difficulty of generating realistic numbers to reflect the value of benefits, is the sensitivity of the outcomes of benefit-cost analysis to the interest rate assumed. Usually, in large capital expenditures, substantial costs are incurred in the early years, whereas benefit streams may begin later and accrue across the entire lifespan of the capital facility. In these typical situations, where costs are incurred in the early years and benefits accrue in the later years, an assumption of a low interest rate biases the analysis toward adoption of the project.

Because of these difficulties in using benefit-cost analysis to measure the efficiency and value of output services produced for captive populations, the approach is used infrequently—even when making decisions about whether or not to expand capital facilities for captive populations. More typically, decisions to expand capital facilities are driven by public opinion and political shifts. For example, the politics surrounding President George Bush's war on drugs declared in September 1989, not benefit-cost analyses, resulted in an expansion of monies for prison construction.

Not always, however, does public opinion result in an expansion of facilities for captive populations. Sometimes the opposite occurs. The deplorable, overcrowded conditions of several state prison systems were widely known in the 1960s, but resulted in little action to upgrade facilities and reduce crowding. Correction of these conditions occurred only after the federal courts took a strong, active interventionist role by ordering some states to reduce overcrowding and other violations of prisoners' constitutional protections against cruel and unusual punishment.

Public outrage over the crowded conditions of many state residential facilities caring for the mentally ill did not result in a substantial expansion of those facilities. Rather, many state governments decided to remove patients from the state mental health system altogether by releasing large portions of that population back into society. While some patients were able to function, the mentally ill street people and homeless increased in most urban areas.

In addition to public opinion shifts, projections of demographic changes frequently affect decisions about the expansion and contraction of capital facilities for captive populations. The baby boom moving through the population pipeline has expanded and contracted the need for primary and secondary schools and then universities. Experts attributed an increase in the crime rate to larger numbers of people in youthful crime-prone years. Part of the pressure on the health care system may be, in part, due to the increased numbers of people approaching advanced middle age, an age when the on-set of illness often increases. Projections of the increased need for nursing home and other senior citizen services as baby boomers continue to age are already being discussed.

These and other demographic changes, interacting with political trends, often cause expansion and contraction of services, rather than more sophisticated and elaborate benefit-cost analysis. Even though projections of need may be as good a basis as any for planning capital facilities expansions and contractions, the projection approach does not address the other question that benefit-cost analysis may answer—that of the efficiency of specific public agencies delivering services to captive populations.

Linking Captive Population Service Expenditures to Social Indicators. A fourth approach suggested to evaluate the impact of service delivery for captive populations is to link program expenditures to broader social indicators that measure quality of life for the populations involved. This approach uses statistics to link the program costs or expenditures as the independent variable to social indicators, which become the dependent variable in a more formal statistical analysis. Examples of social indicators for educational programs would be dropout rates, performance on national tests, and graduates attending college. Social indicators for prison programs would include the recidivism rate, the degree of severity of any additional crimes, and rates of job placement and retention for released inmates. Indicators for hospitals would be the recovery rate and the average length of recovery, while indicators dealing with general morbidity and mortality rates, infant mortality, disease incidence, and lifespan would be appropriate for preventive and more general health programs.

Proponents of using social indicators contend that this approach more closely measures the overall purpose of service delivery programs than does merely counting the units serviced. Critics note that collecting the requisite data for various social indicators is time consuming and expensive. Further, many other factors, besides program expenditures, affect the magnitude of various social indicators. Unless these other factors are also measured and statistically controlled in any analysis examining program impact, the results will present a prejudiced view of the program being examined. For example, the overall state of the economy may influence recidivism and job placement for prisoners. Poverty levels per capita income may influence the success of educational programs. Finally, this approach measures program effectiveness—how well the program achieves its particular stated mission—rather than efficiency.

Consequences of Public Sector Inability to Measure Value of Program Output. The consequences of public agencies being unable to measure the efficiency with which they deliver services are major. Agencies are unable to prove how well they are performing in a systematic way readily accepted by the public. This leaves public sector agencies open to charges that they are less efficient than private firms, or even nonprofits.

The bias against public sector growth and toward private sector activity in the United States is deeply embedded in long-standing attitudes older than the nation itself. When the nation was first founded in the late 1700s, the driving ideology was eighteenth-century liberalism, a philosophy that greatly emphasized individual freedom, rights, and limitations on government power, tyranny, and excesses. Fleeing both religious and political persecution in Europe, many of the early settlers were determined to avoid repeating those negative experiences in the New World. They designed a Constitution that fragmented government power across branches of government and between levels of government. When writers of the U.S. Constitution failed to include specific principles protecting individuals, a Bill of Rights correcting this major omission was demanded during the ratification debate. Following ratification of the Constitution, a Bill of Rights emphasizing individual rights and limiting governmental power was proposed in 1789; two years later it was in force.

The growth of capitalism in the United States during the nation's first century, moving from limited industry to full-fledged industrialism by the beginning of the 1900s, also served to create a pro-private-sector and anti-government-growth bias. The nation flourished under capitalism, and as a philosophy for organizing economic activity, free enterprise obtained many adherents. Only during the dark days of the Great Depression when 25 percent of the labor force was unemployed—in an era before unemployment compensation, welfare, or social security—did socialism achieve a minor flurry of success. Both the excesses of the Soviet Union, viewed as an example of socialism in action, and the recovery of the U.S. economy as it moved into World War II served to crush this flurry of left-wing activism that challenged the limited role allocated to government under capitalism of the day.

During the 1960s, Great Society programs and court rulings provided assistance and relief to the captive populations examined here, as the government struggled to provide a floor or safety net, below which helpless and dependent citizens should not be allowed to fall. During this decade more than any other since the 1930s attitudes toward government involvement in the economy and government provision of services for the disadvantaged shifted to become more favorable.

The economic crises of the 1970s—OPEC-driven oil price increases and stagflation with its double digit inflation and unemployment—served to undercut support for greater government involvement generally, and service delivery for the disadvantaged in particular. Programs that were previously regarded as highly desirable dropped on the national agenda as economic issues became prominent. After the tumultuous decade of the 1970s, confronting a worsening national productivity record, mounting trade and federal deficits, and reduced economic opportunities, citizens embraced the more conservative philosophy of Ronald Reagan and a decade of reductions in social spending.

The Grace Commission, composed of efficiency experts and top private-sector managers, found government excess in abundance and offered many prescriptions for increasing government efficiency so that the public sector could more closely approximate the presumed greater efficiency of the private sector. Without more objective measures of the value of government output, public agencies were subjected to charges of waste, fraud, abuse, and inefficiency. Reagan rhetoric of the era represented a return to the classic emphasis on individualism in the United States. It presented government as the enemy of economic growth and individual freedom, not its protector and the source of solutions for societal ills.

Unfortunately, American mythology has not come to the defense of government programs designed to deliver services to the disadvantaged. Rather, American myths across the history of the nation have typically supported notions that individuals should fend for and protect themselves, and that government is corruptible if not corrupted. Robert Reich (1987) has identified the following four common American myths whose theses have been prevalent in popular culture throughout U.S. history.

The first is the myth of "the mob at the gates." This myth contends that America is a beacon of light representing freedom and democracy in a sea of tyranny and barbarism. As a nation, we are uniquely blessed, but may lose this uniqueness and state of blessedness if we are not ever vigilant against "them"—the forces of evil and darkness that would strive to strip us of our individualism and liberties. Underlying this myth is a darker fear of immigrants, foreigners, and anyone different. Plainly, this myth does little to encourage support for the dependent, helpless, and homeless. Rather, it relies on fear to perpetuate America's unique emphasis on individualism and freedom.

The second prominent American cultural myth is that of "the triumphant individual." This is the Horatio Alger myth, in which the little person works long and hard, takes risks that pay off, and works his or her way up the social and economic ladder, eventually attaining wealth, status, and even fame. According to this second myth, anyone with enough spunk, guts, and hard work can achieve success. The triumphant individual may be rough at the edges, at times a loner and a maverick. Yet this person is outspoken, self-confident, self-reliant, and gets the job done. Implicit in the myth is the belief that people who do not attain economic and social success fail to do so because of personal flaws or limitations. They must lack self-confidence or spunk, be lazy, or accept hard knocks without fighting back. Plainly, this myth directly glorifies individualism at the expense of collective decision making and action.

A third American cultural parable focuses on "rot at the top." Almost libertarian in emphasis, this myth is concerned with the malevolence of powerful elites throughout society, encompassing greedy business leaders and imperious governmental officials. Those concerned about malevolent elites must struggle constantly to guard against corruption, decadence, and irresponsibility among the powerful, including public-sector leaders. Without such vigilance, the powerful will form a conspiracy against the public, abusing their power at the expense of average citizens. This myth draws on a long-standing American suspicion against elites and concern over circumscribing elite power. Its perpetuation has helped to fuel various reform movements throughout U.S. history. Oriented toward eliminating corrupting political influences from public service delivery and program implementation, this myth has contributed as well to a general skepticism of government expansion and involvement in economic and social activities.

Of the cultural myths identified by Reich, only the fourth emphasizes a communal spirit and goals—the parable of the "benevolent community." According to this parable, friends and neighbors help each other in time of need, exhibiting a sense of community pride, national patriotism, and generosity. Modeled on earlier notions of Christian charity, this parable is associated with self-sacrifice for others and compassion. This is the myth behind efforts such as barn raisings, disaster relief efforts, and volunteerism.

Movements to not only extend civil rights to disadvantaged groups but also provide economic support and other services to them have most often been associated with this parable. Yet even this parable does not emphasize government involvement in support for the disadvantaged and for captive populations. Rather, it might just as easily be interpreted as justifying a private sector voluntary approach to such relief as well as systematic governmental programs to achieve service delivery and improved quality of life.

Thus, common cultural myths reinforce notions that undercut increased governmental involvement in the economy, even on the part of captive populations who often do not have the wherewithal to support and defend themselves. These cultural myths provide a bias against greater governmental involvement; the absence of public sector output and efficiency measures fuels the bias. The result is that the United States lags behind most other industrialized democracies in social spending for captive and other populations.

Different Dependencies on the External Environment

Public agencies and private firms differ in the dependence on external forces they exhibit. Some observers contend that private firms have greater control over their immediate environment, including factors that affect production costs, than do public agencies. Private firms depend on the state to grant them corporate charters and to establish rules and regulations for the conduct of business. For example, firms often need permits, licenses, or other forms of government approval or support to engage in business. They may rely on private capital markets to secure monies for new plants and equipment, although the use of federally run or sponsored credit programs to assist businesses is rapidly growing. Typically, private firms also must rely on supply markets to purchase goods used in product production or service delivery, and on the finished goods or service market to sell the firm's output.

Public agencies also depend on many external forces and factors. Public agencies depend on legislatures for authorizing legislation, and subsequently for annual appropriations. Generally public agencies have far less control over personnel issues than do private firms. While private firms are constrained by Title IV of the 1964 Civil Rights Act that prohibits discrimination in employment by firms that engage in interstate commerce, public agencies are even more constrained. Most public agencies are under merit systems with specific guidelines for hiring, promotion, and job classification. Central personnel agencies may also establish refining personnel guidelines that lay out how broad merit system tenets should be implemented.

Usually private-sector managers have greater control over the hiring, firing, and assignment of employees than do public-sector managers. Despite this greater potential for mobility of all personnel in private firms, public agencies must also handle considerable turnover in personnel at the top levels. Within the federal system and most state systems, the four top levels of managers are political appointees who often differ substantially from career bureaucrats in background, experience, and motivation. Often drawn from the private sector, political appointees are short-term managers in the public sector. They frequently lack direct experience in the substantive areas they are selected to administer in the public sector, but rather are picked for loyalty to the political party in power, personal contributions to the campaign of the recently elected chief executive, ideologies and philosophies about the role of government compatible with the president or governor selecting them, and reputations as general managers. Thus with each new administration, most of the top level managers for public agencies turn over.

Below these political appointees, career bureaucrats rarely turn over, but often spend entire careers working within a narrow specialization and developing considerable expertise in that area. Career bureaucrats are typically dedicated to the programs of their agencies and the clients those programs serve. As a result of these divergent backgrounds and particularly during the Reagan era, public agencies at times seem to exhibit schizophrenia with political appointees pulling in one direction and career bureaucrats pulling in another. During the Reagan era, top officials, not unlike those in other conservative administrations, worked to limit public sector growth and reshape service delivery toward the private sector, while some career bureaucrats worked for the reverse. These crosscurrents within agencies further contribute to the popular opinion that public agencies are inefficient and poorly managed compared to private sector firms.

Different Mechanisms for Translating Citizens' Preferences into Action

The mechanisms by which citizens translate their preferences into action have traditionally differed for private firms and public agencies. In the private sector, individuals supposedly express their preferences through their purchases—a form of voting with dollars. When individuals pursue their own self-interest, consuming what they most prefer within income constraints, firms are guided by prices to produce what consumers want.

Yet several limits on the effectiveness of this dollar voting system exist. First, not everyone has the same amount of dollars and the same ability to satisfy individual preferences. People with more money have a greater dollar vote in the private sector than do people with less or no money. This is particularly true of the lower-income sick who must rely on private markets for health care, and the near-indigent elderly who must accept inferior living arrangements in retirement and old age. Nor are all differences in wealth attributed to different levels of effort and risk taking, as the myth of the triumphant individual would imply. Some differentials result from inherited wealth, while others are the consequence of market vagaries and flukes.

Second, monopolies and oligopolies undercut freedom of preference expression by restricting choice of products and services. Parents trying to find day-care services or private schooling for their children often encounter a limited selection of providers. Companies further distort preferences through advertising. In the mental health area, many private psychiatric hospitals have launched major advertising campaigns to convince parents that their teenagers are troubled and need residential psychiatric services.

Finally, technological complexity and lack of information may make it difficult for citizens to evaluate whether corporate products or services are delivering the promised level of quality. In no place is this more problematic than with modern medical care. Technological complexity has become so great that once citizens decide to enter the medical system by visiting physicians, they often lose control over what is purchased to the physicians, who use their greater knowledge to influence the choice of services delivered to the prospective patients (Kronenfeld and Whicker, 1984). Not only do patients often not have the background to ascertain whether the diagnoses are correctly made and the services ordered are appropriate, but they also frequently lack the expertise to determine whether or not reasonable outcomes of medical procedures are achieved.

In addition, the public sector is plagued with limits on how citizens' preferences are translated into programs and services, compounding citizens' frustration with government, and further contributing to alienation and a sense of powerlessness. In theory, each citizen has an equal vote to select any particular officeholder, who once in office reflects majority opinion, constrained by minority rights. Yet despite equal votes, not all citizens count equally in the electoral process.

Under current election laws, members of Congress and politicians at the state level are heavily dependent on contributions from political action committees (PACs) to finance campaigns. PAC influence undercuts the ability of individual citizens to wield clout over politicians. Federal campaign laws limit the direct contributions of PACs and individuals to candidates during both the primary and general election campaigns. The U.S. Supreme Court, however, has ruled that limits on indirect spending not coordinated with the candidate's campaign violate the First Amendment right of free speech. Thus, PACs and wealthy individuals can use indirect spending to continue to wield disproportionate influence over who wins and to gain access to politicians once they are elected.

Prisoners, in particular, lack a vocal interest group to represent them in the election cycle. Nor have the interests of children been particularly well represented, as the absence of a national day-care policy and the deteriorating conditions of many of America's schools attest. The clout of the health care system in the political process reflects more aptly the power of health care providers than the power of health care consumers. And the growth of power of the Gray Panthers,—the organized elderly— has been a fairly recent phenomenon.

Just as in the private sector product ignorance and technological complexity sometimes undercut consumers' abilities to get what they want, citizens who vote for public sector officials may also lack sufficient information to know if the candidate they choose best reflects their own personal preferences for public policies, programs, and services. Some voter ignorance is rational, since political parties frequently hold similar positions in order to capture the majority of voters, most of whom are centrist in their viewpoints (Downs, 1957). Yet lack of information makes voters less likely to achieve their preferences for public sector services. Further, the increase in policy areas in which government is now involved has decreased geometrically the likelihood that in any election a candidate can reflect any particular citizen's preferences, further eroding the incentive to be informed about public policy and increasing malaise and discontent with government (Sigelman and Whicker, 1988). Additionally, politicians' perceptions of voters' preferences may result in short-run expediency, with other preferences being overshadowed or ignored. Elected politicians are often pressured to pursue short-run policies at the expense of long-run planning that would lead to more rational and coherent service delivery.

CHARACTERISTICS OF NONPROFIT AGENCIES

The characterization of all organizations that deliver services to captive populations as either private sector or public sector obscures the middle category, nonprofit agencies. Sometimes, for the purpose of identifying accounting practices and other operating procedures, the term *nonprofit* is used as a broad category that includes both governmental agencies and other types of organizations, although in subsequent chapters in this book, the term will be used to indicate a third category between governmental agencies and for-profit firms. While nongovernmental nonprofits share the characteristic of being in the private sector with for-profit firms, they share an orientation toward broader community service with governmental agencies.

Besides governmental agencies, major types of nonprofit organizations include educational agencies, such as private and public schools, colleges, and universities; and health and welfare organizations, such as hospitals, nursing homes, and orphanages. Other major types of nonprofits are religious organizations that include both churches and church-related agencies; charitable organizations, including those with communitywide service objectives; and foundations, including private trusts and corporations (Lynn and Norvelle, 1984).

Nonprofit organizations must operate within legal or quasi-legal requirements imposed both externally by federal or state statute, ruling, grant stipulation, or judicial decree and internally by charter, bylaw, ordinance, trust agreement, donor stipulation, or contract. While the perception exists that for-profit firms exert stronger managerial control over operations, the reverse is often true—that operational and administrative controls are more strict in nonprofit organizations to assure compliance with legal and other requirements, especially those concerning budgets and funds.

Indeed, nonprofits use the same method of accounting for money that governments do: fund accounting, which disaggregates financial records down to a smaller fund level, rather than aggregating records at the jurisdiction or organization level. The purpose of fund accounting is to assure that records are segregated in such a manner that compliance with legal requirements can be easily monitored. Funds are fiscal and accounting entities with a self-balancing set of accounts recording cash and other financial resources, related liabilities, residual equities or balances, and any changes in each. By contrast, for-profit firms, which typically do not have to demonstrate compliance with various restrictions, limitations, and special regulations affecting the use of funds, use accounting that aggregates information at the organization level and results in a unified financial report.

Discretion for managers of nonprofit agencies is restricted not only in the area of money management, but also in other areas. Nonprofit managers may find it difficult to modify their agencies' structures, even when they are ineffective or awkward. They may also find it difficult to attract qualified employees at prescribed pay rates, to discharge or demote incompetent employees, or to reward outstanding employees. Sometimes nonprofit managers have a hard time acquiring sufficient resources or use of available resources should they deem doing so necessary for effective service delivery. Also, nonprofit managers often have limited discretion to improve existing budgeting, accounting, reporting, and auditing arrangements.

Both governments and other nonprofits differ from for-profit firms in several important ways: They are not driven by the profit motive, and are generally owned collectively by their constituents, unlike for-profit firms where ownership occurs individually, through individually owned equity shares that may be sold or exchanged. For nonprofits and governments, those contributing financial resources to the organizations do not necessarily receive a direct or proportionate share of goods or services, and in the case of some charitable organizations, may not receive any goods or services. Generally, the objective for most nonprofits is to maximize output for a given input; that is, to provide as much service each year as financial and other resources allow. Nonprofits typically operate on an annual basis, raising as many resources as they can and spending them in the same year to service clients. The purpose of nonprofits, as well as governments, then, is to maximize service delivery, rather than to increase their own wealth.

Despite these differences, all three organizations—government agencies, other nonprofit agencies (hereafter, just called nonprofits), and for-profit agencies—share several basic operating characteristics. All three are integral parts of the economic system and are affected by it. All three use similar resources and factors of production to accomplish their goals. All must acquire and convert scarce resources into goods and services.

Even with differences in the level at which financial data is recorded, financial management processes are essentially the same in all three types of organizations. Each of the three must have a viable information system, including an accounting system, to assist managers and other interested parties in receiving relevant and timely data for planning, directing, controlling, and evaluating the use of scarce resources and for making staffing decisions. Because all three types of organizations do confront scarce resources, all use least-cost analytic techniques and other evaluation procedures to assure resources are used effectively. Despite some areas in which one type of organization has specialized, in many areas all three types are striving to produce similar services and products.

PRIVATIZATION OF SERVICE DELIVERY

During the Reagan era, emphasis was placed on both pushing service delivery for captive as well as other populations from the federal government to state and local governments and from the public sector to the private sector. Privatization was in vogue, a trend that some feel reached its zenith in the 1980s and will decline in the 1990s (Bozeman, 1988). Whether or not such predictions are realized, the push for privatization has been an important and potent force in recent American politics.

Besides the privatization of education, social services, medical laboratories, health services, and prisons, advocates of this trend would also apply its philosophy to solid-waste collection, electrical power production, property tax assessment, the development of office space, fire protection, and geological surveys. Indeed, almost no government services and operations—including the U.S. space program—have avoided scrutiny as potential candidates for privatization (Savas, 1982; Moe, 1987; Mikesell, 1987; Levine, 1985; Burger, 1985; Rothenburg, 1987; Morgan and England, 1988).

Provision and Production of Service

Privatization is a concept with more than one meaning, often leading to confusion and heated debate over its desirability (Kolderie, 1986). Some observers have not distinguished between two different meanings associated with the term *privatization*, the primary policy decision of government to provide service and the secondary decision to produce a service, either of which may be turned over to private parties. If either decision may be made in the public or private sector, Ted Kolderie illustrates that four different possibilities arise:

Public Provision and Public Production. Both the decision to provide a service and the decision to produce it may be made in the public sector, so that the government does both. In this case, the legislature writes a law for service delivery and provides the money for the appropriate government agency to run the program. Public schools and police departments are examples of this set of conditions where both provision and production decisions are encompassed within the public sector.

Public Provision and Private Production. In the second case, the government decides to provide a service, but production occurs in the private sector. The government may contract with a nonprofit or for-profit firm for service delivery. Examples would include government health clinics contracting with private physicians for partial services and with private medical laboratories for various medical tests for publicly subsidized patients.

Private Provision and Public Production. In the third circumstance, the government produces and sells a service to private consumers. Consumers presumably have discretion over whether or not to purchase the service since no public sector decision has been made that the service should be universally supplied to all citizens. Before- or after-school care or specialized summer programs for children sponsored and run by the public school system but only available to children on a fee or user charge basis are examples of services in this category.

Private Provision and Private Production. Both provision and production may lie within the private sector, with no governmental decisions about service delivery or role in production. Privately financed and run schools, universities, nursing and retirement homes, and clinics specializing in cosmetic surgery are examples of this case.

Kolderie contends that turning over production decisions to the private sector may increase efficiency and effectiveness, but turning over provision decisions may jeopardize social welfare. Of the two decisions the former is less complicated than the latter. Production decisions can be divided into finer and smaller areas—for example, into questions about line versus support service, how the work will be produced, what is the need ratio of labor versus equipment and facilities, and which style of management is most appropriate for the situation. Each of these issues, in turn, may be divided into even more narrow questions.

Contracting Out Services

By contrast, decisions about whether to provide a service and if so, how to finance it, are more complex. Usually three steps are involved in service provision decisions. First, the government must decide whether and who should be provided the service, and how much of the service is needed. Second, the government must arrange that recipients and beneficiaries of governmental good intentions should not pay for the service in question. Third, the government must select a producer to serve the intended beneficiaries.

Even though the British often mean the sale of government-owned assets and enterprises when they use the term *privatization*, Americans more typically mean contracting out, the most widely recognized form of privatization in the United States. Despite the sale of Conrail to private owners and sales of some government-owned power distribution facilities and selected petroleum reserves, in contrast to Britain the United States has very few government-owned and run enterprises to sell off. Most utilities, although called public, have long been private. Excluding the U.S. Postal Service, the Tennessee Valley Authority, and a few other exceptions, major energy, transportation, and communications systems in the United States are privately owned and run and are only marginally linked to the public sector.

Although contracting out publicly provided services for private production is not new in the United States, the magnitude that was proposed for this form of privatization during the Reagan era was new. The potential and in some cases actual expansion of privatization into new service areas raised several issues and potential problems surrounding contracting out to private vendors (Kolderie, 1986):

The Question of Competition. Often contracting to a private supplier for a previously publicly produced and still publicly provided service just results in the substitution of one monopoly supplier for another. Contracting out does not guarantee that private firms will compete for the privilege of producing the service; without competition, many of the advantages of private sector production may not materialize. The service beneficiaries often continue to have no alternative but to rely on the single source of the service, now in the private sector and more removed from government scrutiny and popular pressure than before. The government that is providing the service must negotiate in weakened position with a monopsonistic supplier.

The Question of Creaming. Another issue related to privatization is that of private firms creaming off the most profitable and easiest to service clients, and leaving the most costly and most difficult clients for government service production. Creaming may occur with or without government consent, as in the case of Federal Express, Emory, and other overnight mail services that compete with the U.S. Postal Service—but only for the most profitable business in the larger markets. Creaming makes government service delivery look inefficient and poorly managed when compared to the "more profitable" private firms, and contributes to the perpetuation of the image of government as an inept supplier of services.

The Question of Corruption. Contracting out presents many opportunities for corruption—ranging from collusion and suppression of competition among contractors to failure on the part of the contract recipient to deliver the services purchased. Governments contracting out must be vigilant to detect and combat these anticompetitive efforts and to guard against other corrupt practices, such as kickbacks and inside information on bidding.

The Question of Cost. The normal expectation is that privatization will reduce costs, driving down total expenditures. Indeed, Kolderie regards this aspect of privatization as its primary advantage. However, these benefits are most likely to accrue if contracts are competitively bid, a condition that often does not hold. Further, in some instances, privatization may have the perverse effect of increasing spending (Butler, 1985). By bringing in contractors and private service providers, privatization increases the numbers and power of spending coalitions that drive up the federal budget.

The Question of Quality and Control. Privatization also raises issues of control. Proponents of retaining service delivery within the public arena fear that moving it to the private sector could diminish public accountability and control. Opponents of contracting sometimes argue that a government has better control over operations that it owns and over permanent rather than contract employees. With loss of daily control of the operations associated with service delivery, opponents contend that incentives to diminish quality in order to reduce costs and maximize profits could mount on private contractors. Without the degree of public accountability that exists when production occurs in the public sector, contractors can succumb to these pressures. Proponents argue that the contract procedure does provide an adequate amount of control over service quality and other aspects of service delivery although opponents challenge this contention, especially when only one private provider is available.

The Question of Affirmative Action. Federal, state, and local governments have been leaders in the area of affirmative action and expansion of employment opportunities for minorities. In the public sector, more than in the private sector, negative stereotypes of ethnic and religious minorities as well as other minorities, such as the physically handicapped, have been challenged. Private employers often offer minorities lower wages. Theoretically, this may curb costs, unless profits for firm owners erase any cost savings; regardless, lower wages reduce upward mobility for minorities (Morgan and England, 1988). At the federal level, Executive Order 11246 mandates affirmative action programs for firms holding federal contracts, but comparable safeguards for state and local governments are sometimes absent.

Opponents of contracting argue that shifting service delivery from the public to the private sector may not only reduce the quality of service for the beneficiaries of captive population programs but also lower the quality of life for many service providers as well. Proponents disagree with both contentions.

The Question of Community. Opponents of privatization, and especially of contracting out, fear that it could undercut a sense of community to mix profit motives with public service. Privatization emphasizes individualism and economic gain for corporations and other units smaller than society as a whole rather than more broadly focused and altruistic motives. Opponents contend that as long as the community is deciding to provide a service, and private firms fulfill predominantly the producer role, the sense of community is not undermined.

Other Approaches to Service Provision

Proponents of a more conservative approach contest the view that provision of services should remain within the public sector, and argue that efficient and reasonable programs would involve some privatization of service production combined with some privatization of service provision. Advocates of such a mix contend that these programs should be selective, targeting eligibility to those in need. Sharing the financial burden between the general taxpayer and program beneficiaries, according to this view, prevents overproduction of the service since it is no longer a free good to recipients, and assures that people receive the service toward which they are willing to contribute. Fees and charges based on income, with assistance for people of low income, should prevent overuse of services. Benefits should be taxed to help restrain expenditures. The introduction of voucher systems and other user subsidies both enhance privatization and depoliticize the vendor-selection process, by increasing the emphasis on finding the lowest cost producer.

Advocates of the mixed program just described, where aspects of both service provision and production are shared by public and private sectors, have also made service suggestions. These include adopting a policy to avoid noncompetitive sole source contracts, regardless of whether the supplier is governmental or private. Service elements should be disaggregated to the extent possible in this framework, to enhance the pool of suppliers and to allow change to occur gradually, affecting one component of service before spreading to other service components. Divestiture would assure that members of a public policy board directly overseeing service delivery to captive populations are not caught in a conflict of interest as they would be if they were also members of producer firms and suppliers.

Other suggestions for changes through privatization of service delivery include adopting capitation as a payment method, where feasible. With capitation, the service producer is paid a lump sum for services to be rendered. The producer is then allowed to keep whatever the organization does not spend to deliver the service. Proponents of capitation argue that this payment method provides an incentive for producers to innovate and that leftover funds will be spent to improve services rather than taken as profits. Yet another suggestion is to involve service beneficiaries through coproduction in providing some of their own services. Presumably, this reduces the amount of money spent on professional services, and encourages strategies of prevention and self-help while reducing costs. For captive populations, the coproduction notion has been used in a very limited sense—such as having prisoners who are mechanically skilled participate in building new prison facilities, and more able students tutor their less able peers. However, by virtue of the fact that captive populations are more dependent than other populations, coproduction as a philosophy of privatization may have limited applicability to the groups considered here.

THE IMPACT OF FEDERALISM ON SERVICE DELIVERY TO CAPTIVE POPULATIONS

Any debate over the respective roles of public, nonprofit, and for-profit agencies in service delivery to captive populations is constrained by the fact that both the decisions to provide and how to produce such services transpire in a federal system. The United States has two constitutionally recognized levels of government—the national or federal government and state governments—each with the power to make binding decisions that regulate the lives of members of captive and other populations.

Expansion of Federal Involvement in Social Services

Traditionally, services to captive populations have fallen more heavily on the state governments and local jurisdictions created by states than on the federal government. Across the twentieth century, however, the role of the federal government in these services has increased, as a result of several factors:

Rising Expectations of Governmental Problem Solving. The changing character of the American family from extended to nuclear and now often to single-parent form has created greater stresses within it, and resulted in increased demands for government services. Unlike the extended family, nuclear and single-parent families have been unwilling or unable to care for the elderly to the same extent as previously. Increased female participation in the labor force as well as more female-headed households have also accelerated demands for day care and on schools. An increase in the complexity of medical technology has contributed to an explosion of health care costs and consequent demands for greater government assistance in the health care area. Fighting wars on drugs has resulted in demands for increased prison capacities.

As demands on government overall have escalated, pressure has been exerted on the national government for additional assistance to states and localities to provide these increased services. Bush's war on drugs including monies for prison expansion, federal assistance to education through the Elementary and Secondary Education Act as well as other legislation, and federal monies for medicare and medicaid are but a few examples of increased federal activity on behalf of captive populations.

Economic Growth. Until the 1970s, the U.S. economy grew at a high rate during the postwar decades—a golden period of rapid economic growth. This growth contributed to federal ability to become involved in areas traditionally left to the states, including services for captive populations.

An Elastic Federal Tax Structure. With the adoption in 1913 of a progressive federal tax structure, federal revenues became *elastic*—a term economists use to denote growth in tax revenues that exceeds the growth in the general tax base. The resulting revenue growth allowed the federal government to become the "rich Uncle Sam" in comparison to states and localities which relied on more regressive and less elastic tax structures. Income-elastic revenue growth allowed the federal government to expand into areas in which it was not traditionally involved.

The Adoption of Keynesian Economics. After the Great Depression, Keynesian economic philosophy was adopted by U.S. presidents and congresses. Accordingly, countercyclical and often deficit spending further contributed to federal expansion. Some federal programs to dependent populations involved entitlements, and became part of countercyclical Keynesian spending at the federal level.

Greater Emphasis on Interpersonal Equity. Increased concern for greater interpersonal equity also enhanced federal power vis-à-vis the states. The federal government, more than the states, became the guardian of dependent and captive populations throughout the nation. Programs for the elderly, sick, and the young were enacted, in part, out of a desire for greater interpersonal equity within American society.

Federalism in the Reagan Era

The trend toward greater federal power and involvement in service delivery was slowed during the Reagan years yet it was not halted. As part of this slowdown, federal funds flowing from the U.S. Treasury to state and local coffers were reduced and changed form somewhat. Prior to the Reagan era, most federal monies flowed to the states and localities primarily in the form of categorical grants, with specific, detailed requirements attached. During the Reagan era, the number of categorical grants decreased and the number of more broadly focused block grants increased, along with a cutback in total intergovernmental subsidies.

Congress accommodated the Reagan administration's request for shifting and consolidated several categorical grants to states and localities into a few block grants, but did make substantial changes in the substance and form of the original Reagan administration block-grant proposals. Congress placed limitations on state discretion, removed a number of categorical grants from block grants, and increased the number of individual block grants.

Reagan had recommended two large block grants in the health area, but Congress created four. The Alcohol, Drug Abuse, and Mental Health Program consolidated categorical programs in these areas; in 1982 this program was funded at 25 percent less than the categorical programs it replaced. Additionally, states were required to totally support community health centers that had previously been funded federally. The states did not have as much leeway as might be expected with this block grant, because many of the funds were earmarked for special purposes. States were mandated to spend at least 35 percent of the monies for alcohol programs, at least 35 percent for drug abuse, and at least 20 percent for prevention and early intervention.

The Health Prevention and Services Program was the second of four health block grants enacted during the Reagan era. This grant consolidated programs in home health services, rodent control, fluoridation, health education and risk reduction, health incentive grants, emergency medical services, rape crisis, and hypertension. The Primary Care Program consisted of the earlier funded community health centers, while the Maternal and Child Health Program consolidated categorical programs concerned with lead-based paint, rehabilitation services, sudden infant death syndrome, hemophilia, genetic diseases, and adolescent health services.

Congress refused to abolish some categorical programs that the Reagan administration sought to eliminate, including those dealing with child abuse, runaway youth, developmental disabilities, rehabilitation services, adoption assistance, child welfare services, and foster care. Congress placed the Community Services Administration in a separate block grant administered by the Department of Health and Human Services, rather than abolishing it as the administration advocated.

The Reagan White House argued for two educational grants, one for states and a second for local educational agencies comprised mostly of programs under Title I of the Elementary and Secondary Education Act. Congress did fold into a single block grant thirty small state education programs designed to improve school performance and the use of resources. It refused to consolidate Title I programs for localities, including emergency school aid, education for the handicapped, and adult and vocational education programs. Congress also resisted adopting the Reagan proposal to consolidate low-income energy assistance and Aid for Families with Dependent Children (AFDC) emergency assistance into one energy and emergency grant, administered by the Department of Health and Human Services.

Block grant requirements for the states were appended to the 1981 reconciliation bill, forcing states to prepare reports that included a statement of goals and objectives; information on the activities to be supported with grant monies and the individuals to be served; and the criteria and method for disbursing funds. States were further mandated to hold public hearings on the report and to provide adequate public notice for the hearings.

Additionally, states were to certify to the relevant federal agency that they were capable of administering the block grant before its implementation. Financial and compliance audits based on standards established by the U.S. Comptroller General were required every two years. Beyond these general requirements, specific requirements were attached to some individual block grants. Even in the Reagan era of decentralization of service delivery back to states and localities, considerable federal guidelines on the expenditure of intergovernmental assistance on behalf of captive as well as other populations remained (Beam, 1985; Wright, 1982; Walker, 1981; Barfield, 1981; Aronson and Hilley, 1986).

Regulatory Federalism

Federal assistance for domestic social spending increasingly has been coupled with regulatory mandates. The U.S. Advisory Commission on Intergovernmental Relations has identified four major regulatory techniques different in character from traditional federal strings attached to categorical service delivery programs (ACIR, 1984).

Direct Orders. Federal regulations involving direct orders must be fulfilled to avoid the threat or reality of civil or criminal penalties. While the technique of direct orders has been used most commonly in the policy areas of public employment and environmental protection, its use has not been restricted to those areas alone. An example of its application is the 1972 Equal Employment Opportunity Act, which prohibits job discrimination by state and local governments on the basis of race, color, religion, or national origin.

Direct orders place the legal authority of Congress and the constitutional rights of states in direct conflict, and thus have raised some legal questions. The U.S. Supreme Court greatly restrained the wage-and-hour requirements directly imposed on states and localities through the 1974 amendments to the federal Fair Labor Standards Act in the 1976 case of *National League of Cities v. Usery*, a ruling that favored state and local discretion. Generally, however, direct orders by the federal government to states and localities have not been challenged or have been upheld, restricting the discretion of states and localities in delivering services to captive populations.

Crosscutting Requirements. To promote desirable national social and economic policies, all federal assistance programs have crosscutting requirements imposed on them. Frequently, crosscutting requirements have prevented discrimination against disadvantaged groups, such as the handicapped and the elderly. By 1984 thirty-six across-the-board requirements had been passed dealing with a variety of social and economic issues; twenty-three more dealt with administrative and fiscal requirements. Nine of these crosscutting requirements were directed to nondiscrimination. Two-thirds of the total of fifty-nine have been passed since 1969, further evidence of increased federal control over service delivery and domestic spending.

Crossover Sanctions. Crossover sanctions link federal assistance in one program area to compliance with federal guidelines in a different program area by threatening to withhold aid in the first if guidelines in the second area are not met. Thus, the penalty for noncompliance crosses over policy areas, causing funds in the first area to be terminated. Crossover sanctions have been applied in the areas of health planning and handicapped education, as well as other areas.

Partial Preexemptions. Partial exemptions is another regulatory technique that allows state regulation to supersede federal regulation if the state adopts standards equivalent to or more stringent than federal standards. Partial exemptions from federal regulation have been used for programs in occupational safety and health, meat and poultry inspection, and environmental protection efforts important for preventive health, such as the 1965 Water Quality Act and the 1970 Clean Air Act amendments.

Federal Mandates. During the 1970s and 1980s, the federal government increasingly relied on federal mandates to states and local governments through the foregoing regulatory techniques but neglected to provide funds to offset increased state and local expenditures needed to comply. Critics of regulatory federalism identified several problems with this approach to service delivery, including the difficulty of measuring mandate costs. Other criticisms focused on the inflexible nature of federal mandates, on how they undercut necessary local discretion, and how sometimes they were inefficient. Opponents also charged that regulatory federalism is ineffective and unaccountable. Crosscutting requirements, in particular, were lambasted as being inconsistent and intrusive. Proponents countered that because the federal system was grounded in

Table 1
Mode of Service Delivery by Type of Provider

CAPTIVE POPULATION SERVICED	PUBLIC	PRIVATE	
		NONPROFIT	FOR-PROFIT
YOUNG	Public schools	Private schools	Day-care chains; local for-profit day care
CRIMINAL	Federal and state prisons; state youth corrections facilities; local jails		Detention immigration centers; juvenile placements in private facilities; services in prisons; prison management
SICK	County hospitals; VA and military hospitals; state mental health hospitals; medical schools	Nonprofit community and religious hospitals; nonprofit HMOs (e.g., Kaiser); Blue Cross/Blue Shield	Hospital chains; for-profit HMOs (e.g., Prucare, Health America, Maxicare); ambulatory outpatient clinics (doc-in-the-boxes)
ELDERLY	VA nursing homes; state nursing homes; public home health services	Religious nursing and retirement homes; adult day-care centers; Meals on Wheels; nonprofit home health services	For-profit nursing and retirement homes; for-profit services (e.g., Johnson & Johnson)

constitutional cement, federal regulations were necessary to implement national standards and goals.

AN OVERVIEW OF SERVICE DELIVERY TO CAPTIVE POPULATIONS

The remainder of this book examines modes of service delivery to four captive or dependent populations—the young, the criminally incarcerated, the sick, and the elderly. With the exception of the criminally incarcerated, all three modes of service delivery—governmental, non-profit, and for-profit organizations have been used to service these populations. (See Table 1.) Experts continue to disagree over which mode of service delivery is most effective and efficient. Plainly each has advantages and disadvantages. Despite the disagreement over the ideal approach, this mosaic of delivery methods presents Americans with an array of choices few other nations enjoy.

REFERENCES

Aronson, J. Richard, and John H. Hilley. *Financing State and Local Governments*, 4th ed. Washington, D.C.: The Brookings Institution, 1986.

Barfield, Claude E. *Rethinking Federalism: Block Grants and Federal, State, and Local Responsibilities*. Washington, D.C.: The American Enterprise Institute, 1981.

Beam, David R. "New Federalism, Old Realities: The Reagan Administration and Intergovernmental Reform," in *The Reagan Presidency and the Governing of America*. Washington, D.C.: The Urban Institute, 1985.

Bozeman, Barry. "Exploring the Limits of Public and Private Sectors: Sector Boundaries as Maginot Line," *Public Administration Review* 48, No. 2 (1988): 672–74.

Burger, Warren E. "Prison Industries: Turning Warehouses into Factories with Fences," *Public Administration Review* 45 (Special Issue, 1985): 754–57.

Butler, Stuart. *Privatizating Federal Spending, a Strategy to Eliminate the Deficit*. Washington, D.C.: Heritage Foundation, 1985.

Downs, Anthony. *An Economic Theory of Democracy*. Boston: Little, Brown and Co., 1957.

Kolderie, Ted. "The Two Different Concepts of Privatization," *Public Administration Review* 46, No. 4 (1986): 285–91.

Kronenfeld, Jennie J., and Marcia Lynn Whicker. *U.S. National Health Policy: An Analysis of the Federal Role*. New York: Praeger Publishers, 1984.

Levine, Arthur L. "Commercialization of Space: Policy and Administration Issues," *Public Administration Review* 45, No. 2 (1985): 562–69.

Lynn, Edward S., and Joan W. Norvelle. *Introduction to Fund Accounting*. Reston, Va.: Reston Publishers, 1984.

Mikesell, John. "Privatization in Public Administration: Quality Effects of Property Tax Assessment Contracting," *Public Administration Quarterly* 11, No. 1 (1987): 101–15.

Moe, Ronald C. "Law versus Performance as Objective Standard," *Public Administration Review* 48, No. 2 (1987): 674–75.

Morgan, D. R., and R. E. England. "The Two Faces of Privatization," *Public Administration Review* 48, No. 6 (1988): 979–87.

Reich, Robert B. *Tales of a New America*. New York: Vintage Books/Random House, 1987.

Rothenberg, Janet. "Privatization of Public-Sector Services in Theory and Practice," *Journal of Policy Analysis and Management* 6, No. 4 (1987): 523–40.

Savas, E. S. *Privatizing the Public Sector: How to Shrink the Government.* Chatham, N.J.: Chatham House Publishers, 1982.

Sigelman, Lee, and Marcia Lynn Whicker. "The Growth of Government, the Ineffectiveness of Voting, and the Pervasive Political Malaise," *Social Science Quarterly* 69, No. 2 (June 1988): 299–310.

U.S. Advisory Commission on Intergovernmental Relations. *Regulatory Federalism: Policy, Process, Impact, and Reform.* Washington, D.C.: U.S. Government Printing Office, February 1984.

Walker, David B. *Toward a Functioning Federalism.* Cambridge, Mass.: Winthrop Publishers, 1981.

Wright, Deil S. *Understanding Intergovernmental Relations*, 2d Ed. Monterey, Calif.: Brooks/Cole Publishing Co., 1982.

2

Schools and Day Care

Children are the first captive population examined. Until children reach the age of legal independence, they are not only dependent on but also potentially restricted by parents, schools, and other caregivers. Two major areas of care that affect children are education and child or day care.

THE INTERRELATION OF ECONOMIC GLOBALIZATION WITH U.S. EDUCATION

During the 1980s, two interrelated trends developed: The first was an ongoing reevaluation of the economic prowess of the United States, along with its role in and competitiveness within the world economy. The second was an outpouring of concern over the quality of American schools (Carnegie Forum, 1986). Even though concern over the welfare of children was possibly the impetus for the second trend, most likely fear that that United States has lost its preeminent position in international markets and politics has been an equal or even more powerful motivator.

The effort to improve the schools in the late 1980s rivaled similar efforts in other periods. It involved many groups, including state political leaders, volunteer business groups, local officials, higher education leaders, professional educators, citizens, and parents. Each became concerned about the noticeable and measurable decline in the quality of American schools, reflected by the performance of students, and sought measures to redress the associated problems. Furthermore, for those troubled by social cohesion, education became even more important as a glue to bind a diverse and pluralist society together.

Traditionally, education has served many functions within society. More than care for any other captive population, education affects both the individual and the well-being of society at large. Economists refer to it as a mixed good, implying that education has both public and private aspects. The private aspect of education is the improvement that results for well-educated individuals in employment opportunities and increased learning potential. The public aspects include social cohesion that results from the inculcation of democratic and humanistic values by schools, as well as the improved quality of the labor force. Productivity gains have been attributed, in part, to improvements in education.

As society becomes more advanced and individuals become more mobile, the public aspects of education become more important. Increasingly during the 1980s, improvements in education were viewed as a way to restore U.S. competitiveness in international markets. Yet globalization has also heightened the importance of the private aspects of education as well. According to Robert Reich (1989), education has become the major, if not the only method, by which individuals can improve their own earning potential and counter global forces that are widening the income gap in the United States between the rich and the poor.

Reich has examined the impact of globalization on income distribution in the United States, and found that between 1978 and 1987, the poorest fifth of American families became 8 percent poorer, while the richest fifth became 13 percent richer. Because many in the poorest fifth belong to the working poor, the drop reflects a change in the wage structure of the U.S. economy as much, or more, than a drop in government spending for social services. During this decade, globalization advanced rapidly, and increasingly, U.S. workers are competing in a global labor market rather than a national one.

Globalization has not impacted all segments of the work force equally; it has positively affected the most affluent and best educated segments, and negatively affected the less educated segments. Reich splits the labor force into three major groups: symbolic-analytic workers, routine production workers, and routine service workers. All must now compete globally rather than nationally, but only the symbolic-analytic workers are doing so successfully and bettering their lot.

Symbolic-analytic workers are typically well educated and have been experiencing high personal income growth. This group may be divided into three subgroups: people who figure out how to produce goods and services more efficiently, such as scientists, managers, engineers, and consultants; people who benefit from market discrepancies or take advantage of slowness in the system, such as corporate raiders, some lawyers, and market arbitrageurs; and people who entertain, including writers, producers, performers, and business managers in entertainment and communications industries. Worldwide demand for the services of U.S. symbolic-analytic workers is high, and the salaries and wages of these groups have risen accordingly.

By contrast, the wages of the second and third groups have fallen. In a global labor market their jobs do not require highly specialized skills or, in many instances, much education; thus, the relative wages for these two groups have fallen in recent years. Routine production workers not only produce physical goods through repetitive actions but may also massage information routinely in such industries as banking and insurance. Routine service workers produce a standardized, labor-intensive service.

In earlier eras, the primary distinction in the labor force was between white-collar professional workers and blue-collar production workers. In such settings, most people were employed in hierarchical organizations, and accordingly, an inherent limit existed on the ratio of white-collar workers to blue-collar workers. Only so many white-collar workers were needed without an increase in blue-collar workers, unless an organization was to become top heavy with "too many chiefs and too few Indians." Thus, an inherent limit was built-in, restricting the individual benefits from education. A primary benefit of education was to get promoted into a white-collar managerial job, but only so many white-collar managers were needed.

By contrast, in the modern labor force symbolic-analytic workers often perform more creative work; they are employed in flat organizations, where a smaller number of employees relate more equally. Because almost everyone in the organization is engaged in brain work of a creative rather than routine nature, with the increasing mechanization of routine repetitive tasks, there are no inherent limits on the ratio of symbolic-analytic workers the economy can absorb, relative to routine workers. Thus, the limits on the value of education to the individual that existed previously have been sharply curtailed if not eliminated. There is no longer a fixed number of educated workers the economy can absorb, and future developments are likely to continue this trend.

Globalization, then, has intensified the debate over what to do about American education, since the outcome of the debate influences a far greater array of people than those immediately working in or attending school. To the degree that education impacts on national productivity, it is a debate in which both the public and private sectors have direct stakes in the outcome. Although greater consensus emerged by the end of the 1980s about the importance of improving the quality of education, dispute continued over the best way to achieve this objective and the most appropriate delivery mechanisms. This dispute over how to organize U.S. education is not new, but the continuation of a long-standing debate.

COLONIAL AND NINETEENTH-CENTURY SCHOOLS

A common myth that the United States has always embraced the notion of universal public schools has been challenged recently by Lloyd Jorgenson (1987) who argues that American schools in the colonial and early national periods were neither public nor wholly private, as we now use the terms. Rather, they were largely voluntary efforts, aided by sporadic government grants. Between 1830 and 1860, the Common School Movement vigorously advocated extending educational opportunities at the primary-school level and bringing elementary schools under civil control. This movement consolidated its power after the Civil War. As a visible manifestation of the extension of civil control over the school, the national flag frequently flew from the roofs of schoolhouses of the period, an uncommon sight in the antebellum period. Despite the efforts of various nineteenth-century church leaders and sponsors of church-related schools to resist the common school movement, by 1900 only 8 percent of primary school children were enrolled in non-public schools.

With the distinctions between public and private schools blurred during the nation's early period, governmental financial support for voluntary schools, including those with a denominational affiliation, was common. Early state constitutions and statutes actively encouraged, rather than discouraged, this practice. Governmental financial support for voluntary schools continued to increase until 1820 (Gabel, 1937).

After 1820 governmental assistance diminished but remained a significant source of school support until after the Civil War. Governmental and denominational support for many colleges also blended during this period. Indeed, the terminology of the period made no distinction between public and private institutions. New England town schools which intermingled public and Congregationalist support were called public by some and parochial by others. Similarly, the public schools of Washington and Georgetown were under private control until the mid-nineteenth century. Nor was this trend prevalent just in the more established regions; it existed in the more recently settled parts of the nation as well. In 1837 Samuel Lewis, the superintendent of schools in Ohio, was forced to concede that although he was committed in principle to public common schools, many of the schools in Ohio at the time were, in fact, private.

Greater definition to the distinction between public and private schools was made by a Massachusetts court in 1866. The court ruled that the terms *public* and *common* referred to a school (1) supported by general taxation, (2) open to all free of expense, and (3) under the immediate control and superintendence of agents appointed by the voters of each town and city. This became the standard definition for a public school, although alternative definitions continued to exist. Even in 1881 a Minnesota court ruled that a Catholic parochial school operated not for profit and open to all children was "wholly public in nature."

The Society for the Propagation of the Gospel in Foreign Parts (SPG), the foreign missionary arm of the Church of England, was the sponsor of the largest number of schools in colonial America (Jorgenson, 1987). Founded in 1701, the SPG sought to maintain an orthodox clergy in the British colonies, and to supply schools, books, and religious training for both colonists and American natives. Some observers of the time called the SPG the most important religious and philanthropic agency operating in the American colonies. The SPG was particularly dominant in the southern colonies, where it sent 197 men, and the middle colonies, which received 149 of its men. Yet it also sent eighty-four missionaries to establish schools in New England, where Puritans were dominant. Most of its revenues were donations. In New York City it offered free schooling to all children; in many colonies, including South Carolina, the government came to its assistance with appropriations.

Yet stirrings from Thomas Jefferson and others for broad dissemination of knowledge served to encourage support for public schools. The Free School Society of New York, a philanthropic enterprise, was formed to encourage the adoption of free public schools in that city. The society, a charitable corporation run by trustees, sought and received support from the state legislature in 1807. The society's efforts were well received, and eventually, all denominations in the city except the Roman Catholic, Dutch Reformed, and Associate Reformed Presbyterian relied on it to educate the children of their poor families. In 1820, however, the Bethel Baptist Church challenged the Free Society by opening a school in a section of the city it claimed the Free Society had ignored. The Baptists also appealed to and received support for their school from the state legislature, alarming the Free Society.

The Free School Society then proposed a city real estate tax to support its schools, and appointed the mayor and other prominent city officials to serve as ex-officio society trustees. The society further urged the state legislature to forbid the use of state funds for any denominational school not located next to the sponsoring church or for the education of any children whose families were not members of the sponsoring church. The Methodists and Roman Catholics submitted petitions to the state legislature supporting the positions of the Free School Society. The Methodist and Roman Catholic petitions argued that if unconditional support for the Baptists was not withdrawn, state financial assistance for schools should also be extended to them. In 1824 the New York state legislature ruled that no public money could be extended to sectarian schools in the future. The ruling, however, resulted from the competition by various religions and concern over equity rather than concern over the legal issues surrounding the principle of separation of church and state.

One major source of early funding for schools in the United States was the lottery. In a period when liquid assets were in short supply, officials used the lottery as a revenue device to fund social services. It was employed to raise monies for public purposes at all levels of government, including at the national level after the outbreak of the Revolution to fund the Revolutionary War. In 1972 Congress authorized a lottery to fund capital projects in Washington; in 1814 James Madison approved this revenue mechanism to fund a federal penitentiary. At the local level, lotteries funded bridges, roads, turnpikes, hospitals, poorhouses, fire equipment, jails, marketplaces, street paving, and water systems, as well as being used extensively to benefit churches and schools (Ezell, 1960). By 1860 at the outbreak of the Civil War, twenty-three out of thirty-three states had authorized the use of the lottery.

Between 1790 and 1860, forty-seven colleges, approximately 300 lower schools, and 200 church groups received funds from lotteries. Both Harvard and William and Mary were among colleges that at times relied on this revenue source. Its use was so prevalent that in 1832, the president of the University of North Carolina declared that any proposal to establish a southern school system supported solely by taxation was doomed to failure. Between 1826 and 1844 lotteries in Rhode Island extensively augmented the state school fund, adding over $200,000 to its coffers. New York conducted the largest lottery of the era to benefit Union College and several smaller schools. In the end, concern over fraud in lottery implementation and mounting opposition from religious groups caused this funding mechanism to fall out of favor. The opposition was moralistic, not the result of concern over separation of church and state.

By 1830 the common school movement gained ground, agitating against sectarian schools aided by public lotteries and for a state-financed and state-run monopoly in education. The common school movement consisted of a series of state movements between 1830 and 1860 that sought the expansion and improvement of elementary schools and education. It lobbied for providing schooling to all white children, partially or fully at public expense. It also sought to require school attendance, to create training programs for teachers, and to establish some degree of state control over these procedures (Church and Sedlak, 1976).

Many of the supporters of school reform were members of, or identified with, the Whig party. The Whigs, an anti-Jackson party, won in some states in the 1830s and ascended to national power in the 1840s, bridging the gap between the Federalists of the early national period and the Republican party. Horace Mann and Henry Barnard, early leaders in school reform, were both Whigs. The party had strong ties to organized protestantism. Jackson Democrats often objected to the centralizing aspects of school reform, most typically enacted by Whig state legislatures. Education reform was supported by the middle and upper classes of the period—industrialists, bankers, and large landowners—who were usually Whig Party members, as well as members of the traditional professions—law, medicine, and the ministry—also heavily Whig. In contrast to the typical positions of the Republican and Democratic parties today, the Whigs favored an active role for the government in stimulating economic activity; the Democrats were more laissez-faire.

Proponents of school reform in the early years perceived it as a basic instrument for achieving social control, and, as they defined it, social progress. Higher education levels were also perceived as crucial to further economic development and greater economic productivity. During the 1830s, many industrialized states passed laws that required children working in factories to attend school at least three months a year. Middle-class children who did not work in factories were not affected by such laws. Eventually, reform goals were broadened to require compulsory attendance of all children, often as a means of securing common values. Prior to this reform, even small "rate-bills"—fees charged to parents in proportion to the number of children they had in school—prevented many poor children from attending.

EARLY BATTLES OVER PUBLIC ASSISTANCE TO PAROCHIAL SCHOOLS

In the 1840s, dramatic population shifts laid the groundwork for changes in the school system in the 1850s. During the 1840s, over seven hundred thousand Catholics immigrated to the United States, tripling the nation's Catholic population during that decade. Political reaction to the growing actual and potential power of Catholics within the nation emerged in the form of a political party called the Know-Nothings, who openly identified immigrants and Catholics as the targets of their attacks.

Know-Nothings first appeared in eastern seaboard cities that contained a large number of immigrants, and represented the culmination of the antebellum nativist movement. Yet Know-Nothing legislative proposals had to be framed in less discriminatory terms. To keep public monies from being dispersed to religious schools, including Catholic schools, as they had been in the past, the Know-Nothings developed a strategy of advocating school aid only to nonsectarian schools. In some areas, the public monies could only be received by schools organized under state school law, a version of the strategy with the same goal and effect—preventing Catholic schools from benefiting from public coffers. Although Protestant religions also lost their access to public monies for schools, the impact was much less because most mainstream Protestant religions had already given up their schools for assurance that any religious instruction in the public schools would be Christian and Protestant in focus. This strategy produced a sharp delineation between public and private schools during the 1850s and afterwards. The Know-Nothing party eventually split over slavery debates, as did the Whigs, but before it did, its campaigns produced a turning point in American education by establishing the precedent that nonpublic schools were not eligible to receive public financial support. At the same time, state laws were passed authorizing or requiring the reading of the Bible in the common schools.

Before the Know-Nothings aligned the common school movement firmly with Protestantism and made it plainly anti-Catholic, Catholic leaders had not opposed common schools, and many were sympathetic to that cause. The Know-Nothing movement, however, sharpened the cleavage between the two religious groups. This cleavage and the school controversy subsided somewhat during and immediately after the Civil War, as national attention shifted first to fighting the war, then to rebuilding the country, and later to industrializing the nation.

During these decades, immigrant labor proved crucial to the nation, first by joining the Union Army and second by supplying factories with the work force needed for industrialization. Mining enterprises, in particular, depended on immigrant labor, and manufacturing was only slightly less dependent. Fear of immigrants among native-born Americans began to diminish, and the notion of the melting pot, with the nation absorbing and assimilating various peoples from different cultures became popular. Melting pot philosophy was espoused before the war by Emerson, Whitman, and Melville, and after the war by Darwin, Spencer, W. T. Harris, and Frederick Jackson Turner (Jorgenson, 1987). Debates over the school question during this age of confidence were more easily resolved in compromises negotiated locally.

Exemplary of this new atmosphere was a compromise worked out in 1862 in the Massachusetts legislature. Because Protestant denominations typically used the King James version of the Bible, scripture reading in the schools was from that version. In Grafton, Massachusetts, a boy who refused to read from the Protestant version of the Bible was expelled from a public school. This and similar cases prompted a Catholic priest to propose a statute to the legislature prohibiting any student from being expelled from a public school against the wishes of his parents for failure to recite any particular form of prayer or to read any particular version of the Bible. During the Know-Nothing era a few years earlier, this legislation would have been handily dismissed. By the early 1860s, the legislature was willing to work out a compromise allowing the school committee in each locality to continue to require daily reading of some portion of the Bible, but forbidding the committee to require any scholar in the public schools to read from any particular version.

Despite a new willingness to compromise, the debate over public aid to church-related schools continued after the Civil War; in 1869 proponents of public aid for parochial schools in New York City won their first major battle of the period. Although political boss William M. Tweed of Tammany Hall was a Protestant, he developed a plan for subsidizing parochial schools to gain the support of the Irish and Germans, most of whom were Catholic and composed a large part of Tweed's political base. Despite his careful attempts to disguise its true intent, the purpose of Tweed's plan was readily perceived by the Republican majority in the New York State Legislature and it was defeated.

Tweed responded by embodying the same proposals in the annual tax-levy bill for the government of New York City. Hidden in the complex, lengthy budget bill, it received legislative approval. Soon Republicans detected the disguise, however, and in 1870 the legislature was inundated with proposals to repeal the "school steal." Tweed salvaged what he could, but the next year, after this fleeting success, the legislature adopted a law forbidding New York City from appropriating money for any institution or enterprise under the control of a religious denomination.

Even though Tweed's attempts to achieve a much-needed social welfare program for his constituents were successful in an era when powerful elites rejected the notion of public responsibility for social welfare, his attempts to secure public assistance for parochial schools were not. Nor was this outcome unique to New York. During the 1870s, several states, most of which already had statutes prohibiting public assistance to schools with religious affiliations, added these prohibitions to their state constitutions. Among the states grounding this separation of church and state into constitutional cement were Missouri, Illinois, Pennsylvania, New Jersey, Nebraska, Texas, Colorado, and Minnesota.

Several local plans were developed in the late 1800s to incorporate Catholic schools into the public schools. Such experiments were tried in Lowell, Massachusetts; Pittsburgh, Pennsylvania; New Haven, Connecticut; and Savannah, Georgia, as well as several New York towns, including Poughkeepsie, Lima, Elmira, Corning, Albion, and Medina. Some of these plans were more successful than others. Often the prospect of combining school systems arose because the parochial system fell on hard times and was to be closed. In at least one arrangement, Catholic children were to arrive half an hour early at the school to receive religious instruction before the formal school day began. Eventually, opposition arose to such shared ventures from both Catholics and Protestants. Catholics feared their children who attended public schools would receive inferior religious training and become less devout. Protestants often contended that the joint arrangements were generally untenable and that public schools should be strictly nonsectarian. Some Protestant leaders feared that public schools would also diminish the devoutness of Protestants and advocated greater emphasis on religious training in public schools. By the late 1800s Protestant opposition to public school Bible reading emerged and began to grow, joining the long-standing opposition of Catholics. Catholics had opposed public school Bible reading because the Protestant version of the Scriptures was typically read in public schools. Despite growing opposition to Bible reading in schools, the National Teachers' Association (later the National Education Association [NEA]) continued to stress the importance of teachers emphasizing religious training and Christian morality in the public schools throughout the remainder of the 1800s. Further, Catholics were often the targets of NEA speakers who accused the Roman hierarchy of undermining the common school to assist the "foreign element."

Even though the early-nineteenth-century consensus on the desirability of public school scripture reading severely eroded, this practice continued in some locales until the mid-twentieth century. A 1949 NEA survey revealed that twelve states required Bible reading in the public schools, and another twenty-five states allowed it. In 1962 in response to another NEA survey, 42 percent of all responding public school officials claimed that the Bible was read in their schools, and another 8 percent acknowledged a devotional service of some type (Dierenfield, 1969). About a hundred years after the common school movement began, one of its principles—Bible reading in public schools—was definitely struck down. In 1963 in the *School District of Abington Township v. Schempp*, the U.S. Supreme Court overturned the laws of thirty-seven states that either allowed or required Bible reading and the recitation of the Lord's Prayer as devotional practices in the public schools.

RECENT CONFLICTS OVER RELIGION IN THE PUBLIC SCHOOLS

Despite a long history of overlap between religious practices and public education in the United States, the U.S. Constitution provides two Bill of Rights guarantees in the First Amendment to limit the influence of religion on American secular life, including education. The two guarantees that concern religion are the "establishment" clause and the "free exercise" clause. Congress is prohibited from "making any law respecting the establishment of religion, or prohibiting the free exercise thereof." The implementation of these principles in recent years has involved a delicate balance, often judicially determined. In 1971 in *Lemon v. Kurtzman*, the U.S. Supreme Court developed a three-part test to ascertain whether the establishment clause had been violated. Laws that meet the Supreme Court criteria must have a secular religious purpose; their primary effect must neither enhance nor inhibit religion; and government must avoid excessive entanglement with religion (Whicker and Moore, 1988).

In 1985 the Supreme Court reinforced its earlier rulings in the *Schempp* case by striking down in *Wallace v. Jaffree* an Alabama law authorizing teachers to hold one-minute moments of silence for meditation or voluntary prayer; the court stated that the law obviously had a religious purpose. The court also ruled that states may not prohibit teaching evolution or discussing Darwin's theory of evolution. And, religious literature may be read in public schools only as part of secular curriculum.

Various court rulings have also refined what is allowable in financing public and parochial schools. Although church property, which is often used for religious schools that serve as alternatives to public schools is tax exempt, until recently parent-paid tuition for parochial and other private schools was not tax exempt. In *Mueller v. Allen* in a close decision, the U.S. Supreme Court upheld a Minnesota law in 1983 allowing all taxpayers to deduct from their state income taxes—up to a specified ceiling—monies paid for tuition, textbooks, transportation, and other school costs for children attending both public and private schools. The reasoning of the Court was that the Minnesota law had a secular not a religious purpose—specifically, to promote a better education population—and therefore the law met the three part criteria it had established earlier.

In other decisions about the permissibility of public funds for parochial and private schools, the Supreme Court has drawn a fine distinction between expenditures that benefit the student and therefore are allowable, and those that benefit the school and therefore are not allowable. In the former category of expenditures benefiting the student, the Supreme Court has allowed tax funds to be used for textbooks, standardized tests, lunches, transportation to and from schools, diagnostic services for speech and hearing problems, and other remedial services in church-operated elementary and secondary schools. In the latter category of expenditures benefiting the school, the Supreme Court has not allowed tax dollars to be used in religious schools for teachers' salaries, equipment, counseling for students, teacher-prepared texts, facilities repairs, or transportation of students to and from field trips.

In recent years, the issues of religion, race, and school funding have overlapped. The 1954 landmark *Brown v. Board of Education* case forced racial desegregation. Actual desegregation did not take place in many parts of the nation, especially the South, until the civil rights movement of the 1960s, and only under federal pressure and with duress. Many white parents who did not want their children to attend racially integrated schools removed their offspring from the public schools and transferred them to private schools. Sometimes called "segregation academies," especially in the South, the private schools that accommodated the demand among white parents for public school alternatives were often sponsored by churches.

With continued racial desegregation of public schools, housing patterns began to shift in metropolitan areas, especially in the North. Public school systems in center cities became predominantly black, as middle-class whites moved to mostly white suburbs with "private public schools." Public schools in affluent suburbs were sometimes labeled private to reflect their rich resources and mostly white enrollment, characteristics similar to many private schools. Unlike private schools, however, these public suburban schools are funded by tax monies. They are protected by court orders from cross-district busing between predominantly white suburban jurisdictions and predominantly black center cities in most circumstances. Judges may not order cross-district busing unless they can establish that school district lines were drawn for the purpose of maintaining segregation and that suburban districts are also being operated in a discriminatory manner. Whites living in center cities where the enrollment in the public school systems is mostly black often opt for parochial or other private schools, so that center-city public schools remain disproportionately minority in enrollment, and suburban schools remain disproportionately white.

Most recently, especially with drug problems sweeping through the schools as well as through other aspects of life, concern has reemerged over the role of the schools in communicating values to students. In a 1984 Gallup poll, 68 percent of public school parents said that schools should place the development of moral standards—traditionally a function of religion—as a top priority. Almost as many parents believed that the schools should teach students the difference between right and wrong as thought the schools should teach students how to read and write (Mathews, 1985). Thus, the old debate surrounding the common school movement has reemerged in different form. A greater number of parents in recent years have challenged the notion that learning can be achieved without discipline and values, forcing educators to struggle once again with methods of introducing ethics into the public school curriculum without offending any group.

DO PRIVATE SCHOOLS PROMOTE PUBLIC CHOICE?

In a 1925 case, *Pierce v. Society of Sisters*, the U.S. Supreme Court held unconstitutional an Oregon law that required every parent, guardian, or other person having control of a child between the ages of eight and sixteen to send that child to a public school. Ruling that the law represented an unreasonable interference with the liberty of parents and guardians to direct the upbringing of their children, the case established the right of parents to choose private schooling, and foreclosed a public monopoly in elementary and secondary education (Hirschoff, 1986).

Today, elementary and secondary education is provided through a mixture of public and private schools. Just as pressures have existed within this mix in the past, today the system confronts demands for both fiscal and regulatory change. Proposals that would diminish the power of the state over education are under debate currently; their supporters favor providing tuition tax credits so parents can choose private schooling for their children, and creating voucher systems for parents with individual subsidies they can use when choosing public or private schools. Proposals that would increase the power of the government have also been made; they include standardization of teacher requirements, higher standards for teachers, and the imposition of more rigorous curriculum requirements on local systems.

As demands for both greater freedom of choice and greater rigor within elementary and secondary education mount, two fundamental questions confront policymakers: (1) What is a desirable mix between public and private schooling, and to what extent should the government try to encourage this mix and the provision of private school alternatives? (2) Which differences between public and private schooling should government promote or prohibit?

Many of the arguments today parallel those made in the 1920s before the ruling was handed down in the *Pierce* case. In the 1920s proponents of laws restricting private schools were afraid that they would harm the acculturation and Americanization of the children of immigrants. Today, opponents of government assistance to private schools contend that private schools exacerbate social, economic, racial, religious, and ethnic divisions within society; therefore, providing public assistance to them is undesirable. Advocates of private schools make a freedom of choice argument, contending that parents have the right to direct their children's education. They further argue that society benefits from diversity in general, and from diversity in education in particular. Nor do they agree that private schools increase social stratification any more than do public schools, or that they are less effective in creating good citizens.

Unlike the 1920s when the debate over the privatization of schools was also carried out in earnest, today great attention is placed on the quality of education. Those who advocate voucher and tuition tax credit systems that would benefit private schools argue that private schools are more efficient, effective, responsive, and flexible than the public schools. Proponents also feel that the presence of private schools as an alternative serves as a competitive spur to public schools and motivates the public schools to become better. Opponents contend that proposals enhancing private schools would erode the already weakened national commitment to public schools, and would not achieve the benefits proponents claim.

Mary-Michelle Upson Hirschoff (1986) suggests four goals for the educational system that might provide guidelines for addressing policy questions concerning the appropriate mix of public and private schools. The goals she posits are

1. *Enhancing Parental Choice*: By this criterion, parents should have the ability to choose the schooling they want and can afford for their children.

2. *Promoting Pluralism*: Pluralism implies diversity, both in schooling and in the larger society.

3. *Achieving Social Unity*: Social unity means assuring that all citizens share values, attitudes, skills, and knowledge considered basic to proper functioning within society. It also means providing equal educational opportunity, so that the positions people assume within society as adults depend on merit rather than accidents of birth. Merit-based systems are viewed as fair and reduce the potential for social division based on perceptions of unfairness in the competition for jobs, power, and income.

4. *Raising Educational Quality*: All schooling should meet minimum standards and the overall educational system should exhibit as much total quality as possible. What is learned (educational effectiveness), what is taught to whom (responsiveness), and the amount of resources devoted to schooling and how efficiently they are used (resource allocation and efficiency) all affect educational quality.

Elementary and secondary education remain primarily a state and local function, so that the legal structure affecting the mix between public and private schools is not uniform, but varies from state to state. In all states, however, the basic form of financing is similar. Public schools are financed through taxes and are tuition free, while private schools depend on tuition payments, donations, and volunteer or low-priced labor for fiscal support, with some, but not much, governmental assistance.

Public regulation of private schools in most states has been minimal, and where it exists, has rarely been enforced rigorously. Thus, private schools have typically enjoyed greater freedom in setting policies, curricula, hiring, and making changes than have public schools. In 1986 about 11 percent of all elementary and secondary school children in the United States attended private schools. Of those attending private schools, 89 percent attended nonprofit schools. Very few for-profit schools exist at these educational levels.

Private schools receive government assistance through exemption from taxation in addition to receiving government services and financial aid in some instances. Nonprofit schools are exempt from state and federal income taxes, and from state property taxes. Donations to private nonprofit schools may be deducted from the donor's taxable income, thus providing a tax incentive to encourage contributions. Even though direct public assistance to private schools has been ruled unconstitutional by the Supreme Court as a violation of the establishment clause, public assistance to parents and their children has been allowed, as discussed previously.

Direct government assistance to private schools may originate at the federal, state, or local levels. State and local agencies administer such aid, even when its origin is the federal government, unless state law prohibits their participation. One important source of federal assistance has been Title I of the Elementary and Secondary Education Act of 1965, which is now Chapter I of the Education Consolidation and Improvement Act of 1981—a Reagan era block grant. This title focuses on aiding educationally disadvantaged children. Compared to the public schools, however, only a small portion of private school children benefit from this program. At the beginning of the Reagan years in 1981, an estimated 3.8 percent of all private school children—most attending Catholic schools—participated in this program for the educationally handicapped.

The funding basis for private schools differs substantially from that of public schools. About 8 percent of all public school funds originate with the federal government. Both state taxes and local property taxes fund public schools. Although local property taxes used to be the primary source of public school funds, recent pressures on states for equalizing resources available to public schools has led to greater emphasis on earmarking a variety of state taxes for education. While state laws vary, many states grant public schools the right to charge fees for extracurricular activities, and may charge tuition for students who live outside the local school district boundaries.

REGULATION OF PUBLIC AND PRIVATE SCHOOLS

Public School Regulation

Typically, states impose regulations on public state-operated schools that are not imposed on private schools, even though the goal of educating students is the same in each. Because public schools are government agencies, they must comply with the constitutional limits placed on governmental action. In addition to the limits on school prayer and

other religious exercises described earlier, the Supreme Court has protected students right to free speech, required segregated public schools
to desegregate, imposed busing to achieve racial balance, and required
that pupil suspensions be imposed in accordance with standards of
fairness under the due process clause. Private schools, by contrast, are
not required to operate under these restraints. Further, in 1982 the Court
established in *Plyler v. Doe* that public schools must be open to all students within their geographic boundaries when it held unconstitutional
the exclusion of children of illegal aliens from free public education in
Texas.

State legislatures and state boards of education share with locally
elected or appointed school boards the power to determine the curriculum, method of teaching, and general operations of public schools. Proponents of public schools argue that these mechanisms assure that the
process of making decisions is controlled democratically, and that there
is accountability to the public. Critics argue that the patrons of any particular public school may not like its operations and may prefer an alternative form of education. Even though federal assistance constitutes a
minor part of total educational funding, much of the enforcement of regulations in public schools, including regulations assuring constitutional
treatment of students, is tied to federal assistance.

Private School Regulation

Private schools are not government agencies; therefore, they do not
need to comply with many of the requirements placed on public schools.
Private schools are primarily affected by constitutional limits on the
government regulation of and assistance to private schools. Because
private monies, not public funds, are the fiscal basis for private schools,
regulatory efforts beyond assuring minimum compliance with compulsory school attendance laws have not been attempted in most states.

Private schools must adhere to the same general laws that apply to
any private business, and when they are nonprofit, as is almost always
the case, may be entitled to special treatment. Private schools must
comply, as any business must, with generally applicable laws such as
building codes, zoning, fire and health codes. They must also comply
with laws governing charitable solicitations and preventing consumer
fraud; these laws do not apply to public schools. Few demands have
been made for special regulations related to education, in exchange for
tax exemptions or limited government assistance. Generally, private
schools meet few government regulations to receive these benefits, other
than a requirement of nonprofit status and, more recently, imposed
restrictions against racial discrimination (Hirschoff, 1986).

The state requirements on private schools may be enforced either directly through mandatory state accreditation or licensing, or indirectly by finding and fining parents who send their children to noncomplying schools. A 1981 survey found, however, that only eighteen states at that time had some form of mandatory accreditation, approval, or licensure. Alabama, one of the eighteen, required licensing only for proprietary schools and not for nonprofit schools, while a few additional states excluded church-related schools from any requirement for licensing or accreditation.

Comparisons of Public and Private Regulation

Important differences in federal and state regulation of public and private schools exist in the areas of school control, teacher hiring and firing, student selection and discipline, and school curriculum.

School Control. Membership on public school boards is typically prescribed within state law, which stipulates whether or not the board is elected or appointed, and whether parents, teachers, and students must be involved in the decision process as well as school board members. States also exert considerable administrative control over local school boards. By contrast, private schools do not even have to incorporate in many states, or must only comply with limited incorporation procedures. Even though private schools are not required to organize as nonprofits, if they do so and meet limited technical requirements, they retain freedom in governing themselves, and may structure the board however they wish, including creating a self-perpetuating board.

Teacher Hiring and Firing. The education requirements and the teacher certification process for public school teachers is also prescribed within state law, as are rules and procedures governing teacher dismissal, tenure, and retirement. Thus, these facets of education have been largely removed from local school board control. Public school teachers also have free speech and due process rights under the Constitution. In most states, where public school teachers have labor organizations, state collective bargaining laws govern negotiations with school administration officials.

By contrast, few regulations in the area of teacher hiring and firing exist for private schools. In the early 1980s, only thirteen states required teacher certification for private school teachers, leaving private schools free to hire whomever they wished to teach. Wherever private school teachers are organized into unions, their negotiations with school administrators would be governed by the National Labor Relations Act; most are not organized and, therefore, are not affected by this statute.

Student Selection and Discipline. Public schools also operate under more regulations and constraints in student selection and discipline. They are required to accept and educate any child living within the geographic boundaries of the school district, and must adopt and enforce rules concerned with discipline, suspensions, and expulsions that follow specified procedures. Private contracts between school officials and patrons govern discipline, suspensions, and expulsions in private school settings.

Racial discrimination has been a particular focus of government regulation and enforcement. Public schools that receive federal funds are restricted from discrimination on the basis of race, color, national origin, sex, or handicap. Private schools are similarly restricted if they receive federal funds; few do. Further, a federal statute (42 U.S.C. 1981) in the Civil Rights Act of 1866 allows private schools to teach only those students they wish to admit, as long as discrimination on the basis of race is not a criterion.

In the 1976 *Runyon v. McCrary*, the Supreme Court upheld this federal statute and repeatedly stated that the prohibition that private schools should not discriminate on the basis of race did not prevent the schools from inculcating the values desired by the parents. The 1983 case of *Bob Jones University v. United States* also upheld regulations prohibiting racial discrimination by private schools. Bob Jones University and a private elementary and secondary school engaged in racially discriminatory practices, claiming religious beliefs as the justification. These schools charged that an Internal Revenue Service (IRS) policy denying them tax-exempt status and charitable deductions because they discriminated racially also denied them free exercise of religion and was unconstitutional. The U.S. Supreme Court rejected this claim and upheld the IRS.

Curriculum. Considerable variation exists in state regulation of private school curricula. Some states impose no curriculum requirements on private schools; others leave that power for state education administrators, while some states delegate it to the local authorities who also enforce compulsory school attendance laws. In those states where requirements have been established, the wording is typically vague, only specifying that private school curricula must be equivalent to public school curricula.

Only recently have some state education agencies begun enforcing state regulations on the curricula of private schools. Frequently, state regulations specify subjects required to be taught, such as U.S. history, civics, government, the federal and state constitutions, reading, writing spelling, and arithmetic. Other requirements, imposed less frequently in the past, may include health and drug education, instruction in patriotism and good citizenship, and recognition of the contributions of women and minorities. Despite the growing size of the U.S. Hispanic population, some states require that all classes be taught in English.

The average state imposes far more regulations on the curricula of public schools than on those of private schools. Often textbooks must be selected from a list of books approved by the state. Public schools may be required to teach sex and consumer education to all students, and to make vocational education available to those students who want it. Both federal and state laws compel public schools to provide education to physically handicapped children. Federal law forces schools receiving federal funds to remedy any language deficiency that prevents equal participation of non-English speaking children in school programs. Some states also mandate local districts to provide bilingual education.

FEDERAL POLICIES FOR PRIVATE SCHOOLS

During the 1980s, the debate over the relationship of the federal government to private education shifted, moving from a focus on requirements in federal legislation for program services for private school students to discussions of new funding devices, such as tuition tax credits and vouchers that would enhance educational choice for parents (Kutner et al., 1986). In contrast to state and local monies, federal assistance is a small portion of the total and is generally targeted for specific populations of students, such as the economically and educationally disadvantaged, the handicapped, or students with limited English proficiency. Sometimes federal assistance is targeted for specific purposes, such as vocational rehabilitation. When aid is targeted for specific students or purposes, private school students may be eligible to receive an equitable share of federally funded services.

Major Statutes

The Elementary and Secondary Education Act of 1965. Several major federal statutes have provided the legal framework for federal assistance to both public and private schools. In 1965 the first of these major statutes, the Elementary and Secondary Education Act (ESEA) redefined the federal role in education. It was the first federal program to contain provisions requiring federally funded services for private schools and students. Before a compromise allowed the passage of ESEA, the unresolved question of federal aid to religious schools had been a stumbling block to federal aid for education.

The ESEA compromise between the interest groups representing public schools and those representing religious organizations sponsoring church-related schools was to adopt a child-benefit approach to federal aid. As reflected in Title I of ESEA, which is now Chapter 1 of the Education Consolidation and Improvement Act of 1981, the agreement focused on educationally disadvantaged children in both public and private schools, and was not considered to be aid to the school system itself. Subsequently, local school districts were required to make educational services paid for by the federal government available to eligible students in private schools as well as in public schools.

Title II of ESEA was concerned with school library resources, textbooks, and other instructional materials. This title authorized federal grants to states for the purchase of materials for both public and private schools. If state law prohibited involvement in the program by private schools, the U.S. commissioner of education was authorized to provide these program benefits directly to exclude private school students, thereby circumventing state law.

The Vocational Education Act of 1968. Since 1965 federal statutes have become more explicit pertaining to private school student participation in federal programs. Private school students have been included in most programs. In Part G of the 1968 amendments to the Vocational Education Act, states participating in cooperative vocational education programs were required to make provisions in their state plans to allow students in nonprofit, private schools to participate. States were also directed to ensure full participation in the program by eligible students in private schools.

The Educational Amendments of 1974. Several provisions were included in the 1974 amendments to ensure Title I services as well as the new Title IV (a consolidation of ESEA Titles II and III) services, were provided to eligible private school students. Under Title I, local education agencies were specifically required to provide for eligible children in private schools to receive special education services and arrangements, such as dual enrollment, educational radio and television, and mobile educational equipment. Should local educational agencies not comply, the commissioner of education was authorized to provide the services directly to private school students.

Title IV dealt with libraries, learning resources, educational innovation, and support. Title IV amendments required that students in nonprofit schools receive an equitable share of these services. As with Title I, the federal government was authorized to provide the services directly if state officials did not comply. Title VII focused on bilingual education; 1974 amendments specified that grant applications submitted to local education agencies were to include provisions for an equitable distribution of bilingual funds to private school students.

Education for All Handicapped Children Act of 1975. Often called P.L. 94–142, the Education for All Handicapped Children Act required states to establish goals of full educational opportunity to all handicapped children by providing free public educations for all handicapped children between the ages of three and eighteen. States were required to submit plans that incorporated private school handicapped students as well as public school students.

Vocational Education Act of 1976. Although the 1968 amendments to the

Vocational Education Act stated that private school students should be included, these mandates had been largely ignored. In 1976 Congress acted by passing additional amendments with greater specificity about how to increase the participation of nonprofit school students in federal educational programs. The 1976 amendments called for basic grants that could support services in private, profit-making vocational schools as well as nonprofit private schools. Both state and national advisory education councils were required to include individuals with backgrounds in and familiarity with nonprofit schools. Further, local educational agencies could only receive program funds for disadvantaged students if provisions were made for nonprofit private schools to participate.

The 1978 Education Amendments. This legislation tightened and clarified earlier provisions concerning participation in federal assistance programs by private school students. Additionally, complaint procedures were established for all federal programs. Local education agencies were directed to provide private school students with equitable services in the areas of compensatory services (ESEA Title I), basic skills (Title II), special projects (Title III), educational improvement resources and support (Title IV), and gifted and talented education (Title IX). Procedures for direct federal provision of services to private school students if state officials did not comply were authorized for Title VII (bilingual education), and were simplified for Title I and Title IV. Participation of private students was extended to include formal procedures for complaints under Title I and Title V, concerning state leadership. Title V also authorized monies for private schools to provide information and technical assistance if the private schools wished to participate in Title I and Title IV.

The Education Consolidation and Improvement Act of 1981. The Education Consolidation and Improvement Act (ECIA) merged earlier legislation to reduce paperwork and regulatory constraints placed previously on state and local education agencies receiving federal funds. Chapter 1 modified requirements in ESEA Title I but did not alter the provisions requiring private school participation, including equitable provisions of program services under certain conditions.

In Chapter 2, twenty-nine smaller categorical programs were consolidated into a block grant for educational improvement, including many programs that contained provisions for participation by private school students: ESEA Titles II, III, IV, V, and IX. Bilingual education, Title VII, remained a separate program with private school participation requirements similar to those existing before 1981. Among these requirements were authorization for state education agencies to provide funds to private school students even if the local education agency did not apply for funds for that use. Further, the U.S. commissioner of education was charged with providing federal aid directly to private school students if state law prohibited state officials from doing so.

Private School Student Participation in Federal Programs

How often have private school students availed themselves of federal aid? At the beginning of the Reagan era, in the 1979–80 school year, private schools served about 193,000 students in Title I programs, or about 3.8 percent of total private enrollments. About 25 percent of local education agencies provided services for students in private schools, a slight decline from earlier years. This drop in Title I participation for private school students has been attributed to a shift in the composition of those students. In recent years, Catholic schools, which were most likely to participate in Title I, experienced a drop in enrollments, reducing the Catholic school share of total private school enrollments. During the same period, Christian-Fundamentalist schools, which were least likely to participate in Title I, experienced increasing enrollments and an increasing share of total private school enrollments (Kutner et al., 1986). Evaluation studies comparing the use of Title I services for public and private schools within the same district found that for private school students receiving Title I benefits, classes were shorter and smaller; the private school instructor had the same average number of years of service as the public school instructor but worked with a smaller pupil/instructor ratio, and that Title I services could be better coordinated with regular classes.

Participation by private school students in ESEA Title IV (now Chapter 2 under ECIA) was more extensive. In 1980 over half of all private schools received services under Title IV-B, but only between one-fourth and one-third of Title IV-C innovation projects were available in private schools (McDonnell and McLaughlin, 1980). Nor were private school principals and superintendents consulted by public school officials in the planning and designing of IV-C programs. Public officials were found to be unwilling to provide technical assistance to private schools to help them seek out IV-C monies, and private schools were found to be generally uninformed about the program and unwilling to devote time and energy pursuing more information. Nor did private schools participate to any significant extent in federally funded vocational education services, because most private schools do not offer vocational education programs.

PROPOSALS TO BROADEN FEDERAL FUNDING OF PRIVATE SCHOOLS

The overall federal role in financing private schools has remained minor, and has been targeted toward specific students and services. During the Reagan era, when privatization was very popular, proposals to extend the federal role in private school financing were proffered, with tuition tax credits receiving the greatest attention. Vouchers were considered less appropriate at the federal level, because over 90 percent of school system funding is derived from state and local governments. In contrast to vouchers, compensatory education grants (direct subsidies to the educationally disadvantaged) could be provided at the federal level, but the political mood was such that proposals for the disadvantaged generated little political support or hope of enactment.

Factors in Parental Selection of Schools

The U.S. Department of Education through its School Finance Project surveyed 1,200 households in 1982 to secure more information about possible public response to tuition tax credits. Parents were also asked which schools their children currently attended and why those schools were selected. The results revealed that most parents with children in public schools did not consider alternative schools within or outside the district, but did consider the quality of schools when choosing a school district in which to live. Over half of the parents of public school attendees, for example, considered school quality when selecting a residence, and for 18 percent of the parents, school quality was the most important factor. Once the choice of residence was made, however, school quality, and whether or not children should be educated in public schools was rarely questioned. For example, 80 percent of all parents never questioned the choice of public schools beyond deciding where to live, a finding that was true for all demographic categories surveyed. These conclusions also matched other studies of parental choice in selecting schools (Nault and Uchitell, 1982).

In this Department of Education survey, the socioeconomic and demographic characteristics of public and private school parents were significantly different. Private school parents tended to be better educated, to have higher family incomes, to be Catholic, to have attended private schools themselves, and to live in large or medium-size cities. Public school parents were more likely to live in nonmetropolitan settings and to have attended public schools themselves. The incomes and education levels of public school parents were lower, and the tendency to be Protestant was higher.

Survey respondents were questioned about the role various factors played in their selection of schools for their own children. Three factors mentioned most frequently by all the respondents accounted for two-thirds of all the answers given. Most important, and mentioned 25 percent of the time, was the assignment of the child to a particular school. Second most important, and mentioned 22 percent of the time, was transportation or convenience. Academic considerations were third in importance and mentioned 20 percent of the time. No other factor influencing school selection was mentioned more than 10 percent of the time.

The relative importance of these selection factors differed substantially for public and private school parents. For private school parents academic quality was the most important factor cited by 42 percent of private school parents. Values or religious instruction was second in importance and was cited 30 percent of the time. Discipline, the third most important factor was mentioned 12 percent of the time. For public school parents, the three most important school selection factors were the fact that a student was assigned to a particular school (28 percent), transportation (24 percent), and academic quality (17 percent).

Despite these differences between the overall groups of public and private school parents, public school parents who had considered but rejected private school alternatives for their children did not differ significantly in selection factors from private school parents. Both of these groups considered academic quality to be the most important factor. Where these two groups did differ was in the greater weight placed by public school parents on the financial costs of private schools, and the greater weight placed by private school parents on values and religious training.

Factors Associated with School Transfers

A subset of students in this Department of Education survey had attended both public and private schools. Almost half of private school students had attended public schools previously, while 17 percent of public school students had once attended private schools. For parents whose children switched from private to public schools, the cost of private schooling was the most frequently cited reason (24 percent in this category). The lack of available private schooling also influenced decisions to switch to public schools. Twenty-one percent in this category changed residences and moved away from the private schools their children had been attending. Nine percent said that the private school their children had attended did not have higher grades. At the kindergarten level, 17 percent said that their local public school district did not provide public kindergartens, so private kindergartens were the only available source of schooling at this level. When public schools became available at the first grade, some parents then transferred their children to the public school system. Thus, financial and logistic factors seem to drive parental decisions to switch from private to public schools.

The reasons parents transferred their children from public to private schools were quite different. The most important factors to this category of parents were academic quality (27 percent), discipline (25 percent), religious instruction and value orientation (25 percent), and quality of teachers (12 percent). Dissatisfaction with various facets of public schools seemed to drive parental decisions to transfer their children from the public system to a private school.

Public and private school parents held different views of the costs of private schooling. Costs were a major inhibition to the selection of private schools for public school parents, particularly less affluent parents, but it was not a major concern to private school parents. Nor did private school parents consider tuition expenses for their children particularly burdensome. Proponents of tuition tax credits for private schools have cited this differential orientation toward tuition costs in arguing that such tax credits would decrease the proportion of parents who do not consider alternatives to neighborhood schools and subsequently increase the proportion of children attending private schools.

Parental Interest in Tuition Tax Credits

About 55 percent of the parents surveyed by the Department of Education had heard about a tuition tax credit, although private school parents were far more likely to have heard about tax credit proposals than public school parents. When parents were asked how likely they would be to change their children's schools if a tax credit were available, over half (55 percent) said they probably would not transfer their children out of public schools to private schools, even if all tuition costs were covered. Proposals for higher levels of tax credit increased the likelihood of parents transferring their children to private schools; only 23 percent said they would be "very likely" or "somewhat likely" to transfer their children for a $250 tax credit. Private school parents were much less sensitive to changing schools in response to varying dollar amounts of tax credits.

Public school parents inclined to switch for a $250 tax credit were disproportionately black or Hispanic, had lower incomes and less education, and were residents of large or medium-size cities. Thus, the group most likely to consider switching to private schools in response to the availability of tuition tax credits is considerably less affluent and nonwhite than either public or private school students as overall groups. Region and whether or not the parents had attended private schools did not influence these responses. Similar patterns held for inquiries about higher level tax credits. Parents who had cited financial issues as a reason for selecting public rather than private schooling were far more likely to consider switching to private schools with a tax credit.

These survey results most likely overestimate, however, the public school parents who would actually switch their children to private schools with the adoption of a tuition tax credit (Kutner et al., 1986).

The decision to switch is a four-stage process, with the potential for not going ahead with the transfer at any stage. It involves:

1. Developing an interest in taking advantage of the tax credit;
2. Applying to one or more available private schools;
3. Being admitted to at least one private school; and
4. Actual enrollment in a private school.

The demand for and supply of private schools influences each of these stages, as do financial costs associated with tuition and tuition tax credits.

PRIVATE SCHOOL ENROLLMENT AND TYPES

Private school enrollment shifted composition during the past two decades, reflecting a significant decrease in enrollment in Catholic schools and a sharp increase in non-Catholic private schools. During the fifteen-year period between 1965 and 1980, Catholic school enrollment dropped by almost half, from 5.57 million to 3.11 million. Non-Catholic private school enrollment rose from 0.73 million to 2.15 million during the same time period (Erickson, 1986).

Catholic Schools

Various factors contributed to the enrollment declines in Catholic schools. In earlier eras, Catholic schools were popular among the devout who often felt that their church was under siege in a predominantly Protestant America. Young Catholics were sometimes attacked in public schools. Because the church did not have the resources to provide the option of attending Catholic schools to all of its students, it worked to reduce the overt Protestant bias within the public schools. These efforts were so successful that public schools became congenial to Catholics, and the need for building or expanding Catholic schools diminished (Ryan, 1963).

Developments associated with the Second Vatican Council, which ended in 1965, also raised questions in the minds of some American Catholics about the desirability of Catholic schools, and the attractiveness of religious communities of nuns, priests, and brothers. Once an esteemed life-style, religious orders diminished. When the Second Vatican Council gave the remaining nuns and brothers greater freedom, many left teaching in Catholic schools to pursue other ministries. Once reliant on the cheap labor of nuns especially, many Catholic schools had to hire more expensive lay teachers as the number of religious available for teaching decreased. Further, as the demographic character of many religious orders aged due to fewer new recruits, many of the remaining nuns and brothers became more expensive because they were now responsible for supporting a growing number of elderly in their orders. As the number of religious instructors in Catholic schools declined, so did the uniquely Catholic atmosphere, and religious reasons for attending Catholic schools, once foremost in the minds of many parents, became secondary.

Many Catholic school superintendents decided to supplant religious instruction with the goal of academic excellence as a motivator for enrollment. In many areas where enrollments were declining, school budgets were limited. Strategies employed by Catholic schools to improve academic quality have been criticized for being unimaginative. Catholic school administrators reduced class size, increased teachers' salaries, and diminished teacher turnover. These strategies increased costs and contributed to the closing of many Catholic Schools (Walberg 1984; Larson, 1972). As white middle-class Catholics left center cities for the suburbs, the church stopped building schools. Proponents of Catholic schools challenged the decisions of American bishops to halt the new school construction, arguing that pent-up demand for Catholic education exists both in the suburbs, primarily from Catholics, and in the inner cities from both Catholics and non-Catholics including non-Catholic minorities. Yet many of the Catholics who migrated to the suburbs lost interest in Catholic education, and many of the minorities in inner cities were unable to afford fees high enough to allow the schools to become financially sound.

Even with the decline in parochial school enrollment as a share of private school enrollments, Catholic schools remained the largest alternative to the public schools, and constitute over half of all private schools. Further, sociologist Andrew Greeley and colleagues (1976) challenged the assumption that the Catholic laity had lost interest in Catholic education, citing figures showing that while only 35 percent of Catholic parents of school-age children surveyed reported children in parochial schools, 38 percent of the remainder said that no parochial school was available.

Eighty-nine percent of Catholics rejected the statement that "the Catholic school system is no longer needed in modern-day life," and 80 percent said they would increase their contributions to save a financially troubled school system. Many Catholics have praised parochial schools for affecting the values of parochial school students to be more tolerant of others, change oriented and flexible, and secure in both their worldview and their loyalty to past traditions. Greeley advanced the thesis that what was needed was for the church hierarchy to get out of the school business and to turn control of parochial schools over to the laity, whom, he asserted were able and willing to run them. The church hierarchy predictably rejected Greeley's advice, and parochial schools remain in a period of flux and transition (Hunt and Kunkel, 1984).

Fundamentalist Schools

In contrast to Catholic schools, Fundamentalist Christian schools have experienced growth during the past two decades. The fact that the public schools became less Protestantlike in character appealed to Catholics, but increased the dissatisfaction of Fundamentalists, who have developed a philosophy of integrating church and school to bring about the broadest possible control over students (Peshkin, 1986).

Before the U.S. Supreme Court ruled in the 1960s that official prayer and Bible reading were unconstitutional in the public schools, many Fundamentalists were opposed to the Christian Day School movement, feeling that children would be stronger if they were not sheltered, and that Christian children had a mission to bear witness to their faith in the public schools. The court rulings, along with controversies over whether schools could discuss creationism and concern over "sex, drugs, and rock and roll" infiltrating the public schools caused many Fundamentalists to reverse their positions and promote separate schools (Carper, 1984). A firm from Lewiston, Texas, called Accelerated Christian Education (ACE) began to sell prepackaged learning materials that greatly reduced the administrative and instructional skill needed to start a school. ACE also sold instructions on how to manage every step of school functioning. Throughout the 1970s and 1980s, the number of Fundamentalist Christian schools continued to grow.

Jewish Day Schools

An upswing in religious sentiment among Jews in the United States after World War II and the creation of the state of Israel, along with discontent among Jewish leaders about what could be accomplished with part-time religious instruction, created interest in expanding Jewish day schools (Rauch, 1984; Erickson, 1986). Postwar immigrants were also intensely religious and held similar interests. Further, concern over waning identification with Jewish life due to intermarriage, a declining birthrate, and a desire to perpetuate the distinctiveness of Jewish life also gave impetus to expand Jewish day schools. Finally, Jews living in urban areas with deteriorating public schools were looking for alternative forms of schooling. Previously unable to afford private schools, many Jews experienced new prosperity after the war, making private schools possible. By 1980 Jewish day schools numbered more than 300 and enrollment had surpassed 100,000. Nonetheless, these schools represent a small part of the total number of private schools and the private school enrollment.

Boarding Schools

Underlying the image of many private schools in America is that of the traditional boarding school or prep school. Just as religious schools have the transmission of values as part of their educational mission, value transmission has also been an important part of education in elite schools (Baird, 1977; McLachlan, 1970). Exactly which values are inculcated is less clear. In an examination of elite boarding schools, including Phillips Exeter, Groton, and St. Paul's, James McLachlan contests the notion that rich parents send their children to these schools to learn upper-class values, manners, and speech. What they learned about such things, he argues, they learned before they left home and from their peers, since most if not all of their instructors were middle-class intellectuals. Rather, the values transmitted by American boarding schools were to educate students so that they would neither drop out nor sit-in. Students were to be formed to the ideals of noblesse oblige, which were classically conservative—concerned about the moral development of society and willing and able to take an active part in that development.

The high cost of American boarding schools makes them primarily accessible to the children of the affluent. When surveying forty-two independent boarding schools in 1976, Leonard Baird found that the family income of attending students exceeded $40,000. Thus, only for the highest income strata do boarding schools represent an alternative to public or other private schools. Interested in whether or not such high-priced schools were worth the cost, Baird devised a survey to compare the responses of public school students to those of students in these independent schools. Survey questions measured perceptions of educational quality. Ten public schools were studied at the same time as the independent schools. The public schools were from affluent areas, with median family income for those attending exceeding $22,000 in 1976, placing the public school students in the sample in the top 90 percent of family incomes. Additionally, the parents of these public school students were well educated, with 43 percent of their fathers and 24 percent of their mothers being college graduates—compared to 80 and 60 percent for the independent school students. The two groups of students, then, were more similar in socioeconomic status than would have been the case if public schools in less affluent areas had been selected.

Compared to 55 percent of public school students, 74 percent of independent school students believed that most of their teachers encouraged classroom discussion and understood the work that was done in class. Forty-seven percent of the independent school students, compared to 27 percent of the public school students indicated that their teachers were understanding of student academic problems. Seventy-two percent of independent school students found that their teachers were friendly outside the classroom compared with 31 percent of public school students.

Few in either group of students indicated that their teachers stimulated students to think and be creative, or that the teachers made classes interesting, but independent school students were slightly less skeptical about these two issues. Nor did the students in the two groups differ in their descriptions of their teachers' clarity, the relevance of class material to current events, the pace at which teachers presented materials, the extent to which they challenged students, their encouragement of independent work, their encouragement of originality, their involvement of students in choosing class goals, their help to students having difficulty with the work, and their overall success in giving students a broad understanding of the subjects. Thus, while the independent school students felt closer to their teachers and had more interaction with them, other aspects of teaching are very similar. Due to smaller class size, the independent teachers had more opportunities for classroom discussions and could provide students with more individual attention; otherwise they performed similarly to their public school counterparts.

In overall environment, a higher percentage of independent than public school students thought that their courses taught them how to analyze and think critically, and that their schools would exert considerable energy to help them get into college. Few other differences, however, emerged in the survey results. Students in neither group would readily turn to any official in the schools for help with any problem other than an academic problem. This included the boarding school housemasters, to whom fewer than 10 percent of the independent school students would turn for help with any problem.

Nor did Baird find any differences in student values for the two groups. Students in both groups were asked to choose the three most important values in life for them from a list of thirteen values. The choices by the two student groups were identical, even in the relatively low values they placed on "working hard to achieve academic honors" and "living your religion in your everyday life." When asked to rank fourteen goals in life, both groups gave the highest ratings to having a happy family life, finding personal happiness, and understanding other people. Both also gave relatively low ratings to engage in the performance or creation of works of art, becoming leaders in politics, making a contribution to knowledge, and working in the world of ideas.

In psychological development, some differences did emerge. Inde-

pendent school students believed their schools helped their development more than public school students did in three areas: becoming
psychologically independent from their parents, developing the ability
to work with people different from themselves, and understanding people of other racial or ethnic backgrounds. Both groups felt their schools
helped them similarly in thirteen other areas of development, including
vocational development, relations with parents, self-confidence, independence, ethical or moral sense, responsibility, thinking and reasoning,
political awareness, the desire to learn, and aesthetic interest. Baird
concluded that while private schools, including elite independent boarding schools, do increase parental and student choices, some of the other
differences from public schools claimed for independent schools have
been overblown.

COMPARISONS OF PUBLIC AND PRIVATE HIGH
SCHOOLS

More recent attempts to examine the differences between public and
private schools have been conducted by James Coleman, Thomas Hoffer,
and Sally Kilgore (1981; 1982) and by Coleman and Hoffer (1987) under
the auspices of the National Opinion Research Center (NORC) at the
University of Chicago. Surveying high school sophomores and seniors
throughout the United States in a study in the early 1980s, the authors
were concerned with examining two basic question: (1) How much do
private schools contribute to social divisiveness or segregation, between
the rich and the poor, among religious groups (because many private
schools are organized by religious groups), and among whites, blacks
and Hispanics. (2) Do differences exist between public and private
schools in achievement in basic skills, measured by standardized tests
in vocabulary, reading comprehension, and mathematics administered
to sophomores and seniors?

Study results were generally more favorable to private schools than
to public schools on both issues, with some exceptions and caveats. One
caveat was that the sample of non-Catholic private schools was insuf-
ficiently large to make any other than tentative conclusions. The second
caveat dealt with selection bias, since families that choose private schools
self-select. Differences between the two school systems may reflect dis-
similar initial characteristics more than differences in schooling, per se.

Coleman, Hoffer, and Kilgore found that students in both Catholic
and non-Catholic private schools showed higher performance on standardized tests than did public school students from comparable backgrounds. The differences between public and private school student
achievement levels were similar for vocabulary, reading, and mathe-

matics. In each area, private school students achieved about a grade level higher than public school students.

Nor did Coleman, Hoffer, and Kilgore find any significant additional increment to racial segregation resulting from private school enrollments. They argued that the increment to segregation caused by the smaller percentage of blacks in the private sector was exactly offset by the decrement to segregation caused by a lesser segregation of blacks and whites than in the public sector. They did find some net increase in income segregation in education, resulting from private schools. While some private schools cater to an upper-middle-class, affluent clientele, only a minority of private school students attend such schools. Most attend Catholic schools. Of those who do not attend Catholic schools, most attend schools associated with some other religion. The income distribution of families sending their children to private schools is similar to that of families who do not, especially in the middle range. The two income distributions differ mostly at the extremes. Coleman and colleagues did find that private schooling increased religious segregation.

Many scholars criticized the Coleman, Hoffer, and Kilgore study for failure to control adequately for background differences between public and private school students. These uncontrolled differences, critics charged, rather than the inherent superiority of private schooling produced the differences in achievement levels. Critics also contend that the study did not examine the impact of schooling on students' formation of life plans and goals—especially on the question of whether or not to go on to college and even on whether or not to drop out or finish high school.

With new data collected in 1982 from the first follow-up of the High School and Beyond Survey and follow-up achievement tests administered in 1982, Coleman and Hoffer (1987) expanded the scope of their earlier work to revisit old questions and to address new ones. Despite differences in median income levels for families with children enrolled in public, Catholic, and other nonprofit schools, Coleman and Hoffer reassert their contention that income differentials between the groups are not great and that private schools are not a bulwark for the elite. In 1982 the median income level for parents of public school students was $18,700, while it was $22,700 for parents of Catholic school students and $24,300 for parents of students in other nonprofit private schools. Overall, private schools are less likely to enroll students from the lowest income levels and more likely to enroll students from the highest income levels, but most of the private school enrollment is from the middle-income range.

Greater differences between the three groups emerge for parental educational level, measured by the mother's education level. Overall, mothers of public school students have less educational achievement. Twenty percent have less than a high school education, compared to 9 percent of Catholic students' mothers and 7 percent of other private school mothers. Only 8 percent of public student mothers have a four-year college degree, compared to 16 percent of Catholic students' mothers, and 24 percent of other private students' mothers.

On ethnic differences, 13 percent of the public school sophomore cohort sampled was black and 13 percent Hispanic. The remainder, 74 percent, was non-Hispanic white. Comparable enrollments in Catholic schools were 6 percent black, 10 percent Hispanic, and 84 percent white. Other private school enrollments were only 2 percent black, 8 percent Hispanic, and 90 percent white. Thus racial minorities constitute a sizable portion of enrollment in Catholic schools, but still represent a smaller proportion of total enrollment than they do in public schools. Minorities constitute a significantly smaller proportion of total enrollment in other private schools.

Family structures and expectations differed for the groups. Twenty-two percent of public school students lived in single parent households, compared to 14 percent of Catholic students, and 16 percent of other private school students. About 5 percent of Catholic and other private school students were likely to have mothers who worked outside the household at each age. Ten percent more of Catholic and other private school students than public school students reported that their fathers paid close attention to their progress in school. Thus, Catholic and other private school students tended to come from families with somewhat higher incomes and educational levels, somewhat greater structural integrity, and higher expectations for their children's educational achievement. Additionally, based on data from a survey of principals, parental involvement in school tended to be greater in private schools. Public school officials were less likely than public school officials to feel that parents were interested in their children's educations and were more likely to have hostile confrontations with parents.

Resources were not equal for the three types of schools. In 1980, per pupil expenditures for public school students averaged $2,016, but only $1,353 per Catholic student. In other private schools, expenditures averaged $2,777 per pupil, and in high performance private schools, $4,648. Because the Catholic proportion of private sector schools is so large, the average for the private sector as a whole was $1,837, about $200 less than the public school average. The lower Catholic average results in part, from lower salaries paid to instructional staff who are nuns and priests living under vows of poverty.

School size also differs across the groups. Public schools are much larger than private schools. The average public school enrolled 1,381 students, compared with 797 students in the average Catholic school and only 533 students in other nonprofit schools. The impact of school size on quality of education, however, is not as obvious. Larger schools should be able to provide more elaborate curricula, programs, and professional expertise. For example, larger public schools often have vocational curricula, programs for the handicapped or gifted, remedial programs, bilingual and bicultural programs, specialized art and music curricula, and a great variety of nontraditional academic courses representing a degree of complexity not found in private schools. Larger size also undermines the intensity of relations between students and teachers and leaves students with fewer opportunities to participate in extracurricular activities.

Reexamining achievement, Coleman and Hoffer continued to find differentials in achievement growth across the three types of schools. As measured by improvements in standardized test scores, greater academic growth occurred in Catholic schools than in public schools in both verbal skills and mathematics. The differential is about one academic year, so that across two years, from sophomore to senior status, public school students improved by two years, while Catholic school students averaged three years' improvement. Catholic schools did not outperform public schools in greater growth, however, in knowledge of science or civics. The achievement results for other private schools are less clear. For students who continued in school in other private schools, the improvement in verbal skills was at least as great as that of Catholic school students, but similar gains were not experienced in mathematics or science. The growth in mathematics skills for other private school students between the sophomore and senior years was particularly poor. Coleman and Hoffer also found that Catholic schools were more effective than public or other private schools in raising the academic achievement of subpopulations that traditionally achieve at lower levels, including blacks, Hispanics, children from families that provide lower levels of parental support, and children from families with lower socioeconomic status.

The probability of dropping out of high school between the sophomore and senior year is highest for public schools, where 14.4 percent of the students dropped out. Non-Catholic private high schools experience an 11.9 percent dropout, compared to just 3.4 percent for Catholic schools and 0.0 for high-performance private schools. Coleman and Hoffer attribute the low dropout rate for Catholic schools to the strong sense of community such schools exhibit which, in part, compensates for family deficiencies. By contrast, the individualistic settings in other private schools increase the likelihood of middle-class students dropping out even beyond the dropout rate for comparable students in public school.

As a result of the follow-up survey and data, performance of graduates of the three types of schools were compared. Success in college was measured by remaining in the first college enrolled in after high school, by reentry into college for those who leave their first college, and by college grades. The differences in the college survival rate among graduates of the three types of schools are small but exist. Slightly higher proportions of Catholic school graduates than other private school graduates survive college, and the survival rates for other private school graduates are, in turn, slightly higher than those for public school graduates. Similar differences emerge for scholastic achievement in college. Among those who did not go to college, success in the labor force is only weakly related to the type of high school attended.

Despite the new data and analysis, Coleman and Hoffer do not fully refute the possibility that variances in performances of students in the different types of schools are caused in large part by selection bias. If this is the case, the greater parental choice of type of school results from adoption of proposals to increase federal assistance to private schools through tax credits, vouchers, and direct subsidies, performance differences between the three types of schools could grow. Although proponents of more private choice argue that doing so would enhance the quality of education for those who wish to pursue alternative schooling, critics contend that allocating public resources to private schools detracts from the increasingly pressing need to elevate student performance through all sectors, especially in the public schools, and to improve the quality of education overall. As yet, this debate has not been fully resolved, and given the flexibility, flux, and change that typifies American politics, it may never be.

DAY CARE

If school-age children are a captive population in that they depend heavily on others for needed services and an overall sense of well-being, preschool children who need child care are even more so. By 1983 half of all mothers with children under the age of six were in the labor force. In the future, the proportion of working mothers is likely to rise even higher (Kamerman, 1986). Providing adequate child care for these younger cohorts is a pressing need. Neglect of this area, however, has even led to an absence of information on how serious the problems is. In 1986 the most recent national survey of day-care centers was almost ten years old—a survey conducted by Abt Associates in 1977. Plainly, the data were dated, because number of day-care centers has increased substantially in response to increased demand over the ten years following the survey. Further, the data did not include programs under educational auspices, such as nursery schools, prekindergartens, and kindergartens, even though child-care programs with educational components are the largest type of child-care service for young children and the most rapidly growing component of child-care services (Kamerman, 1986).

Although initially day care was perceived as inferior to home care, various studies have shown that high-quality care does not appear harmful for young children, and may even be beneficial for some children from low-income families. High-quality care is distinguished from lesser-quality care by smaller groups, high staff/child ratios, and the employment of care givers trained to work with young children. High-quality care costs more than low-quality care.

Enrollments in preschools programs appears income related. Not only are children of working mothers more likely to be enrolled in preschool programs but also the enrollment rates are even higher when mothers have larger incomes and more education. In 1982, 53 percent of three-and four-year-olds in families with median or higher incomes were enrolled in preschool programs, but only 29 percent of children in lower-income families were enrolled. Enrollment is also related to the education level of the mother. Working increases the probability of enrollment for mothers without college educations. However, for mothers who are college graduates, 72 percent had enrolled their children in day-care programs in 1982, a percentage that applied regardless of whether the mother was working in the labor force. Child-care services have traditionally been supplied by private individuals in their homes for profit and by nonprofit agencies, such as churches. More recently, for-profit corporations, including Kindercare and others, have emerged to provide day-care services. Some businesses also provide child-care services for their employees. Generally, day-care workers are poorly paid relative to other workers. For-profit centers often use mothers of young children as caregivers, using the attraction of placing the mother's children in the center for no fee to compensate for working for otherwise low wages.

Traditionally, child care was perceived as a private responsibility with governmental involvement (mostly state and local government) justified only in cases of abuse or neglect and custody disputes. Only in two great national crises—the Great Depression and World War II—has the federal government intervened on a large scale to provide child care for women. In each instance, the purpose was to free women to fill labor force needs, rather than concern over the children or a decision that women should be free to pursue less traditional roles. During the late 1930s, over 1,900 programs were created by the Work Projects Administration (WPA) that provided jobs for the unemployed and care for over 40,000 children. The Lanham Act during World War II funded day-care centers so women could work in defense industries. Federal support for child care was halted as soon as the war ended, and was not resumed for almost two decades (Ruopp and Travers, 1982).

Interest in governmental support for early child care was reawakened during the 1960s as part of the Great Society's domestic policy thrust. The new interest was spurred by a marked increase in single mothers living in poverty and by a growing belief that education could ameliorate, if not eliminate, poverty. Policymakers began to see day care as crucial to reducing the welfare rolls and moving low-income parents into the labor force. Head Start, a nursery school-like early education program, was created in 1965.

The federal role in day care continued to expand during the next two decades into the 1980s. Three types of federal child care assistance were made available:

1. *Title IV-A of the Social Security Act (SSA):* Through Title IV-A of the Social Security Act, working families on welfare rolls may treat day care as a work-related expense. Child-care costs may be deducted from a parent's income before determining the size of an Aid to Families with Dependent Children (AFDC) grant.

2. *Title XX of the Social Security Act:* Title XX of the Social Security Act allocates federal funds for the direct purchase of day-care services for low- and moderate-income families.

3. *Tax Relief:* For working families, modest amounts of tax relief have been provided since 1954 when a small annual child-care deduction was allowed. In 1976 the deduction was shifted to a tax credit. The amounts allowed for tax credits have varied across the years, but continue to cover only a limited portion of what full-time child-care costs.

By the early 1980s, total federal contributions to child care, counting the Work Incentive Program, Child Care Food Program, and a few other direct programs as well as the preceding three major sources of child care support totalled less than $2 billion. Nor has the federal government exerted great regulatory authority over federally funded day care. Since the early 1970s, Federal Interagency Day Care Requirements (FIDCR) have been established, but were poorly enforced (Nelson 1982).

In contrast to education, where concern over monopolistic government involvement has caused critics to argue for decentralization through vouchers and tax credits, in child care, critics have argued for greater federal involvement, primarily through increasing resources available for day care. Richard Ruopp and Jeffrey Travers (1982) have advocated maintaining a consumer orientation, and encouraging a diverse supply of providers as desirable goals for a national day-care policy. To achieve these goals, they suggest several strategies, including:

1. Maintaining current day-care support programs for low- and moderate-income families;

2. Expanding tax relief for middle-income families;

3. Integrating support programs and tax relief;

4. Developing more adequate day-care information and information distribution systems; and

5. Creating a short-term day-care economic development authority.

The last proposal would entail a development agency whose primary mission is to stimulate the supply of day-care facilities and services. Among its primary functions would be providing information about the alternative ways to become a day-care provider for a variety of service delivery agencies, including center and family day-care homes, profit and nonprofit agencies, and corporations as well a proprietorships. A day-care development agency would provide guidance about the market research that needs to be done to make sound business decisions about starting a day-care operation. It would also provide information about day-care programs, administration, personnel management, staff development, costs, financing, cash-flow management, accounting, and other aspects of running a business. Such a national development authority might provide start-up, facility, and operating loan guarantees to increase the prospects of stable growth in the day-care market.

Rochelle Beck (1982) has advocated greater governmental involvement in child care. She suggests slightly different criteria for evaluating new proposals for enhancing child care:

1. Does the proposal recognize child-care services as a legitimate need of different families and define a role for public support?
2. Is accessibility to child-care services increased?
3. Does the proposal ensure that use of services is voluntary?
4. Are funds targeted to protect children most in need and for programs that work well?
5. Are diverse child-care arrangements encouraged?
6. Is parental involvement encouraged and, to the extent possible, ensured?

Major child-care legislation to achieve these goals would include heightened federal regulation and establishment of standards, greater public monies for child care, and potentially the development of locally based child-care councils similar to local school boards to oversee program expenditures and to survey local child-care needs. Other suggestions for expanding child care have included greater use of public school facilities during times school is not in session. Although proponents of the development of a national family policy, including a child-care component, wish to see greater governmental involvement, many existing child-care providers, including day-care corporations and some individuals who care for children in their own homes do not.

The current debate over the proper governmental role in the provision of child care, similar to those controversies surrounding governmental assistance for other captive populations, remains unresolved.

REFERENCES

Baird, Leonard L. *The Elite Schools.* Lexington, Mass.: Lexington Books, 1977.

Beck, Rochelle. "Beyond the Stalemate in Child Care Policy," in Edward F. Zigler and Edmund W. Gordon (eds.), *Day Care: Scientific and Social Policy Issues*, pp. 307–37. Boston: Auburn House Publishing Co., 1982.

Carnegie Forum on Education and the Economy. *A Nation Prepared: Teachers for the 21st Century.* New York: Carnegie Corporation, Task Force on Teaching as a Profession, 1986.

Carper, James C. "The Christian Day School," in James C. Carper and Thomas C. Hunt (eds.), *Religious Schooling in America*, pp. 110–29. Birmingham, Ala.: Religious Education Press, 1984.

Church, Robert L., and Michael W. Sedlak. *Education in the United States: An Interpretation.* New York: Free Press, 1976.

Coleman, James S., and Thomas Hoffer. *Public and Private High Schools.* New York: Basic Books, 1987.

Coleman, James S., Thomas Hoffer, and S. Kilgore. *Public and Private High Schools.* Washington, D.C.: National Center for Education Statistics, 1981.

———. *High School Achievement.* New York: Basic Books, 1982.

Dierenfield, Richard. *Religion in American Public Schools.* Washington, D.C.: Public Affairs Press, 1969.

Erickson, Donald A. "Choice and Private Schools: Dynamics of Supply and Demand," in Daniel C. Levy (ed.), *Private Education: Studies in Choice and Public Policy*, pp. 82–109. New York: Oxford University Press, 1986.

Ezell, John H. *Fortune's Merry Wheel: The Lottery in America.* Cambridge, Mass.: Harvard University Press, 1960.

Gabel, Richard J. *Public Funds for Church and Private Schools.* Washington, D.C.: Catholic University of America Press, 1937.

Greeley, Andrew, William C. McReady, and Kathleen McCourt. *Catholic Schools in a Declining Church.* Kansas City, Kan.: Sheed and Ward. 1976.

Hirschoff, Mary-Michelle Upson. "Public Policy toward Private Schools: A Focus on Parental Choice," in Daniel C. Levy (ed.), *Private Education: Studies in Choice and Public Policy*, pp. 33–56. New York: Oxford University Press, 1986.

Hunt, Thomas C., and Norlene M. Kunkel. "Catholic Schools: The Nation's Largest Alternative School System," in James C. Carper and Thomas C. Hunt (eds.), *Religious Schooling in America*, pp. 1–34. Birmingham, Ala.: Religious Education Press, 1984.

Jorgenson, Lloyd P. *The State and the Non-Public School: 1825–1925.* Columbia: University of Missouri Press, 1987.

Kamerman, Shiela B. "Child-Care Services: A National Picture," in Carol H. Thomas (ed.), *Current Issues in Day Care: Readings and Resources.* Phoenix, Ariz.: Oryx Press, 1986.

Kutner, Mark A., Joel D. Sherman, and Mary F. Williams. "Federal Policies for

Private Schools," in Daniel C. Levy, (ed.), *Private Education: Studies in Choice and Public Policy*, pp. 57–81. New York: Oxford University Press, 1986.

Larson, Martin A. *When Parochial Schools Close: A Study in Educational Financing.* Washington: Robert B. Luce, 1972.

McLachlan, James. *American Boarding Schools: A Historical Study.* New York: Charles Scribner's Sons, 1970.

McDonnell, Lorraine M., and Milbrey W. McLaughlin. *Program Consolidation and the State Role in ESEA Title IV*. Santa Monica, Calif.: The Rand Corporation, 1980.

Mathews, Jay. "The New 'Values' Curriculum," *The Washington Post*, April 22, 1985, p. 33.

Nault, Richard, and Susan Uchitell. "School Choice in the Public Sector: A Case Study of Parental Decision Making," in M. Manley and S. Casmin (eds.), *Family Choice in Schooling: Issues and Dilemmas*. Lexington, Mass.: Lexington Books, 1982.

Nelson, John R., Jr. "The Politics of Federal Day Care Regulation," in Edward F. Zigler and Edmund W. Gordon (eds.), *Day Care: Scientific and Social Policy Issues*, pp. 267–306. Boston: Auburn House Publishing Co., 1982.

Peshkin, Alan. *The Total World of a Fundamentalist Christian School.* Chicago: University of Chicago Press, 1986.

Rauch, Eduardo. "The Jewish Day School in America: A Critical History and Contemporary Dilemmas," in James C. Carper and Thomas C. Hunt (eds.), *Religious Schooling in America*, pp. 130–68. Religious Education Press, 1984.

Reich, Robert B. "As the World Turns: The Global Economy Has Divided the U.S. Work Force Sharply into Winners and Losers," *The New Republic* 200, No. 18 (May 1, 1989): 23–28.

Ruopp, Richard R., and Jeffrey Travers. "Janus Faces Day Care: Perspectives on Quality and Cost," in Edward F. Zigler and Edmund W. Gordon (eds.), *Day Care: Scientific and Social Policy Issues*, pp. 72–101. Boston: Auburn House Publishing Co., 1982.

Ryan, Mary Perkins. *Are Parochial Schools the Answer?* Chicago: Holt, Rinehart, and Winston, 1963.

Walberg, Herbert. "Improving the Productivity of America's Schools," *Educational Leadership* 41 (May 1984): 19–30.

Whicker, Marcia Lynn, and Raymond A. Moore. *Making America Competitive: Policies for a Global Future*. New York: Praeger Publishers, 1988.

3

The Incarcerated

The history of punishment and prisons in the United States is not pretty. The American colonies in the late 1600s were governed by British law and used similar legal codes. Capital and corporal punishment were common, including branding, flogging, the stocks, the pillory, and the brank. William Penn, the founder of Pennsylvania and leader of the Quakers of the era, brought a concept of more humanitarian treatment of offenders to America (Allen and Simonsen, 1986). This concept envisioned hard labor as a more effective punishment than death for most serious crimes, with only premeditated murder punishable by death.

Further, Penn's Great Law abolished most religious offenses as legal violations, and restricted itself to criminal jurisprudence. A "house of corrections" was charged with meting out hard labor as a punishment itself and not as a prelude to some other form of punishment. Shortly after Penn's death, his concept of punishment and prisons was replaced; the new English code was even more harsh than the earlier code of the Duke of York. The new code prescribed death for thirteen offenses and mutilation, branding, and other corporal punishments for many other transgressions. Using "hulks" or old transport ships to house prisoners was another English practice that was adopted, albeit more briefly, in the United States.

With the upheavals of industrialization, both the demand for prisons and for their reform increased. A modern prison built at Auburn, New York, in 1816 became a model for prisons in over thirty other states during the next half century. Early on, several rules of old prison discipline emerged. These rules included hard labor for prisoners ranging from productive work for prison industries to nonproductive punitive labor, such as use of a treadmill or carrying cannon shot from one end of the prison yard to the other. Other disciplinary concepts included depriving prisoners of everything but the bare essentials; monotony in dress and daily routine; uniformity; mass movement and living in communal arrangements; and degradation through a loss of identity, confinement, and verbal abuse. Prisoners' wishes were to be subservient to rules, and corporal punishment was frequently administered to keep prisoners in line. Isolation and noncommunication, through silence or solitary confinement, limited news, visits, and contact with the outside was also a frequently used disciplinary technique. The first warden at Auburn, Elam Lynds—who later founded Sing Sing—was a strict disciplinarian who thought that convicts were cowards and would not be reformed until their spirits were broken, if necessary by brutal punishments and degrading procedures. Lynds' philosophy has been the dominant one in American prisons until recent times.

Prison industries began as handicrafts and activities in solitary cells. Concern over making prisons self-sustaining, rather than the need for vocational training or earnings for inmates, provided the impetus to expand prison workshops. By the 1860s production was a primary goal of prisons that were, in the view of critics, guilty of exploiting the available free labor for the purpose of perpetuating the institution. One report of the era noted that not a single prison system at that time placed reforming the convict as the primary goal, above that of production and institutional preservation (Killinger and Cromwell, 1973).

During the mid–1800s, penal philosophy developed outside the United States. In a British penal colony offshore of Australia, a Captain Maconochie implemented the concept of the indeterminate sentence in 1840. Under the prior system of a flat sentence, prisoners had no hope of release until the full time had been served. Under Maconochie's mark system, a convict could earn freedom by hard work and good behavior. Even though Maconochie's system did not survive his departure from the penal colony, his ideas were implemented in Ireland by Sir Walter Crofton. Crofton devised a series of stages through which convicts could pass, each bringing them closer to free society. While the first stage consisted of solitary confinement and monotonous work, the second stage included assignment to public works, and a progression through various grades, with each grade shortening the length of stay and providing greater movement in and out of free society. The final stage was a "ticket to liberty"—the precursor to modern day parole.

The ideas of Maconochie and Crofton were first implemented in the United States in 1876 at a newly built youth reformatory in Elmira, New York. Most of the sixteen states that built prisons between 1870 and 1900 were in the north or west. None adopted the newer penal philosophy. The penitentiary system in the South had been virtually wiped out during the Civil War; for decades afterwards, the region remained poor. States such as Georgia, Florida, Mississippi, Louisiana, and Arkansas "privatized" their entire prison population by leasing out all of their convicts to contractors. Other prison systems took in contract work, or combined contract work within the prison with leasing prisoners out for work on the outside. Exploitation of the free labor of convicts within the South was easy and desirable as the South remained an agrarian economy long after the rest of the nation has industrialized. The system was rife with corruption, abuse, graft, and racism. A disproportionate share of southern convicts after the Civil War had been plantation slaves before the war. Eventually, prison farms replaced leasing of convicts in most southern states, although the practice of leasing was not completely erased until the 1920s.

The period from 1900 to 1935 represented the era of industrial prisons in the United States. The prison population increased by 140 percent, and ten new prisons were constructed (Allen and Simonsen, 1986). Industrial prisons were inspired by the profits earlier state prisons had earned. By the mid–1880s, earlier prison industry profits prompted private mechanics and cabinetmakers to complain about the unfair competition they faced from prison workshops using free convict labor. The emergence of labor unions, along with growing awareness of the abuses in prison contract and leasing systems led to a series of investigations in 1886 that obtained national prominence. By the end of the 1800s, contracting and leasing had been abolished in most northern states. They were replaced by state-account systems, where all convict employment and activity was under the direction of the state. Products were sold on the open market, and the profits were returned to the state. The prisoner received a small wage, but very little if any training, because only labor-intensive products requiring little or no technology, such as binder twine, rope, and hempsacks, were produced under the state-accounts system. A few states used a piece-price system, which represented a variation of the contract system. Under the piece-price system, the contractor supplied the raw material and paid a price for each finished product delivered. These reforms forced many convicts to be unemployed and eliminated the possibility of being self-sustaining for most prisons.

Throughout the twentieth century, organized labor has opposed any expansion of prison industries. Two federal laws controlling the character of prison products precipitated the beginning of the end of large-scale prison industries that kept most inmates employed. In 1929 the Hawes-Cooper Act was passed requiring that prison products be subject to the laws of any state to which they were shipped. An even more stringent law, the Ashurst-Sumners Act, was passed in 1935; its impact was to essentially halt the interstate transport of prison products.

The Ashurst-Sumners Act required that all prison products shipped out of the state be labeled with the prison name and prohibited interstate shipment of prison products anywhere state law forbade them. Due to the economic strains of the Great Depression, thirty three states had laws prohibiting the sale of prison products on the open market. In 1940 the act was amended to prohibit all interstate shipment of prison products. These acts virtually ended the industrial prison, with the exception of a few license plate and state furniture shops. Prisons reverted to their earlier, more primitive purposes of imposing punishment and maintaining custody of convicts.

Between 1935 and 1960, prison administration was marked by turmoil and tension. Administrators were stuck with the large prison fortresses built during the 1800s and were deprived of the ability to provide meaningful work for inmates. Further, both the Great Depression and the well-publicized criminal excesses of the bootlegger and gangster era hardened public attitudes toward penal reform. J. Edgar Hoover, director of the Federal Bureau of Investigation (FBI) and a highly visible public figure, railed against "hoity-toity professors" and the "cream-puff school of criminology" (Allen and Simonsen, 1986). During this era, the Federal Bureau of Prisons built one of the world's largest maximum security prisons, Alcatraz. Situated on a twelve-acre island in the middle of San Francisco Bay, the prison was considered escape-proof, and was seen as a fitting place for such notorious criminals as John Dillinger, Bonnie and Clyde, and Ma Barker. Eventually, the Federal Bureau of Prisons abandoned Alcatraz as a failure in 1963. Also during this period, the Federal Bureau of Prisons became a national leader in corrections, introducing the diagnosis and classification of convicts and the use of professional personnel, such as psychiatrists and psychologists, to help rehabilitate inmates. Both ideas were eventually copied by state prisons. The federal system also led the way in establishing more humane treatment and better living conditions for inmates.

Idleness and harsh conditions both have been related to prison riots in the past. When prison industries provided extensive work for inmates during the mid-nineteenth century, few riots took place. Riots began to occur more regularly as prison industries died out. Between 1929 and 1932, as the Great Depression fueled the attack on prison industries, a wave of prison riots occurred. Another explosion of rioting occurred between 1950 and 1966, with over 100 riots or major disturbances in American prisons. After investigating that wave of riots, the American Corrections Association reported that the major causes were inadequate financial support, official and public indifference to prison conditions, substandard personnel, and enforced idleness. Additional causes were the lack of professional leadership and programs, excessive size and overcrowding of institutions, political domination and motivation of management, and unwise sentencing and parole practices (Barnes and Teeters, 1959). The prison structures of this era—many built in the previous century to house masses of convicts in silence and hard labor—now house increasingly vocal inmates forbidden to compete with outside labor. By the 1960s prison practices and structures were becoming increasingly outdated.

MODERN PRISONS

The 1960s represented a decade of social change and turmoil for those affected by prisons as well as for the society in general. The U.S Supreme Court made an extensive series of sweeping and significant judicial interpretations that extended the basic rights of those in the criminal justice system. As prisons became more secure, escape became less common, and frustrations within prisons mounted. Prison populations were disproportionately black and Chicano. As civil rights movements were launched outside of prisons, the demands made by those within prison shifted from demands for basic conditions to demands for basic rights. As large prison riots became common, many had racial overtones including riots in the Maryland Penitentiary in Baltimore, the California State Penitentiary at San Quentin, and Philadelphia's Holmesburg Prison. The most violent of these occurred in September 1971 at the New York State Penitentiary in Attica where thirty-two prisoners and eleven guards were killed. As a result of these riots, many states formulated new prison policies including inmate councils, new grievance procedures, the adoption of a collaborative model with inmates serving on prison committees, and the use of ombudsmen as links between prisoners and prison administration.

Federal courts became active agents for prison reform. During the 1960s under the Warren Court, nearly all the constitutional guarantees of the Fourth, Fifth, Sixth, and Eighth Amendments were incorporated into the Fourteenth Amendment and made binding on the states. While the Fourteenth Amendment with its equal protection and due process clauses plainly applied to the states, the Bill of Rights had applied only to the national government. In this series of cases and others, the Fourteenth Amendment's equal protection and due process clauses were interpreted as including many of the Bill of Rights protections, and therefore were ruled as applying to the states as well as the federal government.

U.S. Supreme Court Rulings

Several major cases during this period had notable impacts on criminal law and corrections, including the following:

Mapp v. Ohio. A 1960 case, *Mapp v. Ohio*, developed the exclusionary rule of evidence. The case made inadmissible in both state and federal courts evidence obtained during an illegal search or seizure. Even though the case had little direct impact on prisons, it expanded criminal rights for the accused, using the Fourteenth Amendment.

Robinson v. California. In 1961 the Supreme Court ruled that the Eighth Amendment's prohibition of cruel and unusual punishment was binding on state proceedings. In particular, a majority on the court found that a state law that imprisoned a person for being sick inflicts a cruel and unusual punishment, violating the Eighth Amendment and the Fourteenth Amendment due process clause. This case involved a defendant charged with being a drug addict who had not used drugs in the state or exhibited irregular behavior. Subsequently, other issues have been considered under the Eighth Amendment, including the death penalty.

Furman v. Georgia. The death penalty issue in 1972 was decided by the U.S. Supreme Court, whose members ruled that any statute permitting a jury to demand the death penalty is unconstitutional. The Court wrote that leaving the choice of the death penalty to a jury violated the Eighth Amendment, not because the death penalty itself was inherently intolerable, but because it was so likely to be applied "wantonly and freakishly" by juries, that it served no deterrent purpose and therefore became cruel and unusual punishment.

Several states immediately passed mandatory death penalty laws to meet the objections of the U.S. Supreme Court. However, the Court also declared these new death penalty laws unconstitutional in a series of decisions in 1976, including *Roberts v. Louisiana* and *Woodson v. North Carolina*. Many death row prisoners at the time had their death sentences revoked as a result of these Supreme Court rulings. The Court used three other cases to firmly establish that a state's death penalty laws would be constitutionally sound if they provided specific guidelines to sentencing authorities, if sentencing took place in a separate procedure from that determining guilt or innocence, and if mitigating or aggravating circumstances were considered. After a period when no prisoners were executed, the 1980s saw new state laws that did meet these capital punishment guidelines and an increase in the number of prisoners executed.

Gideon v. Wainwright. In 1963 the Court ruled in *Gideon v. Wainwright* that defendants in noncapital cases are entitled, as a matter of right, to the assistance of counsel at their trials. Under the Fourteenth Amendment, this right was extended to state court proceedings. *Morrissey v. Brewer* extended this right to counsel to parole board revocation hearings.

Johnson v. Avery. The ruling in the 1969 case provided prisoners in state penal institutions with legal assistance in preparing habeas corpus proceedings. Subsequently, law libraries were set up in many state correctional institutions with the help of the Law Enforcement Assistance Administration, to allow prisoners in states that did not otherwise provide adequate legal assistance to act as jailhouse lawyers, by researching and conducting their own appeals, as well as the appeals of fellow prisoners. After *Johnson v. Avery*, some states accommodated prisoners' habeas corpus rights through the use of law students and trained lay personnel. This and subsequent decisions placed the responsibility for prisoners' right to counsel on correctional administrators.

Miranda v. Arizona. In a preceding case, *Escobedo v. Illinois*, the Supreme Court supported certain procedural safeguards against self-incrimination during an interrogation at a police station house. Confusion around the case was clarified in the 1966 *Miranda v. Arizona* ruling, one of the most famous cases in criminal and corrections law. In this case, using the Fourteenth Amendment due process clause as the constitutional basis, the Court required that a detailed set of police warnings be read to the arrested person.

The *Miranda* case plainly stated that privilege against self-incrimination is available outside of criminal proceedings, and arrestees must be informed of this right. Miranda warnings that police must give to arrestees are: (1) You have the right to remain silent. (2) Any statement you make may be used as evidence against you in a criminal trial. (3) You have the right to consult with counsel and to have counsel present with you during the questioning. You may retain counsel at your own expense, or counsel will be appointed for you at no expense to you. (4) Even if you decide to answer questions now without having counsel present, you may stop answering questions at any time. Also, you may request counsel at any time during the questioning.

Although law enforcers feared that Miranda warnings would "handcuff" their ability to obtain confessions, it does not appear to have done so to any appreciable sense. Subsequent rulings in 1976 and 1984 have tempered the application of Miranda.

Legislation and Evaluation

Omnibus Crime Control and Safe Streets Act of 1968. In addition to federal reform of crime enforcement and the criminal justice process through U.S. Supreme Court rulings, Congress enacted legislation to this end. The Law Enforcement Assistance Act of 1965 was designed to test the value of granting federal funds to local law enforcement. It was followed by a major block grant, the Omnibus Crime Control and Safe Streets Act of 1968, which replaced direct grants to local governments with block grants to states.

Implemented by the Law Enforcement Assistance Administration (LEAA), this act provided billions of dollars to states for action programs, research, education, evaluation, training, and administration of the criminal justice system. Amendments in 1970 earmarked funds for corrections. LEAA represented an attempt to broaden policy focus from earlier emphasis on police and enforcement to the entire criminal justice system, including corrections. This shift in part recognized that when too much emphasis was placed on police and enforcement, without an equivalent emphasis on the judicial and correctional components of the criminal justice system, the courts and prisons were overwhelmed with an increased workload. The relative deterioration of the courts and prisons resulted in recycling of the same people again and again through the criminal justice system. LEAA was ended during the Reagan administration, with mixed reviews as to its success.

Commission on Law Enforcement and Administration of Justice. In the face of mounting national concern in the 1960s about crime, Lyndon Johnson used the executive order power of the presidency to establish the Commission on Law Enforcement and Administration of Justice, and gave it a mandate to examine every aspect of the criminal justice system. The commission completed a massive study by 1967 that found deficiencies in prisoner classification, employment, education, parole, and probation. Some federal and state prisons, reformatories, workhouses, and county and city jails were characterized as having outdated physical facilities, untrained and inadequate staffs, and inmates with little to do to fill idle time. The commission report prompted greater federal funds for criminal justice problems, including corrections, and contributed to a new activism on these issues by many of the nation's governors.

Challenge to Conventional Assumptions about Corrections as a Result of Evaluation Studies. During the 1970s, many evaluation studies were conducted to test the effectiveness of alternative methods, programs, treatments, and facilities designs that this era of corrections reform spawned. Several longstanding assumptions about the impact of incarceration on prisoners and the value of incarceration to society were shown to be false (Allen and Simonsen, 1986). Among the findings were:

1. Long sentences were found to have a self-defeating impact on rehabilitation.

2. A majority of offenders—possibly as high as 85 percent—did not need to be incarcerated and could function better back in the community under supervision.

3. The first two years of incarceration produce the most rehabilitative benefit for most inmates; with incarceration for longer periods, the probability that inmates who return to society would function as productive citizens drops significantly.

4. Community-based corrections are more realistic, less expensive, and at least as effective as incarceration.

5. To be effective, corrections must incorporate rehabilitative services, including mental health, employment services, education, and social services.

6. Dangerous offenders must continue to be incarcerated at secure prisons, staffed extensively

7. Most prisoners are not mentally ill but are limited by a variety of educational, medical, psychological, maturational, economic, and interpersonal handicaps that are seldom addressed or resolved in modern prisons.

8. If inmates are to be kept off public assistance rolls, they must be given an opportunity and the capacity to earn living wages, both to compensate their victims and to support their own families.

9. The pay for inmates currently incarcerated is too low to be considered wages and should be raised to the minimum wage level for outside labor.

10. Laws prohibiting meaningful prison industries should be replaced. The private sector should be encouraged to provide both training and work programs for prisoners to produce employable workers at the end of the corrections cycle.

The 1980s saw a reversal of many of the findings from earlier evaluation studies, as fear of crime—especially crime associated with drug trafficking, wars, and use—continued to mount. Indicative of this new anticrime mood are many provisions in the Comprehensive Crime Control Act of 1984 (Trott, 1985). For federal crimes the act strengthened the ability of prosecutors to use pretrial detention, established a new sentencing system that abolished parole, created guidelines to aid judges in imposing consistent sentences, and narrowed the insanity plea. Many of the provisions, such as those that allowed increased use of forfeiture were oriented toward drug traffickers. The act did not directly affect state courts and prisons, however.

By 1985 direct and indirect costs of crime in the United States exceeded $90 billion a year. In response to growth in crime, America's prison population more than doubled from a decade earlier. The nation embarked on a major prison construction program to accommodate this increase. By 1989 George Bush's proposals to combat the flow of illicit drugs into the nation, along with the violence the drug trade spawned, promised to increase the number of prisons and overall prison capacity even more. Yet prisons—traditionally a state and federal monopoly—remain overcrowded, leading some to call for increased competition.

CORRECTIONAL IDEOLOGIES

Three ideologies underlay correctional efforts and institutions in the United States—punishment, treatment, and prevention. Sometimes, but not always, the ideologies overlap. Each has implications for the type of correctional facility and its prison rules, programs, and procedures.

Treatment and prevention were more popular as philosophies of penology during the sixties and early seventies. By the mid 1970s, a reversion to a punishment orientation toward prisoners was in evidence, in part due to funding issues. Corrections facilities became increasingly overcrowded and had to use monies to add basic necessities for new inmates, rather than for more expensive treatment and rehabilitation programs.

Various justifications have been offered for punishing prisoners, including retribution, deterrence, and incapacitation. Retribution holds that society deserves the right to punish criminals because they have broken the law. Others contend that punishment has a deterrent effect on offenders and on others who might consider a similar criminal act (Grasmick and Bryjak, 1979). Yet prisons based on the punishment ideology—using punishment as a deterrent—have often failed in part because of the application of the philosophy.

Researchers have found that to serve as an effective deterrent punishment must be swift and closely linked to the criminal action so that it discourages future recurrences. Further, if offenders who have been punished face a continued stigma or other overpunishment, the deterrent effect diminishes. With overpunishment, when the prisoners' compliance points are passed they cease to care. With continued stigma, exprisoners reason that nothing can remove them from the category of being stigmatized, and so they might as well continue their criminal activities.

Incapacitation, especially of career criminals, is yet another rationale for criminals. This rationale is in direct opposition to rehabilitation, and contends that if there is no hope for the individual's rehabilitation, selective incapacitation through isolation and removal of the individual from society is appropriate. Various studies have shown that career criminals, although few in numbers, account for most crime (Zawitz, 1983).

Experts recognize that punishment, when applied in the right amounts at the right time, can alter behavior. In corrections institutions, however, the implementation of this philosophy rarely achieves significant behavioral change. In punishment-oriented prisons, the emphasis of administration and staff is on administering a complex set of rules, that are typically prohibitions against various activities. Positive feedback is not given. Any number of additional factors undercut the effectiveness of punishment in reducing crime. If punishment is overly severe, it arouses public sympathy for the offender. The persons most likely to be imprisoned and punished are those who have already experienced and may be relatively desensitized to deprivations and frustration in routine daily living. Developing appropriate and legal yardsticks that link the severity of the crime to the severity of the punishment so that the punishment deters crime is hard, if not impossible. Even though compliance is achieved when coercion is applied, it may not continue to be forthcoming once coercion is removed. Also, the chances of committing various crimes vary with environmental conditions that impact on behavior.

PROJECTING PRISON GROWTH

The total number of prisoners in state prisons over the last thirty-five years has varied considerably, increasing the stress on prison administrators to meet sudden fluctuations in demand for capacity. Prisons and corrections institutions are the last phase of a three-phase criminal justice system. The first phase is law enforcement and police actions. The second phase is judicial actions, involving decisions made by state prosecutors as well as court workloads and rulings. For each part of the system, decisions made in the previous phase become input for the next phase. Thus, demand for criminal incarceration is determined within phase one, in part, based on the number of arrests, and in phase two, based on the number of cases prosecuted, whether or not they go to trial or are plea bargained, and what type and length of sentences the judges impose. These become the outputs of phase two that determine the demand for prison space—a factor over which prison administrators have very little control.

Considerable shifts have occurred in demand for prison space, as measured by the number of inmates. During the 1950s, the size of the inmate population grew slowly but steadily. It remained fairly constant during the 1960s and early 1970s. From the mid–1970s to the present, however, the number of prisoners has grown at an unprecedented rate so that by 1984, the state prison population has doubled to 420,000 people (Rich and Barnett, 1985).

As a result of recent rapid growth, most prisons are operating beyond their capacities. In addition to short-run measures, in the 1980s state legislatures began a massive capital program to expand prison capacity with 200 new corrections-related buildings under construction by 1983 and 80,000 new prison beds projected to be available by 1990. Ironically, the expansion coincided with the first downturn in reported serious crimes in years. In part, these opposing statistics reflect that prison expansion entails executive and legislative authorization, site-selection, and construction of atypical facilities—a very time-consuming process. More than a decade often passes between a proposal for more prison space and the opening of a new correctional facility. Because of the long lead time involved in prison construction, accurate projections of future prison populations are highly desirable. Projections of growth are also important to the "privatization of prisons" debate, because rapid growth would place extra stress on the corrections system and increase demands for privatization as well as other innovative alternatives. Accurate projections are difficult to obtain, however, due to the impact of multiple interactive factors on the actual number of prison inmates, including the state of the economy, the proportion of the population in prison-prone cohorts, and other external factors, such as drug epidemics and gang wars. The intensity of enforcement especially in areas where enforcement has previously been light, such as white-collar and industrial crime, as well as sentencing standards and patterns also impact on the number of inmates.

Despite these difficulties, Thomas Rich and Arnold Barnett (1985) developed a computer-based mathematical model to project prison populations for eight states and the nation as a whole through 2020. Crucially, these authors assumed that changes in sentencing policy do not affect the size of the chronic offender class, the offenders' crime commission rates while they are active, nor do they cause given offenders to hasten their retirement from criminal activity. Results from the model predict that if present sentencing policies are maintained, prison populations will stop growing around 1990. The drop in demand, however, will result primarily from short-term abnormalities in the age distribution, especially the numbers and proportion of the population in prison-prone cohorts. Growth in prison demand should resume toward the end of the twentieth century or the start of the twenty-first century. Only states actually losing residents will see their inmate populations peak around 1990.

If get-tough policies are enacted and the average length of the prison term grows as a result of more stringent policies toward drug dealers, drug distributors, and violent criminals, upward pressure on prison populations will increase. A three-fifths rule of prison growth posits that if the percentage increase in mean time services is X, then the percentage rise in the inmate population is about $^3/_5$ X. Therefore, a 50 percent increase in mean sentence would cause approximately a 30 percent increase in the total number of inmates. This rule assumes that prison terms have little deterrent impact on criminal activity.

THE COST OF CRIME

The social costs of crime extend far beyond just the costs of prisons and police salaries, and include social costs as well. Among these more difficult to measure social costs are expenditures for home and business security systems, victim losses, and prematurely abandoned buildings. Thus, crime costs may be divided into three categories: (1) harm to the victims; (2) the costs of combating or preventing crime; and (3) the costs of punishing criminals. These three costs are interdependent. The philosophy of punishment holds that punishment costs should be inversely related to victim and prevention costs, so that as punishment costs increase the costs to victims and for prevention should decrease. The difficulty is in obtaining an appropriate balance between these costs at any given time.

The custodial costs of a year in prison were estimated by the American Correctional Association to average $15,000 per inmate in 1985. The General Accounting Office estimated that construction costs per new prison bed average about $50,000. These capital costs may be amortized across several decades just as mortgages are. Using a 10 percent interest rate on state bonds, the cost of capital adds another $5,000 per year to construction costs. When a net social loss of about $5,000 for removing someone from the labor force is added into the total annual costs of incarceration for one inmate, total costs are approximately $25,000.

The total social cost of incarcerating an inmate for one year exceeds the costs of providing a year's education at the nation's most elite universities. The high costs of incarceration have led critics or prison expansion to advocate several reforms and innovations:

First, in making sentencing decisions judges should employ selective incarceration by weighing the likely future criminality of those found guilty by the courts. Prison construction costs would be reduced if long terms were meted out to frequent offenders, and short terms or non-prison sanctions were used for lesser criminals. Opponents of selective incarceration argue that accurate predictions of future criminality are difficult to obtain. Even comprehensive sentencing investigations that document employment history, family structure, and criminal records have not proved to be good predictors of recidivism (Petersilia et al., 1985). Nor does the concept of selective incarceration provide guidance to judges making sentences for various criminals, including juveniles and first-time offenders.

Second, increased use of parole and probation have also been suggested as alternatives to prison expansion. In 1983, 73 percent of all offenders were in the community as parolees or probationers, not in prison. Opponents of greater use of parole and probation argue that these criminal justice measures have been applied sufficiently and should not be extended. Proponents argue that greater use of parole and probation is preferable on both efficiency and effectiveness grounds.

Third, other alternatives to incarceration, especially for first time offenders, include fines, restitution, forfeitures, community service, and suspended sentences. Whatever the alternative employed, it uses one of two approaches—expropriation of assets or monitoring subsequent behavior in the community. If the former approach is used, what is the appropriate level of fine or asset appropriation? Gary Becker (1968) and others have argued that fines are socially efficient, because they punish offenders without being costly to administer. Yet fines are only effective if the convicted has an ability to pay and the government has an ability to force the convicted to pay. The Supreme Court somewhat limited the latter in *Tate v. Short* (1971) when it ruled that fines could not be set beyond a defendant's ability to pay and then converted to imprisonment. In 1983 in *Beardon v. Georgia*, the Court ruled that unpaid fines could not be converted to imprisonment unless the state determined that the defendant had not made a bona fide effort to pay. Although these decisions restricted fines, they continue to be used heavily for lesser offenses, including nontraffic violations in courts of limited jurisdiction (Hillsman et al., 1984).

Finally, a fourth cost, considered by some and discounted by others because people are presumably sentenced to prison for voluntarily committing acts against the state or other individuals, is the cost of disrupting and dislocating the lives of those incarcerated. In the United States, one out of every 350 persons is behind bars (Borna, 1986). It is the high financial costs of incarceration rather than the high total social costs that drove inquiry into privatization of prisons during the 1980s. Concern over efficiency and cost-cutting fueled the privatization debate.

PRIVATIZATION IN PRISONS

Many criminal justice experts regarded the rekindling of interest in prison privatization in the 1980s as a potential shift backwards to a time when jails and prisons were run by private individuals for profit (Munro and Toy, 1987; Travis, et al., 1985). In earlier times, various private systems of incarceration became so corrupt and were so rife with graft and abuse that the establishment of public prisons were hailed as an important and needed reform. Besides references to earlier eras where prison privatization proved a failure, very little data on modern applications exist to back up arguments that privatizing corrections would improve the system.

Methods

Privatization in corrections may assume three different aspects (Munro and Toy, 1987): investment, contracting out, or use of private management firms.

Venture Capital for Prison Construction. Privatization may refer to using venture capital to construct facilities, a funding strategy encouraged by the Reagan tax reforms of 1981 (Carlson, 1986). These reforms made lease-purchase agreements profitable to investors, and provided incentives for private capital to seek new outlets, including, at least in theory, prison construction.

Contracting Out Services. Privatization may also refer to private companies providing services to correctional facilities and running halfway houses in the community for correctional agencies. Services that may be contracted out include providing food, medical care, and specialized rehabilitative programs (Logan and Rausch, 1985). Contracting for selective services is a longstanding practice in corrections and is relatively noncontroversial. Its use predated the current debate over the usefulness of privatization.

Managing and Operating Entire Prison Facilities. The third notion of privatization, and the one that during the Reagan years stimulated debate over its applicability, is contracting to private corporations to manage and operate entire corrections facilities (Robbins, 1986; Saunders-Wilson, 1986). This notion generated considerable excitement and enthusiasm as well as opposition. It was first implemented in modern times with the takeover in 1975 by RCA of the Intensive Treatment Unit at Weaversville, Pennsylvania, a small, twenty-bed, expensive facility costing $40,000 per inmate per year. In 1983, the Eckerd Foundation took over the Okeechobee School for Boys. Subsequently, private firms acquired management contracts for facilities run by the U.S. Immigration and Naturalization Service, and jails and medium security prisons in Bay County, Florida, and Hamilton County, Tennessee. Prisons and jails in Texas and Wyoming were added to those managed by private corporations. By 1987 approximately 1,200 adults were held in secure, privately run correctional facilities. Many more were in privately run nonsecure detention space, such as work release centers and halfway houses (Munro and Toy, 1987).

Of the total $9.5 billion spent in the United States for corrections in 1987, the private enterprise proportion of these expenditures remained very tiny, yet was large enough to have enticed several private corporations into the field (Travisons, 1988). The largest private firm in 1987 was Corrections Corporation of America, which planned an 8 to 12 percent return on revenues. Behavioral Systems Southwest earned revenues of $6 million annually from housing 600 to 700 prisoners a day, while Buckingham Security Limited, of Lewisburg, Pennsylvania, was developing a protective custody facility. Despite the entry of a limited number of firms into the private corrections market, however, the growth of prison privatization has been slow, due to legislative restrictions, opposition by local communities to proposed prison sites, and opposition by unions as well as other factors unique to the corrections field.

Concerns about Privatization

Three criticisms or concerns have been voiced about the efforts to reintroduce privatization into corrections (Munro and Toy, 1987): economic, legal, and ethical or political.

Economic Concerns over Prison Privatization. While some reports enthusiastic about the cost-savings potential of prison privatization have argued that savings could approach one-fourth of the total costs for a publicly run facility, critics question that figure as too optimistic. A January 1986 cost figure for a privately run facility at Marion, Kentucky, showed inmate costs running $25 per day, compared to $22.74 and $26.83 per inmate day at two similar state-run institutions. While Pennsylvania reported costs at the privately run Weaversville facility to be about 11 percent less than costs at state-run facilities, not all of the figures were fully comparable. Other attempts to compare privately run and publicly run facility costs have also been handicapped by the lack of comparable data, as well as the small number of privately run facilities. Existing data indicate cost-savings claims are exaggerated.

Legal Concerns over Prison Privatization. Privatization of prisons raises four important legal issues: First, there is the issue of granting private firms the authority to operate a private corrections facility. Police powers may not be delegated to private individuals or firms for private purposes, but they may be delegated for public purposes. In most states, enabling legislation allowing private firms to enter the corrections field must be passed. In those states that have such enabling legislation, the language of the statutes typically makes it impossible for the states to give away their full power.

Second, there is concern about the use of force by employees of a private corrections facility. When and how should employees of a private corrections facility use force against inmates? Most of the private facilities are minimum security operations, and this question has risen infrequently. Yet some experts believe that recent court cases imply that only in the event of escape or when a guard acts in self-defense or in defense of another person could deadly force be used. Guards using excessive force at any other time would be liable under criminal law, and the guard, contractor, and possibly the state would be liable under civil law.

Lack of clear-cut standards on how to apply force has contributed to the slow growth of privatization in corrections. Some proponents of privatization have advocated that contractors seek special statutory authorization for the use of force in their facilities. Precedents for such provisions exist in California, for transit guards, and in New York, where special authorization to use force has been granted contractors connected with the drug abuse commission.

Third, there is the question of the right to participate in the classification and disciplinary proceedings of the corrections system. Most experts respond in the negative to this legal issue, contending that the state cannot delegate its power to define and create offenses. Thus, in privately run facilities the state would have to retain control of disciplinary proceedings and hearings, or, minimally, at least review procedures so that determinations by private employees are not binding and final. This additional review costs time and money, but is an expense not usually included when the costs of privately run versus publicly run facilities are compared.

Fourth is the problem of the liability of the state and correctional agency in the event of suit. Some proponents of privatization have implied that by the act of contracting prison management to private firms, state liability will be reduced, resulting in additional cost savings. Jim Munro and Larel Toy (1987) strongly disagree with this supposition, contending that there is no legal principle that allows public agencies to avoid or diminish their liability by contracting with a private operator. Further, they argue that the very contract may increase a jurisdiction's exposure to liability, because prisoners claiming injury from negligence or deliberate acts by private contractors may use the contractual provisions as additional grounds for a suit against both the contractor and the state corrections agency.

Proponents counter that the state can be protected by including an indemnification clause in the contract with the private firm, so that the firm would repay the state for any awards made against the state as a result of the contract. Opponents counter that if an award forces a firm into bankruptcy or financial insolvency, the state will receive no reimbursements from the contractor, despite the inclusion of an indemnification clause. The comparatively small size of some contractors in corrections increases the likelihood of financial difficulties if successfully sued.

Ethical and Political Concerns over Prison Privatization. Critics of privatization in corrections contend that questions concerning people's freedom and basic rights should not be contracted out to the lowest bidder. Others further argue that doing so is encouraging "profit-making from human misery" (Munro and Toy, 1987). Privatization removes and diminishes accountability, critics contend—an unacceptable alternative in a democratic society.

Much of the support for the privatization of corrections is managerial and cost oriented; it includes arguments that contractors are more flexible, that red tape will be less in private facilities, and that inefficiencies will be reduced. Critics argue that while public facilities are encumbered with many problems, energy and effort would be better spent by focusing on the reform of public corrections facilities. The questions of legality, accountability, and life and death decisions involving force are too weighty to contract out. Nor is the profit motive the appropriate one to use in such situations. Thus, although continuing contractual arrangements for minimum security institutions, juvenile justice programs, and a variety of specific food, medical, and counseling services may make good programmatic and economic sense, contracting out for the management of entire medium and maximum security facilities does not. The uniqueness of corrections, contend critics, implies that its management must be the responsibility of the state, and the slow growth of privatization in these areas implies they are right.

PRIVATE AND PRISON INDUSTRY

Rarely have those advocating privatization of prison management pursued the greater introduction of both public and private production-oriented industry into the corrections system. Yet such a union may provide the greatest as yet untapped opportunity for privatization of prisons.

Former Supreme Court Chief Justice Warren Burger has been among those strongly advocating a refocusing and reemphasis on prison industries. Burger (1985) attributes the doubling of the prison population between 1974 and 1984 to greater detection of crime and longer sentences, as well as increases in crime. Burger argues that recidivism can be greatly reduced if prison programs are reoriented toward education and skills acquisition, especially through prison industries. Currently, an illiterate and unskilled person imprisoned for even a short time and then released has a strong incentive to become a recidivist, even immediately, because no one hires unskilled illiterates, especially those with prison records. Burger advocates several measures to achieve rehabilitation and reduce recidivism, including:

1. Converting prisons into places of education and training, and into factories and shops for the production of goods;
2. Repealing all statutes that limit the amount of prison industry production;
3. Repealing all laws discriminating against the sale or transportation of prison-made goods; and
4. Encouraging the cooperation and active participation of business and organized labor leaders in programs to permit wider use of prison production facilities. Even modest production facilities in some prisons currently lie idle, due to laws that limit the sale of prison-make goods to cities, counties, and state governments, an insufficient market if more inmates are to be employed.

Burger recognizes that private industry fears competition from prison industries, but he argues that the competition should be slight, and that the economy should be able to accommodate the output of all inmates without displacing private workers. Prison industries, he argues, not only increase inmates' skills in some instances but also improve inmates' self-esteem and encourage work habits that would enhance the probability of successful adjustment to outside jobs in the labor force on release.

The United States lags far behind other countries in providing inmates with opportunities to work. In U.S. prisons, only about 10 percent of the inmate population is employed in prison industries. This contrasts with a full employment rate in Scandinavian prisons. In the People's Republic of China, prisons become production units, and in essence, are formed into a factory enclosed by a fence.

An alternative to prisons as self-contained work units producing finished goods is to have prisoners produce machine parts rather than finished products. If this partial production is contracted with private industry, then production equipment needs, inmates' skill levels, and capital investment required are all reduced. Burger cites as an example of this union of private and prison industries a Minnesota prison that previously produced farm machinery parts and currently assembles computers for Control Data Corporation.

Unlike other experts, Burger also does not advocate paying inmates full union scale wages with a deduction for room, board, and keep. He does advocate, however, increasing the rate of pay somewhat, tying pay to hours worked, providing bonuses based on quality and volume of production, and deducting a reasonable amount for room and board. By allowing prisoners to work and pay for some of the cost of their incarceration, the financial burden prisons place on taxpayers should be reduced.

PRISON REFORM

Privatization of prison management as an issue focuses on saving marginal dollars and cents by more efficient inmate care, according to proponents, or potentially reducing the quality of care, according to critics. Yet the two most important problems in corrections and prison governance are not addressed directly by the privatization debate and await more direct reform efforts. These are the issues of prison overcrowding and recidivism.

Reducing Prison Overcrowding

In severe cases of prison overcrowding, the courts have on occasion ordered mass releases of large numbers of prisoners to reduce populations so imprisonment does not constitute a violation of the Eighth Amendment prohibition against cruel and unusual punishment. In other instances, state corrections facilities, plagued with overcrowded conditions, have allowed posttrial state prisoners to remain in county and municipal jails, institutions created as short-term detention facilities, not prisons.

This prisoner backup in local jails has, in turn, created great stress and overcrowding in those facilities, leading some frustrated local administrators to engage in dramatic actions, such as carting posttrial state prisoners to the nearest state correctional facility, handcuffing the prisoners to the fence, and leaving. Other administrators have deposited posttrial state prisoners at the feet of lawmakers in the state legislature. While such actions gain attention and may temporarily solve the overcrowding problem in one local facility, they do not address the problem of overcrowding throughout the entire corrections system.

Prison populations have increased to an overcrowded level, in part, due to a rise in the crime rate as national demographics changed and the baby boom generation moved into and through the crime-prone years. Yet even with a growth in time, a coordinated criminal justice system could still manage the expansion, by sentencing only those with the most serious offenses to long terms, and reducing the terms of other criminals according to the severity of their crimes. Many experts contend that surety and swiftness of punishment are more important as a deterrent than severity. Two major factors, however, diminish the degree to which the prison system is coordinated and greatly exacerbate prison overcrowding—mandatory sentencing laws, and the total lack of coordination between judicial sentencing and the capacity of the prison system to accommodate new inmates.

Judges are the intake for the prison system, yet they are not required to consider prison capacity in their sentencing. Most state laws give judges broad ranges within which they can administer a sentence. Although in theory this flexibility produces independently tailored sentences resulting from the judges' exercise of discretion, on occasion it also creates great inequity and prison overcrowding. Further, judges greatly resist any attempt to erode their discretionary sentencing power, even though their exercise of it independent of the capacity of the prison system places great stress on corrections facilities.

Even though new prisons are being built at a phenomenal rate, they, too, will soon become overcrowded if lack of coordination between the intake to the prison system (judicial sentencing) and the capacity of the system persists. The solution is to make judges more aware of and accountable to prison capacity in their sentencing. In the ideal world, only the harm caused by and conditions surrounding the convicted would weigh in sentencing; however, nothing else about the criminal justice system is ideal. Like all real systems, the intake to the prison system must be coordinated with the capacity.

Minnesota addressed this problem in the 1970s in its community-based corrections act. The act authorized judges to use certain prisons (or a specific number of prison beds) for their sentencing. The allocation of prison beds to judges was based on the workload and type of offense judged in each court. Once judges filled the prison beds they were allocated, they could no longer easily sentence a convicted person to prison. This forced judges to manage their bed allocations. Judges who sent convicted felons to a maximum security prison were required to send along funds collected through court fines to help pay for the incarceration of such prisoners. For political and other reasons, Minnesota abandoned this system and adopted more stringent sentencing guidelines to reduce prison terms, hold down prison populations, and reduce overcrowding. The idea of making judges more accountable to and concerned about prison capacity in their sentencing, however, remains promising, and is, indeed, crucial to long-term reductions in overcrowding.

In the 1980s, as in other more conservative eras, state legislatures sometimes opted for mandatory sentencing laws, usually stiff in nature, as an option for combating crime. These mandatory sentences also increase prison populations and overcrowding. Yet they are politically popular, especially at the time of passage, because they allow politicians to contend they are "hard on crime" and "tough on criminals." Such politicians can point to the mandatory sentence as evidence, without being immediately confronted with the taxpayer costs of longer and tougher sentences. Yet such sentences do have considerable costs— prison overcrowding, new prison construction, and ultimately, higher taxes.

In 1985 Tennessee addressed this problem, not by abandoning statutorily set mandatory sentences, but by requiring that any legislation proposing such a sentence have a detailed fiscal note attached to it. The fiscal note would analyze the projected increase in prison population caused by the mandatory sentence, the added stress to the prison system, and the financial costs to the state treasury. Mandatory sentencing legislation in Tennessee has been sharply curtailed since the adoption of the fiscal note requirements.

Reducing Recidivism

An increase in education and training, coupled with full employment of all inmates in some form of prison industries may alleviate recidivism. Should it fail in this mission, the intermediate goals of reducing taxpayers' burdens and reducing riots and other internal violence in prisons caused in part by inmates' boredom and idleness may be alleviated. As noted by Burger and others, private industry has opposed prison industries in the past, fearing competition in domestic markets.

In the future, innovative leaders from both sectors may work together to find products suitable for export markets. With the globalization of the economy, and the increasing interdependence of domestic and foreign markets, exporting prison-made products would provide a means for reducing private sector resistance to this important aspect of prison governance and potential reduction in recidivism. Any contribution prison-produced exports make to reducing the U.S. trade deficit would be no doubt small, but would be an added gain. The lower wages paid to prisoners would allow U.S. products to be more competitive in low-wage countries.

Prison industries might also be directed toward manufacturing products that the current private markets in the United States do not find sufficiently lucrative to provide, such as houses for the homeless and low-income groups. In these instances, some other governmental agency—sometimes federal, sometimes state—might contract with a state corrections agency to produce low-income housing. Prefabricated as well as more conventional housing methods might be used. Other government agencies might contract for assistance in rebuilding the nation's badly eroded infrastructure.

Inmates who proved competent at performing low-skill jobs might be advanced to jobs requiring greater mastery of technology and equipment, thus better preparing them for jobs in the labor force. Identification with a technologically sophisticated work unit (such as one using computer-assisted production) could become both a reward and an incentive. Workers who did not demonstrate a sufficient aptitude or discipline would not be advanced, which would benefit them less but would still result in a saleable, more labor-intensive product.

When prison industries worked with private corporations, production of saleable products would be the common goal binding private firms to prison industries. The primary benefit from this effort, however, should remain focused on improving inmates' skills, self-esteem, and work habits. But the secondary goals of lowering public costs of incarceration and reducing prison violence might also be facilitated. Unlike prison management, if properly structured, prison industries might be a public/private partnership that would work.

REFERENCES

Allen, Harry E., and Clifford Simonsen. *Corrections in America: An Introduction.* New York: Macmillan Publishing Co., 1986.

Barnes, John V., and Negley K. Teeters. *New Horizons in Criminology,* 3d ed. Englewood Cliffs, N.J.: Prentice-Hall, 1959.

Becker, Gary S. "Crime and Punishment: An Economic Approach," *Journal of Political Economy* 76 (March 1968): 169–217.

Borna, Shaheen. "Free Enterprise Goes to Prison," *The British Journal of Criminology* 26, No. 4 (1986): 321–33.

Burger, Warren E. "Prison Industries: Turning Warehouses into Factories with Fences," *Public Administration Review* 45 (Special Issue on Law and Public Affairs, 1985): 754–57.

Carlson, Norman A. "Congress Studies Privatization," *Corrections Digest* 17, No. 7 (1986): 1–4.

Grasmick, H. G., and G. J. Bryjak. "The Deterrent Effect of Perceived Search of Punishment," *Social Forces* 59, No. 2 (1979): 471 96.

Hillsman, S., J. Sichel, and B. Mahoney. *Fines in Sentencing: A Study of the Use of the Fine as a Criminal Sanction.* Washington, D.C.. National Institute of Justice, 1984.

Killinger, George C., and Paul F. Cromwell, Jr. *Penology.* St. Paul, Minn.: West Publishing Co., 1973.

Logan, Charles H., and Sharla P. Rausch. "Punish and Profit: The Emergence of Private Enterprise in Prisons," *Justice Quarterly* 2, No. 3 (1985): 303–18.

Munro, Jim L., and Larel Toy. *The Privatization of Corrections: A Note with Readings and Bibliography.* Pensacola: University of West Florida, 1987.

Petersilia, J., S. Turner, J. Kahan, and J. Peterson. *Granting Felons Probation.* R-3186–NIJ. Santa Monica, Calif.: Rand Corp., 1985.

Rich, Thomas F., and Arnold I. Barnett. "Model-Based U.S. Prison Population Projections," *Public Administration Review* 45 (Special Issue on Law and Pubic Affairs, 1985): 780–89.

Robbins, Ira P. "Privatization of Corrections: Defining the Issues," *Judicature* 69 (1986): 324–31.

Saunders-Wilson, D. "Privatization and the Future of Imprisonment," *Prison Service Journal*, 62 (April 1986): 7–9.

Travis, Lawrence F., III, Edward J. Latessa, Jr., and Gennaro F. Vito. "Private Enterprise and Institutional Corrections: A Call for Caution," *Federal Probation* 49 (1985): 11–16.

Travisons, Anthony. "Celebrating the Past, Anticipating the Future." *Corrections Today* 50 (1988): 1–4.

Trott, Stephen S. "Implementing Criminal Justice Reform," *Public Administration Review* 45 (Special Issue on Law and Public Affairs, 1985): 795–800.

Zawitz, Marianne W. (ed.). *Report to the Nation on Crime and Justice.* Washington, D.C.: U.S. Government Printing Office, 1983.

Zedlewski, Edwin W. "When Have We Punished Enough?" *Public Administration Review* 45 (Special Issue on Law and Public Affairs, 1985): 771–79.

4

The Sick and the Health Care System

The sick in our society are an important group who utilize services. Given the growth of the health care sector of the economy, whether examined over a relatively short period such as the last twenty years or a long period such as since the turn of the century, health care and education have become the major service sectors both in total dollars expended and the numbers of people affected. This chapter examines the debate over the appropriate mode of service delivery to the sick in the most traditional aspects of health care services delivery, ambulatory or outpatient care, and inpatient or hospital care. Services aimed more specifically at the elderly, including health-related services such as long-term care and home-based services are addressed in the next chapter.

We examine changes in both hospital and ambulatory care services in this chapter, although those people ill enough to require inpatient services might be considered a more captive population than those receiving ambulatory care. Even though outpatients may be able to get up and leave care on their own and are not legally constrained to stay and receive services as are school children and prisoners, given the high value placed on health in American society and the protected legal role of physicians and hospitals and other licensed health care facilities as the only legal providers of such services, people who need these services are captive in most cases to the established health care system. Actually, major shifts are occurring in the health care industry, partially due to rising costs and attempts to hold down costs. More and more care is being given in an outpatient setting. Much surgery today, for example, is performed as one-day surgery in which a person goes to a hospital or outpatient surgery center on the day of the surgery and leaves sometime during that same day. This chapter discusses to some extent all of these aspects of health care delivery, although more of the early discussion focuses on hospital care. Later we review outpatient care, including health maintenance organizations (HMOs) and other outpatient care. Much of the initial growth in the corporate for profit sector occurred in the area of inpatient, traditional hospital services.

The hospital service area has had two traditions of health care services delivery: the private sector, traditionally nonprofit, and the public sector. This is particularly true of hospital services. From the 1920s through the mid–1960s, hospital care for the poor has often been concentrated in county or municipal hospitals while care for the paying working, middle, and upper classes has been provided through voluntary nonprofit hospitals. With the introduction of governmentally funded health care for the poor and the elderly through the medicaid and medicare programs in 1965, important groups of people who previously did not have the money or insurance to choose where to receive their health care services obtained that option. Although these programs initially provided enormous amounts of revenue for both voluntary and private-sector hospitals, growing concerns about health care costs in the late 1960s and 1970s led to some restrictions on state and federal funds available to hospitals for medicare and medicaid patients. At the same time, particularly in rapidly growing suburban and Sunbelt parts of the country, the need for new hospitals or hospitals in the suburbs provided a growth area for the emerging for-profit hospital corporations. Part of this chapter examines the changes and shifts in the hospital service area, looking both at private and public modes of service delivery. The private sector includes both for-profit and nonprofit institutions. In the public sector, most of the services are actually delivered by the public sector, although another possibility occurring in the last ten years is publicly owned hospitals in which the management of the service is contracted to another source, typically a for-profit hospital company.

What has been the situation in outpatient or ambulatory care services? To some extent, the traditional dividing lines are less clear. While many in health care might still argue that the growth of a for-profit sector in ambulatory care is new (using as examples a few new for-profit types of urgent care centers or laboratories or HMOs), in reality the bulk of outpatient care as delivered to the typical middle-class patient is part of a for profit system. The major traditional setting of ambulatory care was a private doctor's office, in which that doctor was reimbursed on the basis of a fee-for-service arrangement. Although many doctors now practice with their colleagues in multispecialty groups or more commonly in single specialty group practices, traditionally physicians' practices were solo efforts; as the owners and providers of services, the physicians charged a fee for service. In addition, more recently there has been the

growth of more corporately organized ambulatory care for-profit settings. There have also traditionally been nonprofit ambulatory care settings, especially those connected with private university medical schools
of certain church-owned facilities. Most public outpatient services traditionally were provided by county and city health departments, and
outpatient units of publicly funded medical schools. There was always
a limited amount of contracting out for care to the poor, in which the
government paid private providers to deliver health care services. One
can partially consider medicaid (the joint federal-state funded program
to provide health care services to the poor) to be an example of this
(Kronenfeld and Whicker, 1984). There are many recent aspects of for-
profit and nonprofit private ambulatory care—such as the health maintenance organization in which a preset package of health care services
is available for a standardized prepaid fee—and ambulatory surgery
centers. Trends in this sector of health services delivery are examined
in more detail after a consideration of hospitals and inpatient care.

HISTORY OF FOR-PROFIT AND NOT-FOR-PROFIT
DISTINCTIONS IN U.S. HEALTH CARE

As mentioned in the discussion of traditional care provided by the
typical physician, fee-for-service private practice is not an innovation on
the American scene. Not only medical care provided by doctors but also
most dental care, optometric care, and the production of drugs and
medical equipment have long been private for-profit enterprises as part
of the American health care system. In addition, some aspects of the
corporate practice of medicine were not uncommon in America in the
late nineteenth century. Corporate practice of medicine in the railroad,
mining, and lumber industries occurred because of the remoteness of
those work settings and their high accident rates. These industries contracted for services and often owned hospitals and dispensaries, typically
limiting to serving the company's own workers (Light, 1986). Related
as a for-profit practice different from the currently prevailing patterns
of practice was contract medicine, in which a physician was paid a set
fee by a corporation or a fraternal order such as the Moose to provide
medical services to employees or members (Light, 1989). As organized
medicine gained power in the early nineteenth century with the abolition
of many weak medical schools and the elimination of many of the competing sects such as naturalists and homeopaths, there was also a push
by the American Medical Association (AMA) to eliminate competitive
contracts and contract medicine. In some states, local chapters of the
AMA arranged for the passage of legislation prohibiting the corporate
practice of medicine or the practice of medicine by organizations run by
nonphysicians. This legislation limited the growth of that for profit entity

in medicine and led to the fee-for-service private practice of medicine which had become the overwhelmingly prevailing mode of practice by the end of World War II (Light, 1989).

As with the practice of medicine and the early presence of for-profit organizations in the delivery of ambulatory care, medical education in the mid-to-late 1800s and beginning of the twentieth century included a large proprietary component in the for-profit medical school. Many of these early proprietary (for-profit) medical schools were run by prominent local physicians in cities across America (Rosenberg, 1987; Starr, 1982). As late as 1910, Abraham Flexner, in a study prepared for the Carnegie Foundation, found that 28 of the more than 150 medical schools in operation in the United States were for-profit. Some of these were stock companies operated by people whose prime goal was to make money. As part of the Flexner reforms in medical education and medical practice designed to upgrade American medicine, most of these proprietary medical schools closed in the decade following World War I.

Medical education was not the only area of for-profit enterprises. As detailed in the next section, even though there were some for-profit hospitals and institutional facilities at the turn of the century and the early 1900s, hospitals of that period were predominantly religious or voluntary, nonprofit institutions or publicly funded, especially if one included in the total numbers state tuberculosis hospitals, state-owned mental health hospitals, and county-run municipal hospitals for the poor. In addition, there were other publicly funded facilities, such as ambulatory and public health clinics, and old-age homes. There was some growth around the turn of the century in the numbers of for-profit hospitals and in their role in U.S. health care. While growth in the number of U.S. hospitals occurred after World War I, there was some earlier growth in the number of small, for-profit hospitals started in small towns. Often these hospitals were started by local physicians to provide for themselves an institutional setting in which to practice medicine. Most of these hospitals were very small, so that even though in 1928 they accounted for 38.9 percent of the nongovernment general hospitals (a much higher percentage than today with the growth in the 1980s of for-profit national chains), these for-profit hospitals accounted for only 16 percent of nongovernmental hospital beds (Light, 1986).

Other health-related industries also included for-profit components. The young pharmaceutical industry, the patent medicine industry, and the medical supply industry were all organized and operated as for-profit firms in those times. Even at a point that we now think of as before the growth of for profit influences in the health care system, such as 1965, the presence of for-profit corporations was felt in the manufacturing sector and in the sale of drugs, medical equipment, appliances, and health insurance policies. Estimates are that in 1965 these activities accounted for over $8 billion, or just over 19 percent of total national health expenditures (Ginzberg, 1988). In fact, pharmaceuticals, whether prescription or over-the-counter (the outgrowth of the patent medicine industry) and equipment provision have always been for-profit industries in the United States and in many of the other countries (such as Switzerland and Germany) with major pharmaceutical industries. Perhaps the need to develop new products and to plan the marketing of such products with the requisite large amounts of capital make the providers of drugs or equipment particularly likely to be for profit firms and conducted as more typical businesses than the direct providers of health care services to patients.

Prior to 1965 and the modern growth of the for-profit sector, there were nonprofit acute care hospitals, psychiatric hospitals, and nursing homes. The ratio of nonprofit to for-profit hospital beds was eleven to one (Ginzberg, 1988; American Hospital Association, 1987). If one adds in hospital expenses to pharmaceuticals, equipment, appliances, and health insurance, the for-profit share of national health expenditures in 1965 was 22 percent. The government sector accounted for 26 percent of expenditures, leaving 30 percent for professional expenses (almost all fee-for-service care by physicians or dentists), and 22 percent for nonprofit hospitals, nursing homes, and marketing and administrative outlays of the nonprofit Blue Cross-Blue Shield organizations (Ginzberg, 1988; Health Care Financing Administration, 1987).

What has happened in very general terms since 1965? Today about 15 percent of private acute care hospitals are for-profit, while a majority of nursing homes and psychiatric hospitals are for profit. Investor-owned, for-profit businesses have been expanding into outpatient areas such as HMOs, ambulatory surgery centers, urgent care centers (sometimes known as doc-in-a-box centers), dialysis centers, and laboratories. Some experts have characterized the current American health care delivery system as one with weak public provision of services, active private nonprofit provision of services, and a rapidly growing for-profit sector (Gray, 1986; Bergthold, 1988).

What are the distinctions between public, nonprofit, and for-profit sectors in the U.S. health care system today? More so than some of the other service sectors discussed in this book, health care is characterized by an extensive, active private nonprofit sector. This has been an important sector since at least the turn of the century, and some would argue even earlier. Health and social services together are the major component of the nonprofit sector, accounting for 62 percent of its annual resources (Hodgkinson and Weitzman, 1986). When split out further by specific sectors, social services make up 9.9 percent of the nonprofit sector expenditures. Health services account for 52 percent of current operating expenditures in the nonprofit sector. Within health services, hospitals account for 88 percent of the total (Bergthold, 1988).

Some researchers now argue that the growth of the state has had a significant impact on the nonprofit sector, although it is difficult to quantify that impact (Bergthold, 1988). The period since 1965 and the adoption of the medicare and medicaid programs has been one of rapid growth of the public sector. Many nonprofit service agencies have become dependent on state funding for their survival and growth. In any case, the role of the federal government as a financier of services has become more important; this has implications on operations and rules even for the for-profit sector such as for-profit hospitals and private doctors' offices, as well as for nonprofit and governmental facilities.

Many theorists argue that the differences, especially in the health care sector, between for-profit and voluntary nonprofit institutions are relatively minor (Pauley, 1980). This is particularly true for hospitals, as discussed in more detail later. One example of ways in which the institutions have similarities in their operations would be in the area of oversight or governance boards. Both for-profit and nonprofit hospitals typically have a board of directors or trustees, although how this governance board is selected may differ between the two institutions. Similarly, although under the laws in most states nonprofit institutions are prohibited from distributing net earnings to any individuals who exercise control over the institutions, such as members or directors or trustees, this prohibition does not apply to the collection and retention of surpluses (Hansmann, 1980). Generally, nonprofit organizations can earn profits (typically labeled as surpluses) from operations, although there may be restrictions about how these surpluses can be used. A typical requirement in many states is that surpluses be devoted to financing and production of services similar to the original goals of the organization. If there are many aspects of similarity, why has there been such concern and outcry about the intrusion of the for-profit sector into health care?

EARLY CRITICISMS OF FOR-PROFIT HEALTH CARE

The early warning against for-profit intrusion into the health care system was sounded by Arnold Relman (1980) in an article in the *New England Journal of Medicine*, the most prestigious medical publication in the United States today. In this article written primarily for an audience of fellow physicians, Relman warned against the growth of for-profit medicine and raised alarms about the negative implications of such growth for physicians and also for their patients. He made a distinction between the old for-profit types of health care (such as pharmaceuticals and the medical supply industry) which he did not see as alarming and the new for-profit medicine (termed the new medical-industrial complex in the article). Examples of the new for-profit facilities included for-profit hospitals and for-profit specialized ambulatory care facilities, such as ambulatory dialysis centers for kidney patients. He was particularly concerned about the implications of physicians as stockholders in such corporations, fearing that having a fiduciary interest in the source of further treatment would affect the judgment of physicians and inhibit their ability to serve as the protectors of patients' interests.

Even though some aspects of Relman's argument can be convincing, the most interesting aspect is what was missing. There was not any real discussion or acknowledgment of the fact that most of typical health care as delivered by the average physician in a private office to a fee-for-service patient is an example of for-profit medicine. Critically, the physician often has a fiduciary interest in further care, such as in requiring a repeat visit to resolve a minor health problem. Although this may often be necessary to be sure a problem is resolved (as in the case of checking the ear of a small child with an ear infection), it nevertheless also increases the volume of visits in the doctor's office and thus the total revenue (and typically profit) coming into the office.

Relman's answer to this would be clear from this early article, as well as later editorials in the *New England Journal of Medicine* on this topic (Relman, 1987; Relman, 1988). He believes that the established code of ethics in the medical profession requires physicians to look out for patients' health and interests first, rather than considering their own financial gain. This is accurate, in terms of medical codes of ethics, and is probably followed by most good physicians (who clearly are the vast majority of physicians in the United States). There are cases in the traditional for-profit medicine represented by the fee-for-service system, however, in which some physicians did not and do not act only in the patients' best interests and without concern for their own financial interest.

HOSPITAL SECTOR

History of For-Profit Hospitals

For-profit hospitals have a long history in the American health care system. What is new is not that for-profit hospitals exist, but rather the important role of investor-owned hospital corporations controlling large numbers of hospitals. Related to this, a new trend is also the growth of multi-institutional arrangements within the not-for-profit hospital setting. This section traces the early historical roots of the for-profit hospital in American health care. Later sections explain in more detail the different types of for-profit hospitals in the United States today and the growth trends over the last several decades, focusing especially on differentiation within the for-profit sector.

When did the growth of hospitals in the United States begin to increase and the public image of hospitals become more positive? In the early part of the century, most of the for-profit hospitals were run by physicians and often were set up in smaller and rural communities to provide an individual doctor or a few doctors in town with a modern site in which to practice their profession. Major advances in surgery and in the control of infection were very important in the growth of American hospitals in the late nineteenth and early twentieth centuries. These same advances were critical in forming a changing image of the hospital from a place to which the poor would go to receive custodial care and eventually to die to a place to which the middle and even the upper classes would go to receive the most up-to-date medical care, and especially to receive surgery. Prior to the development of modern anesthesia and asepsis, surgery had very high mortality rates. As surgery became more successful, the role for hospitals as specialized places to receive health care treatment grew, making them desirable sites for paying as well as charity cases (Rosenberg, 1987).

By the beginning of the twentieth century, over half of hospitals in the United States were proprietary. This proportion decreased over the next sixty years, so that by 1970 the for-profit proportion had decreased to 13 percent and actually remained fairly stable over the decade of the 1970s, increasing slightly up to 15 percent of all hospitals today (Steinwald and Neuhauser, 1970). By 1928 the numbers of for-profits were already decreasing and for-profit hospitals were down to slightly less than 40 percent of all hospitals. Because they were located in small areas, however, they tended to be smaller hospitals and represented only about 16 percent of nongovernmental hospital beds (Light, 1986).

Even prior to World War II, some trends were beginning to change. Most notable was some beginning of the role of corporate ownership of for-profit hospitals rather than ownership by one physician or a very small group of local physicians. One indication of this is that in 1934 the American Medical Association included a new category in its annual survey of hospitals (Light, 1986). The category of "corporations unrestricted as to profit" was added, to reflect the growth of a class of hospitals owned by stockholders rather than one individual doctor or a small group of doctors. Even though it was a new addition to the survey, this category was not brand new, as evidenced by 32.4 percent of the proprietary hospitals in that year being in that category (Light, 1986). Even then, in the middle of the Great Depression, this category was beginning to represent larger (and probably more modern) facilities,

Table 2
Investor-Owned Hospitals and Beds: Number and Percentage of U.S.
Nonfederal Short-Term General and Other Special Hospitals, 1975–1984

	Investor-Owned Hospitals[a]	Percent of U.S. Hospitals[b]	Investor-Owned Beds[a]	Percent of U.S. Beds[b]
1975	378	6.3	51,230	5.3
1976	396	6.6	54,744	5.7
1977	420	7.0	58,357	5.9
1978	437	7.4	61,499	6.2
1979	464	7.8	66,039	6.7
1980	531	9.0	74,012	7.5
1981	580	9.9	79,002	7.8
1982	682	11.6	90,328	8.9
1983	767	13.1	99,958	9.8
1984	878	NA	113,122	NA

[a]Community, psychiatric and specialty hospitals owned by corporations that own or manage three or more hospitals.
[b]Nonfederal short-term general and other special hospitals.

Source: Bradford Gray et al., *For Profit Enterprise in Health Care*, c. 1989, by the National Academy of Sciences, National Academy Press, Washington, DC. Used by permission.

since over 50 percent of the for-profit beds were from this type of for-profit hospital.

In the United States, the impact of the Depression and World War II meant that little new construction of any buildings occurred, including hospitals. This was not a period of growth in the hospital sector, whether one focuses on for-profits, nonprofits, or government facilities. The decade of the 1950s and early 1960s saw great growth in community-sponsored nonprofit hospitals, due to the impetus of the Hill-Burton Act, passed in 1946, which provided federal aid for the construction of community hospitals. At this time some of the small, for-profit hospitals were changed to nonprofit facilities as Hill-Burton funds were used to construct new facilities. Individually owned for-profit hospitals experienced a period of decline from which they have not recovered. The 1950s and 1960s were the low period for U.S. for profit and investor-owned single hospitals.

Since the inception in the 1960s of investor-owned hospital systems, their rate of growth has exceeded that of nonprofit systems. Previously corporate ownership mostly involved one or two local hospitals held by specially created corporations. When medicare and medicaid legislation was enacted in 1965, there were no investor-owned hospital systems or chains in the United States. By 1970 twenty-nine investor-owned systems had been formed with 297 hospitals (Ermann and Gabel, 1986). There has actually been steady growth in investor-owned hospitals in the

United States since the mid–1970s as well as in the percent of U.S. hospitals and beds that are part of such systems. As Table 2 illustrates, by 1975 the investor-owned hospitals in the United States had declined; this was particularly true of the percent of all U.S. hospitals and hospital beds that were for-profit. From 1975 to 1984, the number of for-profit hospitals doubled, the percent of all beds in such facilities doubled, and the percent of all beds that are in for-profit hospitals has almost doubled. Recent growth trends in the for-profit hospital sector and the differentiation between types of hospitals and hospital systems are addressed in the next section.

Types of Hospitals

What are the major sources of differentiation within the for profit sector of the hospital industry? In the current period, most of the investor-owned hospitals are part of large corporate structures and are involved in multihospital systems. A move to systems of care is not unique to the for-profit sector, since not-for-profit systems have also been developing. The for-profit systems tend, however, to be substantially larger both in numbers of hospitals owned and number of beds involved in the system. In fact, for-profit systems are concentrated in a few very large companies. Within these companies, one source of differentiation is the focus on general versus specialized hospitals. Of the specialized hospitals, the most important group is the psychiatric hospitals. Another source of difference between for-profit and not-for-profit hospitals is geographic location. Hospitals in the for-profit sector are concentrated in the Sunbelt (southern and southwestern states) and California. In fact, almost half of all investor-owned hospitals are in three states, Texas, California, and Florida. The percent of investor owned facilities by state varied from none in New York, Rhode Island, North Dakota, and Vermont in 1984 to 44 percent in Florida and 50 percent in Nevada. Other states with high percentages of investor-owned hospitals were Tennessee (38 percent), Texas (32 percent), and Louisiana and California (31 percent each). Five other states had 20 percent or more of their nonfederal short-term general and other special hospitals that were investor owned in that year (Gray, 1986).

The representation of for-profit hospitals in these states correlates highly with either a high rate of growth in per capita income or in population growth rates. In addition, for-profit hospitals have preferred to locate in states in which the proportion of people covered by health insurance is fairly high. The older industrial parts of the county (sometimes called the Rust Belt, such as the Northeast and the urbanized Midwest) have not been attractive to the for-profit companies, despite the relatively high levels of income and insurance coverage in these states. Two important factors explain the lack of attraction of such parts of the country: These areas have not been experiencing rapid population growth and thus there is not a newly increasing demand for hospital beds driven by population growth. In addition, these are parts of the country in which hospitals have been relatively more plentiful initially; thus, there has been slow growth in new hospital beds in the decades of the 1970s and 1980s. In fact, in a city such as New York, hospital beds were being closed or recommended for closure up until the time of the AIDS epidemic. At this point, hospital beds in those areas of the country are beginning to fill more rapidly due to the presence of AIDS patients. Typically, these patients are not adequately insured (in the Northeast they are increasingly intravenous [I.V.] drug users) and represent sectors of the society that obtain care from public facilities. Thus despite rising occupancy rates in the Northeast and Midwest, AIDS patients make growth in numbers of for-profit hospitals unlikely.

Within any given sector of the country, for-profit hospitals are more likely to locate in suburban areas rather than in the central parts of cities. This is true because suburbs tend to be the parts of metropolitan areas experiencing growth in population and because they are, on average, more affluent than the central cities and have a greater proportion of the population with health insurance.

The world of corporate-owned large hospital chains is a fast moving world. Since 1985 the largest corporations have undergone periods of growth, retraction, growth again, expansion away from the hospital market and reconcentration on the hospital market. The next section provides some information on patterns of growth and trends, although which corporation is the largest and how many hospitals or other facilities are owned or managed can vary greatly over even a six-month period. In general, and for the time period since 1985, the major large chains have been Humana, Hospital Corporation of America (HCA), National Medical Enterprises (NME), American Medical International (AMI), Charter Medical Corporation (Charter), and Republic Health Care Corporation (Republic) (Hoy and Gray, 1986; Wallace, 1986). Some of these companies focus on general short-term hospitals, while others have expanded into outpatient care and insurance; a few focus on psychiatric (mental health) and specialized hospitals and others focus on nursing home components. There is variability—some large corporations have grown through building their own facilities; others through building and taking over already existing facilities. In addition, some of the corporations have focused on the United States predominantly, while others have built (and in several cases, sold in recent years) large international components of their corporations (Berliner and Regan, 1987).

Based in Louisville, Kentucky, Humana has traditionally focused more on general short-term hospitals than have some of the other corporations. In addition, Humana has built many of its own facilities, in addition to buying existing facilities. Compared to some of the other chains, Humana has expanded greatly into non-inpatient institutional lines as well as into other service lines, with HMOs and outpatient urgent care clinics. Their experiences with these endeavors are discussed more in the section on ambulatory care; overall, they have not contributed to the financial strength of the corporation, however, and cutbacks in these areas have been underway the last few years. Humana, as with several of the largest for-profit hospital corporations, also has some hospitals abroad, although this has not been as important a part of their market plan as for some of the other corporations.

A Nashville, Tennessee, corporation, HCA has been the largest of the for-profit hospital corporations, although it has been going through a period of selling off hospitals, both smaller hospitals within the United States and foreign hospitals. Before this company began contracting, it built a number of new facilities, took over existing facilities, and ran a very large management sector that operated nonprofit and public hospitals in a number of states. At one point, this company owned more foreign hospitals than any other United States corporation. They have owned hospitals in Latin America, Great Britain, and in Australia. This company at times has included large psychiatric and clinical laboratory divisions.

NME is a Los Angeles-based hospital chain that concentrates on psychiatric, specialty, and long-term care facilities, although it has also owned some general, short-term acute care hospitals. This corporation includes a small number of internationally based hospitals, especially in the Pacific Rim area.

AMI, a Beverly Hills-based corporation, has a strong international base. AMI has not been as involved as other for-profit chains in building their own U.S. facilities as they have acquired them through mergers or individual acquisitions of existing hospitals. At times, this company has included a large health insurance subsidiary. They have operated specialty facilities such as psychiatric health care, alcohol treatment centers, a head injury clinic, and primary care centers in Great Britain. This corporation has been a major provider of hospitals in Great Britain, including the operation of the famous Harley Street Clinic which attracts the wealthy and world leaders from many countries, especially some of the less-developed countries, Arab countries, and Iran under the Shah.

Two of the other largest companies are either more specialized or much smaller. Charter is predominantly a psychiatric and specialized care company. Although it has a small number of international hospitals, Charter is noted for psychiatric care as well as drug and alcohol treatment in recent years. Republic is a smaller, much newer company founded in 1981 by former executives of Hospital Affiliates, International, Inc., a group bought out by HCA during their expansion. They have purchased hospitals from other chains, added some psychiatric facilities, and bought out a smaller substance abuse chain.

Psychiatric hospitals are different facilities from general hospitals, although many of the for-profit corporations own both general and psychiatric hospitals. In the nonprofit sector, whether overseen by governmental or community or church-based boards of directors, psychiatric hospitals have traditionally been viewed as very different facilities that should not be operated as part of a system. The ownership status of such hospitals is particularly unusual. Half of all psychiatric hospitals in the United States are government owned, and most of these are part of state-run mental health systems. For the last 100 to 150 years, most states have maintained a system of large, inpatient mental health hospitals which have served as the provider of last resort for psychiatric care. In the last thirty years, two major trends have occurred in this sector of care. The deinstitutionalization movement has led to the closure of some of the largest state hospitals and to a trend of community care and smaller state-run facilities. Part of the reaction against large state-run hospitals has been a growth trend in smaller, for profit psychiatric facilities, both general ones that focus on all types of mental illness and specialized ones that focus on particular problems, such as alcohol or drug addiction.

In the nongovernmental sector of psychiatric hospitals, investor-owned hospitals have become a major factor, increasingly as parts of systems. Over half of all the private psychiatric hospitals affiliated with the National Association of Private Psychiatric Hospitals are part of investor-owned systems. Another 20 percent are independent for-profit hospitals, leaving only less than 30 percent of the membership of this organization in not-for-profit facilities (Gray, 1986).

Three major chains are important in psychiatric hospital care: Hospital Corporation of America (which also owns general hospitals), National Medical Enterprises (a chain with a large number of nursing homes), and Charter Medical Corporation, a chain specializing in psychiatric care. One major change in the for-profit psychiatric hospitals over the last thirty years is the growth of these few large chains. Although in the past private psychiatric hospitals tended to be small facilities run by a psychiatrist or a group of psychiatrists, most today are part of these larger chains.

Trends in Growth, Diversification, and Chains

A number of aspects of growth and change must be considered in the examination of for-profit hospital corporations. Before discussing the experiences of the major for-profit health care corporations specifically, some aspects of general trends in growth and diversification should be reviewed. Important concepts are horizontal and vertical integration and diversification (Gray, 1986).

A common distinction made in many types of businesses and increasingly made in health and hospital care is whether growth is occurring along the dimension of horizontal or vertical integration. Generally, horizontal integration implies growth with more units of a similar type. Specifically in the hospital and health care field, horizontal integration implies expansion of a system by having more units of the same type (typically general short-stay hospitals).

Vertical integration or growth, by contrast, implies adding units of different types. In a general industrial setting, a typical example would be a manufacturing concern that not only adds outlets to sell its products but also buys up and incorporates a major supplier of raw materials into the manufacturing concern. Although the analogy into health care is not as direct, vertical integration in health care usually implies movement to encompass other levels of care. In essence then, vertical integration occurs across the care continuum, going backwards from the hospital to the care that precedes hospitalization—that is primary care, care in a HMO, and provision of health insurance—and forward to the care people often need after (or perhaps in today's health care environment in lieu of) hospital care. This includes care in a nursing home, home health care services, or sometimes special equipment. Even though a more complete examination of trends in outpatient care follows later in this chapter and long-term care and aging related services are discussed in Chapter 5, to examine the growth trends in the for-profit hospital corporations, we need to briefly talk about their strategies of integration for growth. In addition, the types of integration have traditionally been distinguishing features between for-profit and nonprofit hospital systems. Increasingly, however, nonprofit hospitals have been adding for-profit subsidiaries (whether as parts of chains or as separate hospitals). These for-profit subsidiaries have often expanded into health promotion services and laboratory services.

A related term is *diversification*. As used in health care, it generally refers to selling of other services such as contract management or the addition of nonhealth businesses. Together, vertical integration and diversification are useful strategies for for-profit hospitals. Through the generation of new revenue sources, these strategies can help control the flow of patients—and even more critically, dollars—into the hospital. A strategy of vertical differentiation into some aspects of long-term care, such as a hospital purchasing and running an affiliated nursing home, can provide the hospital with a place to which to discharge elderly patients, especially those who live alone. By being able to discharge its patients more quickly, a hospital is able to keep more of the revenue for visits if the reimbursement of that visit is based on diagnostic related group (DRG) reimbursement methodology. Examples of the most common types of vertical integration undertaken by for-profit hospitals are the operation of a psychiatric facility, a nursing home, a lifecare center, an HMO, and freestanding facilities such as surgery centers, urgent care centers, and wellness or rehabilitation facilities (Gray, 1987).

Contract management is another very common activity for the for-profit hospitals. This has been an important activity for these hospital chains for almost ten years. Donald Johnson (1985) reported that in 1984 investor-owned systems operated many facilities under contract grant arrangements. At that point, 76 multihospital systems had contracts for the management of 537 hospitals. Both not-for-profit and public hospitals were operated by the for-profit chains under a contract management arrangement. The major advantage usually given for such management arrangements is that management skills are improved and updated, while preserving to some extent the original goals and autonomy of the hospital and its board. For county-owned hospitals, another advantage sometimes given has been the ability of the new management (depending on the type of contract) to hire its own employees, often at a lower cost and with fewer benefits than under government and civil service employment. Less often similar advantages have accrued from for-profit management of nonprofit facilities if union contracts have been renegotiated at a more favorable rate to the management.

A recent study by Hoy and Bradford (1986) has examined the growth of six of the largest investor-owned corporations (HCA, Humana, AMI, NME, Republic, Charter), using data through September 1984. That report together with more recent reports of trends in some of the for-profit companies provide a partial picture of trends among these corporations. Many changes are currently in various stages of discussion, however, and restructuring in the form of consolidations, sale of some units, and even of aspects of ownership has occurred in the last four to five years (Billions in New Debt, 1989; Davis, 1989; David Jones, 1989; Leberto, 1989; Multi-Unit Providers Survey, 1988; Traska, 1987; Wallace, 1986). Thus any discussion is at best a partial representation of the situation, with many changes occurring over even a few months.

The six major investor-owned companies have concentrated on growth through purchases (68 percent), and leases (12 percent). Construction of their own facilities has accounted for only 20 percent of 6 major corporations' growth, on average, with a range in this category from no growth for Republic to 27 percent for Humana. Most of the growth from construction occurred in the 1970s, with lower percentages in the decades before or after. The decline in the percentage due to construction from the 1975–1979 period as contrasted with the 1980–1984 period resulted primarily from an increase in acquisition activity. The actual amount of construction in this period did not change greatly (Hoy and Gray, 1986). While in the early period most of the growth in the major chains occurred due to purchases of small proprietary hospitals—typical proprietary hospitals in the decades prior to 1960—by 1980 more of the purchases were of not-for-profit and governmental hospitals. In general, purchased hospitals tended to be smaller than hospitals constructed by the companies. One major shift from 1969 to 1984 was in the geographic locations of hospitals that were part of investor-owned systems. The six largest chains owned hospitals in ten different states in 1969; however, three-quarters of them were in just four states: California, Texas, Alabama, and Tennessee. Much more dispersion of the location of hospitals had occurred by 1984. In that year the six major chains owned hospitals in thirty-five different states, although there was still geographic concentration in a relatively small number of states. Seven states (the four from 1969 plus Florida, Louisiana, and Georgia) contained about three-quarters of the hospitals owned by the major for-profit corporations. States with a larger presence of for-profit hospitals are in the South and Southwest, with some expansion into the Midwest and Rocky Mountain states. New England and the Middle Atlantic states are least likely to have any for profit hospitals, whether from the major for-profit chains or smaller for-profit corporations. Two trends reported by Elizabeth Hoy and Bradford Gray (1986) for the period up to 1984 are the frequency of further changes in ownership once a hospital is acquired by a for-profit chain and the rarity of closure of a hospital after acquisition. Although the data on closure since 1984 still indicates a reluctance by for-profit chains to close a hospital once they own it, a trend of change in ownership and the selling off of smaller (and typically less profitable hospitals) has begun to emerge in the last half of the 1980s for many of the larger corporations.

Since 1985 several companies have been engaged in downsizing and decreasing the hospitals and beds they own. AMI, which owned 114 general acute care and specialty hospitals in 1984, has recently sold 37 of its acute care hospitals (representing about 4,200 beds) to an employee group formed through an employee stock ownership plan. This period of contraction and selling off of hospitals contrasts sharply with earlier patterns of growth. In 1981 and 1982, for example, AMI acquired the Hyatt chain of eight hospitals and the Brookwood Health Services chain of eleven hospitals. Twenty-seven more hospitals were added to the chain in 1984 as the Lifemark Corporation was absorbed through a merger. During part of this period, the corporation also experimented with expansion into other aspects of care, especially outpatient surgery centers. Part of this move was an attempt by the corporation to diversify away from inpatient care which was viewed as more subject to financial controls by the federal government and into less regulated care areas.

Although a number of facilities were built, they were not financially successful for the company. The downsizing now leaves AMI with forty-eight acute care hospitals and 11,279 beds. In addition, the company continues to own some specialty hospitals, including five psychiatric hospitals in the United States and twenty-five facilities in seven foreign countries.

In general, part of the strategy of downsizing is not simply to sell off hospitals and beds, but to selectively sell off the weaker and less profitable hospitals in the chain. As with other companies that have engaged in downsizing, AMI sold off the smaller hospitals in its group. Before the sale, AMI hospitals averaged 182 beds per facility. After the sale, the average size is 235 beds. In general, hospitals with a larger number of beds are considered more economically viable in today's more competitive health care market. They have greater total facilities and higher total utilization making it easier to absorb large capital expenditures for new equipment. Small hospitals are generally unable to have the newest equipment. This often leads to fewer physicians having their primary affiliations at these hospitals, which eventually contributes to a cycle of lowered utilization with resulting financial problems, a tarnished reputation due to the financial problems becoming public, even lower utilization and, in the worst scenario, to closure. Thus by leaving themselves with only the larger hospitals, AMI is left with the hospitals that are more likely to be successful financially. What this implies for the survival of the new company as a group or for each individual hospital is less clear.

AMI is not the only major for-profit hospital corporation to have engaged in major downsizing in the past five years. The largest chain in 1984, HCA, has undergone a very major change in its scale since 1987. In 1984 HCA had 202 hospitals, both short-term and specialty, of which over a quarter had been constructed specifically for the corporation. This chain had periods of consistent growth from the early 1970s well into the decade of the 1980s. Between 1970 and 1972, only two years, the corporation added twenty-seven hospitals to its total, of which thirteen were specifically constructed for the corporation (Hoy and Gray, 1986). HCA added another fifty hospitals between 1973 and 1979, of which twenty-seven were constructed. In addition, a major source of growth for HCA in the late 1970s and early 1980s was the acquisition of other investor-owned chains. Three smaller chains (General Care Corporation; General Health Services, Inc.; and Hospital Affiliates International, Inc.) were purchased in 1980 and 1981 (Hoy and Gray, 1986). Altogether, the acquisition of these three corporations added forty-eight hospitals to the HCA total. In the large acquisitions of 1980–81, most of the acquired hospitals had been independent proprietary hospitals before their first acquisition by the chain that was bought out by HCA. One major pattern of growth for HCA from 1978 through 1985 was an increasing expansion into the international market. HCA is particularly involved in Latin America, owning six hospitals in Brazil and many in other Latin American countries (Berliner and Regan, 1987).

In 1985 HCA management discontinued buying hospitals particularly due to nationwide trends and predictions of declining occupancy and admission rates. Within the HCA hospitals, this became a problem, as occupancy in the first quarter of 1987 was only 51 percent, down from 56 percent in 1985 (Traska, 1987). In 1985 the decision was to concentrate on reinvesting in the hospitals it owned and to cease growth. A few years later, however, corporate managers decided to downsize. By 1987 plans were for HCA to sell 100 of its 180 general acute care hospitals to a new, affiliated company. Following a strategy that AMI would emulate a year later, the 100 hospitals were sold to an employee stock ownership plan. HCA kept the financially stronger hospitals that were market leaders in their geographic areas. In general, these also tended to be the larger hospitals. HCA has still remained a very large corporation, with fifty psychiatric hospitals in the United States and forty hospitals in its international division, in addition to the eighty general acute-care hospitals being retained. HCA has also been the largest of the firms in contract management, with 215 hospitals owned by others but managed by HCA's contract management division in 1987 (Traska, 1987). The corporation engaged in more downsizing in 1989, however, and sold ten hospitals and seven nursing homes in the United Kingdom during 1989. In addition, in late 1989 HCA was negotiating to sell its major stake (69 percent) in its Australian hospital division in Melbourne; it appears that this deal will become a reality.

Humana has probably been the chain most involved in vertical integration and diversification, especially in the 1980s. A more detailed description of Humana's move into outpatient care is discussed in the sections under ambulatory care; however, some appreciation for the role of vertical diversification strategies in Humana, Inc., are important to understand the downsizing in this chain in the last few years. Before the experience of this corporation between 1973 and 1977 can be understood, its growth patterns in the 1960s through 1984 need explication.

Humana began with a single nursing home in 1961 and was a very small health care corporation for the next five to nine years. The company bought its first hospital in 1968 and sold its nursing home division to concentrate on hospital care in 1973 (Interview with David Jones, 1989). Humana began one period of expansion in 1970. For the next two years, the chain added thirty-six hospitals, of which four were newly built. As with HCA, Humana began a move toward building more of its own hospitals as part of an expansionary strategy from 1973 to 1977. All but two of the twenty seven hospitals added to the chain in this time period were newly constructed as Humana Hospitals. While 1978 was a major growth period for Humana, Inc., merger was the strategy used for growth. In that year, a merger with American Medicorp added thirty-nine new hospitals to Humana and almost doubled the size of the chain Compared to the other companies in the period up to 1984, Humana had the largest number of divestitures. They sold thirty-eight hospitals and closed one—a total of 31 percent of all the hospitals acquired through 1984 had been divested by 1984. By 1984 Humana had 124 hospitals, of which 26 percent were constructed, 56 percent were purchased, and 18 percent were leased (Hoy and Gray, 1986).

Compared to HCA and AMI, Humana has concentrated more on the domestic market. In 1978 it owned only three hospitals outside of the United States and this increased only to a total of four by 1985. In 1984 Humana started a group health division, partially to help steer patients into its hospitals. Another major reason for the initiation of a group health division was that the company was convinced that the impending implementation of the medicare DRG reimbursement system, a prospective system which switched reimbursement for hospital care from the previous cost-based retrospective system, would seriously limit the potential profits for inpatient services. They saw more room for growth and profit in expanding into outpatient services. At one point this division was involved in HMOs, preferred provider organizations (PPOs), some indemnity insurance, and urgent care facilities. By 1986 Humana had expanded into urgent care or ambulatory care centers (known in the company at that time as MedFirst) with 153 clinics, of which 70 were then sold (Wallace, 1986).

Another area of diversification for Humana is its being the first of the for-profit corporations to take over the management of a university hospital. The University Hospital in Humana's headquarters town was part of the medical school at the University of Louisville; it was losing over $4 million in 1982. The corporation took over the management of the hospital and rented the facility for $6 million a year. As part of this arrangement, Humana took over care of indigents in the Louisville, Kentucky, area for a set fee. In 1988 the hospital earned $9 million. Twenty percent of this was returned to the University of Louisville Medical School as had been prearranged (Interview with David Jones, 1989). Another aspect of this arrangement that has brought notoriety to Humana is setting up a major cardiac surgery experimental unit. The best-known part of this effort was a program in the development and clinical applications of the artificial heart. Many within health care have believed that this effort was more related to public relations than to profitable business, and separate figures on the financial aspects of that program have not been released.

Humana today is a company with fewer hospitals in 1989 than in 1984

(124 then versus 83 in 1989) and less interest in HMOs and urgent care facilities than a few years ago. It is a company that still operates managed care plans with nearly one million enrollees; however, in terms of diversification by type of care (vertical diversification) Humana is one of the more complex of the large hospital and health care chains. It also is one of the chains that appears to be looking again at growth and expansion and may have plans to add both hospitals and HMOs, depending on the location, the market at that time, and the price (Interview with David Jones, 1989).

There has been a great deal of change, growth, expansion, and contraction in many of the other companies. In general, it is beyond the scope of this chapter to trace these shifting patterns among the many other for-profit hospital and health care corporations. Some, such as Charter and National Medical Enterprises (NME) are corporations with more interests in psychiatric, specialty, and long-term care facilities than in short-term general hospitals. As of 1984, NME had fifty hospitals in the chain, of which only twelve percent had been constructed for NME. More of its growth since 1986 has been in the specialized areas, as has also been true for Charter. One other of the largest chains—Republic— is of some interest because it is newer and has had some very unusual patterns of growth. The fate of Republic may be important in assessing some of the negative aspects of the rapid growth and large numbers of buyouts of related companies that have occurred in the for-profit hospital industry in the 1980s.

Republic was organized by four former executives of HAI, a chain that sold out to HCA in 1981. The group did most of its expansion in the early 1980s by purchasing two-thirds of its hospitals from other chains. For example, it purchased sixteen hospitals from HCA in 1983. Next, Republic purchased six general hospitals from three different chains as well as acquiring Horizon Health, a group of twenty-three hospitals with 1,111 beds focused on substance abuse. By 1984 it had grown to the fifth largest investor-owner of general hospitals (Hoy and Grace, 1986). One of Republic's major approaches was a tight control of costs and personnel. It was also noted for aggressive marketing, especially of services such as cataract surgery, foot care, and upgraded maternity care and amenities through fancy facilities for upscale couples.

In 1985 Republic became one of the earliest of the for-profit chains to begin to negotiate a private status through a leveraged buyout in which the Health Resources Corporation merged with Republic, partially to provide an infusion of cash. By 1986 the census of hospitals in the Republic group was only 38 percent for its acute care beds. The leveraged buyout became a reality by August 1986. Despite the specter of future problems, Republic was a profitable company in 1986; however, the company was in major trouble by February 1987. The census of its hospitals fell even lower and interest payments of $95 million on the company's $800 million debt each year were a major problem for a corporation with a cash flow of only $91 million. Employees of the company sensed the chaos, and Republic had a 67 percent turnover in administrators and an 80 percent turnover in comptrollers. Top management resigned in July 1987; a subsequent audit indicated that Republic lost $283 million in the year it went private. The company was forced to suspend payment on its debt and close and sell a number of hospitals. As other ways to raise needed capital, doctors were encouraged to own or lease expensive pieces of equipment, whole departments, or if they were interested, whole hospitals. The company is now under new management; aggressively restructuring its debt to extent the terms of payments, and trying to reorganize the company so that it can survive (Davis, 1989).

Financial Capital and Financial Health of Chains

As the Republic situation indicates, the issue of financial capital is very tied to the financial health of chains; many of the chains have been experiencing problems since 1985. Some of these problems are due to poor management and over ambitious managers as in the Republic case. Others are due to overly ambitious expansions either of a general nature or expansions into aspects of health care in which the companies had insufficient expertise; still others are due to shifts in government and other payers' reimbursement strategies that have a deleterious impact on the potential profitability of inpatient hospital services (especially the move to DRG payment). At times problems occur due to insufficient capital. Access to capital has often been considered one of the major advantages which for-profit hospitals may have over either nonprofit or governmental hospitals. This section first addresses the general issue of access to financial capital and its impact on for-profit versus other types of hospital services. Then we discuss the financial health of some of the larger chains (already partially addressed in the previous section) and especially a recent move by many of the larger for-profit hospital corporations to become part of leveraged buyout attempts that make the company a private for-profit rather than a public for-profit corporation.

Access to capital is crucial to health care institutions, even though it typically represents only from 5 to 10 percent of health care costs because it determines the availability of new equipment and new buildings. Equipment is particularly important, as the rate of growth in new technology in health care is very high, the obsolescence of equipment occurs rapidly, and access to the newest technology is considered an important sign of quality and up-to date health care both by physicians and by consumers of health care.

Financial capital is used by health care institutions to purchase or rent space, to buy equipment and supplies, to meet labor costs, and to modernize and renovate older facilities. In a hospital, as in any other organized activity, capital is used to prepay for inputs that are eventually used to produce the good or service. In a hospital, the service produced is the delivery of health care. The money paid in advance for the essentials needed to provide this service is then recovered through the revenues the institution earns.

Capital assets typically include both real assets, such as movable and fixed equipment, buildings, and land, as well as supplies, prepaid interest or rent, cash in accounts, marketable securities, and accounts receivable. Accountants differentiate between current assets for which recovery or prepayment is expected within a relatively short time frame (usually a year) and fixed assets for which recovery of costs occurs only over a long time. Land, buildings, and major equipment fall into this category.

Sources of capital can vary and, historically, have varied greatly for hospitals. Major sources of capital include philanthropy or an endowment from past philanthropy, grants or specifically appropriated money from governmental units, money from past operation of the facility, selling of debt instruments (typically short-term or long-term bonds), and sale of stocks or ownership in the corporation. Less frequent sources of capital funds might be sale of land or buildings.

The relative importance of these various sources of capital has changed historically and also varies by type of ownership. Philanthropy was the initial major source of capital for most hospitals in the United States. It is typically still a source, though increasingly less major over time, for community nonprofit hospitals. Philanthropy is not generally a capital source for governmental hospitals and is never a source for for-profit hospitals. Grants from governmental units were once a major source of funds for new building and expansion of hospitals in most parts of the United States, as part of the Hill-Burton Act, which was in effect from the late 1940s through the 1970s. With its demise, government grants for capital purposes are available only to governmental units. For-profit hospitals have never been able to use Hill-Burton funds for capital expenditures, so the expansion, described in the previous section, by the largest for-profit hospital corporations was predominantly funded by the sale of bonds, stocks, or funds accumulated from past operations. To get a more complete picture of the shifts in sources of capital funds over time in the hospital industry, philanthropy and governmental funds and appropriations accounted for more than 30 percent of the capital used for hospital construction funding in 1973; this percentage was even higher in the 1950s and 1960s (Cohodes and Kinkead, 1984). By contrast, for projects begun in 1984, debt was the source of 76 percent of the funding, while philanthropy and governmental grants and appropriations together were responsible for only about 8 percent of funding (Metz, 1983).

There are several explanations among the not-for-profit hospitals as to the declining importance of philanthropy and government grants as sources of capital funds. The gradual decline and eventual ending of the Hill-Burton program of government grants for construction is the major reason for the decline in the importance of the government grant source. Reasons for the decline in philanthropy are more complex. Because they now covered at least part of the expenses of care for those uninsured before 1965, medicare and medicaid ended up reducing the importance and dependence of hospitals on philanthropy. When these programs gave hospitals greater stability in their base of funding, hospitals became a sounder risk, thus making the possibility of obtaining debt financing at attractive rates more likely (Ermann and Gabel, 1986).

Currently, most for-profit and not-for-profit hospitals finance their major capital expenditures through debt instruments, though the type of debt instrument frequently varies between profit and not-for-profit hospitals. Tax exempt bonds are a major source of funding for not-for-profit hospitals, while this is not an available source for for-profit hospitals. Instead, they use taxable public offerings and sale of stock as major ways to raise capital (Metz, 1983). While this may appear to be a standard way for corporations to raise funds and thus a logical way for hospitals to be financed in the United States, most countries in the world do not finance their hospitals in this way. Specific capital appropriations through governmental funds and separate capital budgets for countries in which all health care is provided through the government are more typical (Reinhardt, 1984; Glazer, 1987). The heavy reliance of all U.S. hospitals on debt financing makes the U.S. health care sector conform to the expectations of the financial markets. An increasing concern is that concentration of debt financing for both for-profit and not for-profit hospitals makes them operate more similarly, with a concentration on the bottom line to obtain capital funds for new equipment or replacement equipment. Too much charity care (which typically shows up as bad debt/uncompensated care) hinders the ability of the hospital to gain access to capital (Wilson et al., 1982). This may be a factor in the rising problem of uncompensated care in the 1980s. While the uninsured have increased during the Reagan era, hospitals are also increasingly less willing to give much uncompensated care, trying in many localities to shift all of these patients to publicly funded facilities.

A major source of controversy in the past ten years in the health care industry has been the issue of return on equity payments to for-profit hospitals. Under cost-based reimbursement, for-profit hospitals received a return on equity from medicare that was set at 1.5 times the rate of return earned by medicare's Hospital Insurance Trust Fund on its investments. In 1982 legislation reduced the return on equity to the same rate as trust fund investments (Gray, 1986). A major debate which continues about the DRG reimbursement system is how return on equity and capital cost payments are handled. Related to this has been a traditional advantage in the tax code for for-profit hospitals. These companies are eligible for investment incentives that allow corporations to recover investment costs more quickly by deferring a portion of corporate income taxes. In 1983, for example, companies varied in the actual taxes paid as a percentage of statutory rates. Humana paid 77 percent while NME paid only 29.4 percent, mostly due to differences in the amount of investment in new facilities in that year (Gray, 1986). In the last several years, some researchers have also argued that not for-profit hospitals receive an unfair tax advantage due to the tax exemption of their facilities. An article in the *Harvard Business Review* argued that not-for-profit hospitals do not return benefits to society commensurate with the privilege of tax exempt status (Herzlinger and Krasker, 1987). This position was critiqued and rebutted by other experts in health care finance and health economics (Reinhardt, 1987). However, some states have raised questions about the tax exempt status of for-profit hospitals if they fail to continue to provide charity care and run substantial for-profit subsidiaries. One move being discussed by some states is to require nonprofit hospitals to demonstrate some commitment to charity care.

Several other approaches to raising capital have become important both in the for-profit and not-for-profit sector in the last few years. Joint ventures between hospitals and physicians have been described as a move toward privatization by not-for profit hospitals (Coleman, 1986). These ventures provide a way for hospitals to build facilities without affecting their capital resources. Joint ventures have been used to help build physicians' office buildings, diagnostic imaging centers, outpatient rehabilitation centers, hospices, and drug and alcohol abuse treatment facilities. Typically, physicians provide long term capital and credits for the building program, while at the same time increasing utilization of the facilities. Despite the attractiveness of joint ventures for hospitals as a way to expand or acquire expensive new equipment without using up capital resources, some of these ventures do raise major ethical questions about the role of physicians as agents for the consumers of care.

Debate is also occurring about the role of equity financing through the issue of new stock certificates. One line of argument has been that this is a major financial advantage of the for profit hospitals because the issuance of new stock certificates is cheap relative to debt financing. This idea has at times been promulgated by executives within the for-profit sector. In an interview with a senior vice-president of HCA reported in one of the many newsletters relating to health care trends in 1985, the executive gave an example: If a for-profit chain has $1 million in earnings, and if the stock is selling at a 12–1 price-to earnings ratio, the company can issue new stock and gain $12 million in new equity capital. Using the $12 million in new equity, the company could borrow an additional $12 million from the debt market. By contrast, the not-for-profit hospital would have to use the same $1 million in earnings to borrow only $1 million (Lefton, 1985). More responsible analysts in equity financing would increasingly argue that equity financing is at least as expensive as debt financing and represents a money pump of the type the HCA executive described only if financial analysts in the market were incompetent (Gray, 1986; Reinhardt, 1986).

The issue of debt and its relationship to sound management is a major issue in all parts of the hospital industry. To some extent, Republic's problems described in the last section are an example of the problems for-profit hospital corporations can encounter if equity financing is used irresponsibly and many different mergers occur. Debt has become a problem for several of the largest of the for-profit health care corporations. A new trend, as exhibited by AMI and HCA, is a leveraged buyout and taking the company private. In July 1989, it was announced that AMI had accepted a $28 per share offer to take the company private from IMA Holdings Corporation, an investment group that includes the wealthy Pritzker family. If the buyout is completed as planned, AMI will sell off its thirty foreign hospitals and possibly its psychiatric units. Whether those moves and private for-profit status will help to heal a company racked by dissension among managers and shareholders and by a drop in net revenues is not yet clear (Leberto, 1989).

HCA is planning a similar move, although in this case the buyout arrangement is being led by the managers of HCA. The corporate CEO of HCA, Thomas Frist, Jr., is leading a drive to make HCA a private company. In July 1989 he was arranging a $3.6 billion deal that was reported to include $65 million of his own resources (Billions in New Debt, 1989). Many experts question the advantages of this deal, although one major reason for such a deal to be completed appears to be the need for the company, no matter how reorganized and refinanced, to combine asset sales and operating improvements to service a huge amount of debt. It appears the company will need to sell assets to deal with its debt. The price they receive for the assets may determine how well going private works. It appears that HCA will sell off its psychiatric hospitals. Some believe it will sell off all but its eighty medical-surgical hospitals, which might still leave HCA with $300 in debt service per patient day in 1993. In contrast, Humana is paying only about $60 per day in debt service (Billions in New Debt, 1989). Not all restructuring plans are currently experiencing as many problems as Republic or AMI. In a different earlier restructuring which also involved HCA, the restructuring in 1987 in which 100 HCA hospitals were sold and reorganized as HealthTrust through an employee stock ownership plan, there is some more positive news. In May 1989 HealthTrust was ahead of its debt repayment schedule and had strong cash reserves (Billions in New Debt, 1989).

Financial capital and access to it are a very important part of how well many of the for-profit companies are faring in today's marketplace. It is an increasingly critical issue for the not for-profit sector as well; new and innovative ways to obtain capital have been one of the trends of the 1980s that appears likely to continue into the 1990s. Private capital is increasingly being used by both sectors of the hospital industry through debt financing. In addition, private capital is sometimes being used now to build new hospital facilities that are then leased to the not-for-profit or even the governmental sector. There is one counter trend whose impact is not yet clear on the growth in use of private capital. The Tax Reform Act of 1986 taxes capital gains at the same rate as ordinary income, which could have the effect of slowing the use of capital for public and nonprofit facilities except through the mechanism of tax-exempt bonds. There have been proposals in Congress, however, to change the treatment of capital gains.

Costs of Care

One of the most hotly debated questions within the debate in health care about the growth of for-profit corporations is whether for-profit ownership has a major impact on the cost of care (Gray, 1986; Coelen, 1986). Within this debate are several competing and conflicting answers as to the role of the for profit sector. One line of argument is that the for-profit hospitals increase total health care costs. Experts from this side believe that for-profits exploit any inadequacies in the system of paying for care to their advantage and earn higher dollars for similar procedures than a different facility would earn. They also argue, based on some of the evidence presented in the previous two sections, that the need to maintain consistent earnings growth and, thus, a high stock value will lead to cost increases, and that several components of care are more expensive in the for-profit sector, namely taxes, the need to pay divi-dends, and the high salaries of top executives in for-profit corporations.

The opposite argument is that for-profit hospital corporations help to alleviate and control the problems of high and rising costs. Experts on this side argue that corporate forms of organizations have some advan-tages in operating and that the general business know-how of private-sector management can be applied in the health care sector to produce care delivered more efficiently and thus cheaper. Specific aspects of this approach are the economies of scale due to multi-institutional arrange-ments, the more rapid response to change which a corporate form allows, the better management that results from more diverse career paths and thus the associated ability to recruit better managers, and cost advantages in operation due to more careful selection of market.

A large number of studies in recent years have examined the impact of investor-owned systems on the cost of care. In a recent review article, Ermann and Gabel (1986) summarized twelve studies on this topic. Most of these compared investor-owned systems of care with a comparison group of independent nonprofit hospitals. Some of these studies pooled systems together and compared them with independent hospitals; however, some compared for-profit and not-for-profit hospitals. Seven of the twelve studies reviewed indicate that investor-owned systems increase the cost of care. In contrast, three show that costs are lower for system hospitals and two indicate no difference.

In a study specifically conducted for the Institute on Medicine's Committee on Implications of For-Profit Enterprise in Health Care, Craig Coelen (1986) tried to improve on some other studies by using data for a generalizable sample of community hospitals in forty-eight states—he excluded Hawaii, Alaska—and Washington, D.C. He also explicitly adjusts for cross-sectional differences in case mix and presents the dispersion of costs per patient among hospitals. Coelen reports that independent hospitals are less expensive than chain hospitals and that within the group of independent hospitals, for-profit hospitals are 4 percent less expensive than nonprofit hospitals. Nonprofit chains are roughly 2 percent more expensive than independent nonprofit hospitals, and proprietary chains are the most expensive, 6 percent more than nonprofit independents and 10 percent more than proprietary independents. Thus, it does not appear that for-profit chains benefit from economies of scale in costs or from profit-related incentives for minimizing care.

In further analysis, Coelen (1986) shows that after adjusting for case mix and other factors, few differences are found in average length of stay across the four groups of hospitals. He finds, as is typically true in most reports, that occupancy rates are lower in proprietary chains. He confirms the findings of two previous studies that hospital charges per discharge are higher for the average for-profit hospital than in an average nonprofit hospital (Lewin et al., 1981; Pattison and Katz, 1983). On another issue, the after-tax margins on patient revenues, Coelen's (1986) results are between those of two other published studies (Lewin et al., 1981; Sloan and Vraciu, 1983). He reports margins on patient revenues 3 to 5 percentage points higher in for-profit than nonprofit hospitals. Frank Sloan and Robert Vraciu (1983) have argued that the true test of performance is after-tax margins on total income. Using this measure, proprietary hospitals in the study have one to two points differential in net income as a percentage of revenue.

How can these different studies, generally published in reputable journals and by respected researchers, come up with such different conclusions? Which studies are more accurate? Overall, Gray (1986) concludes that prices of for-profit chain hospitals are substantially higher than not-for-profit hospitals, whether chains or independents. One study compared specific procedures at six for-profit hospitals and an appropriate comparison group. For three common procedures (hysterectomy, cholecystectomy, and normal deliveries) Coelen found that charges at the for-profit chain hospitals ranged from 6 to 587 percent higher except for one for-profit chain's charge for normal deliveries (Gray, 1986). There seems to be strong evidence also that ancillary services on for-profit hospitals are marked up (Pattison and Katz, 1983). If profitability measures are used, all but one study show that for-profit hospitals are more profitable than nonprofit hospitals. If multiple measures of profitability are used, differences are greatest for margins on patient care revenues (Gray, 1986; Watt et al., 1986; Coelen, 1986). The one study with contrary findings included only hospitals in Florida (Sloan and Vraciu, 1983). One of the sources in variability in studies is whether only a small number of hospitals in one or a few states are studied or whether attempts were made to collect data from a more representative sample of hospitals. One point that does seem clear is that for-profit hospitals do not have management or cost control secrets that make them more efficient.

Access Issues

Along with the major question of the impact of for-profit hospitals on quality of care, the other two major areas of debate concern the role of for-profit hospitals on access and quality. A major concern about the growth of for-profit hospitals has been that their emphasis on profit and the bottom line would make those hospitals unwilling to provide services to the uninsured. In a typical business, this indeed would be the orientation. Anyone who cannot pay for a good or service does not receive it. However, health care services and all of the services discussed in this book traditionally have not been treated by society as typical consumer goods. There is a notion that people have at least some limited right to receive health care services, even without health insurance, and that health care institutions have a certain social responsibility to meet individual and community needs, even if they cannot be met profitably. In terms of the captive populations theme of this book, the willingness of different hospitals (for-profit, not-for-profit, and governmental) to provide health care services to the indigent is a critical element for assessment of the trend to a greater role by for-profit institutions.

This is such an important issue partially because of the nature of other aspects of health care delivery in the United States. Unlike many European countries or Canada in which there is a national health care system or national health care insurance, the U.S. government does not provide health care insurance for all. Most Americans receive their health care insurance through their places of work, but that is not mandated by government except in those few states that recently enacted legislation that most businesses must provide all employees with some health insurance. The most common current estimate is that 35 million Americans do not have health insurance or access to the medicare and medicaid programs. Given this large number of people with no health insurance, along with many people who have coverage for basic services but not for more catastrophic illnesses or specialized types of services (such as certain rehabilitative, home health, or long-term care services), the issue of access to care is very important. And, the impact that the growing hospital care corporations have on access needs to be examined.

The most straightforward aspect of access is whether for-profit hospitals are willing to serve patients without money or health care insurance. Other important aspects of access are whether for-profit hospitals are more likely to attract patients with high insurance levels and thus make it more difficult for other hospitals to be able to treat uninsured or indigent patients, whether the proprietary hospitals only offer those services that are profitable without concern for the needs of the community, and whether for-profit hospitals are more likely to close and leave a whole community without access to health care services (Gray, 1986).

Given the lack of adequate coverage for health insurance in the United States, hospitals on average, spend about 5 percent of their gross revenues on uncompensated care (charity care and bad debts together) (Gray, 1986). Historically, private hospitals have been a major provider of free care (about 60 percent), as well as care to medicaid patients (about 75 percent), that, depending on the state, may be reimbursed at rates below market rates (Feder et al., 1984). More recently, however, a 1981 survey of data on admissions of uninsured patients from all types of hospitals over a two-week period reported that public hospitals accepted the greatest burden of uninsured patients (16.8 percent of their admissions), followed by not-for-profit hospitals (7.9 percent) and for-profit hospitals (6 percent) (Gray, 1986). Similarly, about 4 percent of nonprofit versus 3 percent of for-profit hospitals reported that more than 25 percent of their admissions were uninsured. In admissions to emergency rooms, there was no difference in the percentages uninsured (22 percent) between for-profit and not-for-profit hospitals. Two studies reported that for-profit hospitals are less likely to offer services to low-income patients at a reduced rate (Schlesinger and Dorwart, 1984; Schlesinger, 1985) and another reported that for-profit hospitals, on average, offer less uncompensated care (Sloan et al., 1986).

Some limited data were obtained from five specific states as part of the Institute of Medicine's (IOM) examination of for-profit service delivery in health care. They obtained information from California, Florida, Tennessee, Virginia, and Texas for the 1981–83 period. Except in California which had a well-functioning system of public hospitals during the study years, for-profit hospitals have substantially lower bad debt and charity care deductions than do not-for-profit hospitals. There was no difference in California. In the other states, not-for-profit hospitals gave from 50 to over 150 percent more uncompensated care than their for-profit counterparts (Gray, 1986). In both the IOM study and other studies (Sloan and Vraciu, 1983; Pattison and Katz, 1983), system-affiliated hospitals provided less uncompensated care than their independent for-profit counterparts.

How do physicians in a particular hospital perceive limitations on uncompensated treatment? Mark Schlesinger and colleagues (1987) surveyed physicians in 1984 and asked them whether the hospital with which they maintained their primary affiliation discouraged admission of potentially unprofitable patients (defined in the study as either uninsured or medicaid). Twenty-one percent of the physicians reported that their hospitals discouraged admissions of uninsured patients and 6 percent reported restrictions on admissions of medicaid patients. Physicians who primarily practice in for-profit hospitals were more likely to report restrictions for both medicaid and uninsured patients. The most discouragement came from for-profit hospitals that were part of multihospital systems. In addition, private nonprofit hospitals discouraged such admissions more than did public facilities. A measure of the competitiveness of the local medical market was also constructed as part of this study and entered into the regression equations. When this variable was entered into the regression equations, it indicated that the more competitive the local hospital market, the more likely are both for-profit and voluntary not-for-profit hospitals to place restrictions on the admissions of unprofitable patients.

These results reflect the impact of for-profit institutions on other institutions in the area. In addition, there are some studies on patient dumping, that is, the transfer of undesired patients to another hospital (often a public facility) for economic reasons. In Chicago the major urban public hospital, Cook County, receives almost 75,000 patients each year dumped from private Chicago hospitals (Schiff, 1985). A major public hospital in Dallas, Parkland Memorial, has instituted a policy to try to ensure that all patients receive some care before being transferred there and that economics are not the only reason for transfers (Sloan et al., 1986).

Are access concerns related to the maintenance of specific hospital services that are losing money? In many hospitals, accident cases frequently admitted via the emergency room and maternity patients are disproportionately represented among the self-pay and bad-debt patients. In contrast, a recent marketing ploy of many hospitals has been to create separate women's hospitals with special amenities to attract paying obstetric and gynecological patients. Humana operates several of these and finds these services profitable. Overall, there is no major difference by type of ownership in the frequency of a hospital maintaining these services. Although there are some differences if one examines American Hospital Association data in services offered between for profit and other hospitals, it is difficult to discern an overall pattern. Premature nurseries are much less common in investor-owned hospitals, but one cannot tell from available data whether this is a conscious marketing decision to minimize uncompensated care or simply because such nurseries are typically already available in the local area and there is no need for an additional facility (Gray, 1986).

Are for-profit hospitals more likely to close and does this have a negative impact on access to care? It would, if a for-profit hospital were the primary provider of services in a given area. Past studies of hospital closure found that for-profit hospitals were more likely to close, but much of this closure was due to smaller, independent proprietary hospitals and is not really the major policy question currently (Sloan et al., 1986; Mullner et al., 1982). Of the hospitals built as part of investor-owned chains or taken over by investor-owned chains, only 12 of 540 had closed in the recent time period (Gray, 1986). There is little evidence that for-profit hospitals are more likely to close or that this contributes seriously to an access problem.

Overall, the evidence is mixed on the role of for-profit hospitals and access to care. They do provide fewer of certain services and are more likely to discourage admission of uninsured and medicaid patients. On balance, however, for-profit hospitals do pay taxes and some experts argue that because not-for-profits receive a tax break and for-profits do not, not-for-profits have a greater obligation to provide charity care (Gray, 1986). One fact on which most experts and health care institutions—whether governmental, for-profit, or not-for-profit—would agree is that health care institutions alone cannot solve the problem of access for uninsured patients. This is a much broader issue of public policy.

Quality of Care

As with access and fears that for-profit hospitals would restrict access in ways different and deleterious in comparison with not for-profit hospitals, a related concern about the growth of for profit hospitals has been that they have a negative impact on quality of care. Fears have included that these hospitals emphasize economic efficiency rather than quality or that an emphasis on economic efficiency leads to less attention on other aspects of the hospital and has an unintended negative effect on quality of care.

The traditional approach to the assessment of quality in health care is that promulgated by Avedis Donabedian (1969) and emphasizing structure, process, and outcome. Structure includes physical aspects of the facilities and equipment along with characteristics of the organization and qualifications of the health professional employees. Process refers to care of patients as reflected in the activities of the health professionals. Outcome includes health and patient satisfaction. Few studies have examined quality by comparing types of hospitals, although previous work by Harold Luft (1980) and Richard Scott and colleagues (1979) have all established that there are differences in hospital mortality rates and that such differences are related to hospital organizational attributes.

One recent study has explicitly examined the issue of differences in quality between types of hospitals (Gaumer, 1986). This study was commissioned by the Institute of Medicine panel studying for profit enterprise in health care. The commission report included a chapter on quality (Gray, 1986). These are the two major sources for the following discussion of quality.

Gary Gaumer (1986) examined postoperative mortality for medicare elective surgical admissions, ninety-day post-discharge readmission rates for medicare elective surgery admissions, status as to accreditation by the Joint Commission on Accreditation of Hospitals (JCAH), and two measures of medicare case mix. His data bases included: (1) a 25 percent simple random sample of all continental U.S. hospitals with a median length of stay of fifteen days or less from 1970 to 1978, and (2) all other similarly defined short-stay hospitals in fifteen states with some form of prospective payment at that time.

Even though the study reports extensive means on patient outcome data that is unadjusted, these unadjusted data often have large differences between types of hospitals and great instability from year to year due partially to small samples of patients in some procedure groups. More important are adjusted differences to account for ratios of actual to expected death rates at discharge. In these analyses, proprietary status is often associated with lower inhospital mortality and chain affiliation is often associated with higher mortality. These results may be confounded by severity, because it appears that proprietary hospitals have a less complex case mix. In contrast, the results on 180 days postadmission mortality are reversed, but less consistent, with investor-owned hospitals having higher 180–day mortality.

In terms of JCAH accreditation, Gaumer (1986) found that regardless of ownership status chain affiliated hospitals are more often accredited.

Within the for-profit hospitals, proprietary chains have higher rates of accreditation than single investor owned hospitals. Thus there is little evidence from the Gaumer study of quality differences in care by ownership category.

In its overall review, the IOM committee was also unable to find many clear areas of quality differences between for-profit, not for-profit, and governmental hospitals. There was some limited evidence that investor-owned hospitals may be less selective in approving physicians for staff privileges. In general, based on their practicing in various types of hospitals physicians did not believe that ownership was an important factor in quality of care. For those physicians who did report qualitative differences, they generally favored the for-profit hospitals.

Education and Research

The history of the for-profit chains reviewed in previous sections gives some indication that for-profit hospitals have traditionally not been large teaching hospitals and have not been major research facilities, although Humana has recently been experimenting in this area. Another concern about a negative impact of for-profit hospitals has been their lower rates of participation in teaching and research. Concerns about this include that for-profit hospitals are draining away paying patients who might have gone to such facilities and helped to subsidize teaching and research activities that typically are not self-supporting. It has been true that for-profit hospitals traditionally had little involvement in research or teaching. In 1983 only 2 percent of hospitals in investor-owned chains and 2 percent of independent investor-owned hospitals had residency programs. The average number of medical residents per bed was much lower in investor-owned hospitals (Gray, 1986).

New changes currently underway in this area make it difficult to assess what the future will be like. In addition to Humana operating the Louisville teaching facility, AMI operates the teaching hospital of Creighton University and has been working with the HMO of George Washington University. HCA has undertaken some responsibilities with teaching facilities in Oklahoma and Kansas and discussed others in Tennessee. NME has been participating with the University of Southern California on management of a teaching facility.

Several of the larger corporations have begun to contribute to research through their own research programs, as has Humana, and also by establishing company foundations to make grants. The rate of change within the for-profit companies and the restructuring and downsizing currently underway make predictions of future trends in this area very difficult.

Takeover of Special Situations

This final section on hospitals examines one special situation, the decision of local governments to contract out service delivery of county and local hospitals to for-profit chains. Typically in these situations, local government retains the responsibility for providing and especially financing the service but does not actually produce the service. The main advantage to contracting out has been the potential cost savings. In some ways, this issue of contracting out of services within the hospital industry bears more similarity to some of the other service sectors, especially those relating to criminal justice in which the issue is not major corporate growth in provision of services to the general population, but rather the influence of corporate and for-profit entities in assisting governmental units to provide a service to a specialized sector of the population.

Where do the cost savings of this approach come from? These cost savings usually come from scale economies and labor advantages due to location in the private sector. Scale economies relate to savings in input prices; for example, large-scale companies may be able to purchase goods at more advantageous prices (Schulz et al., 1984). Labor advantages often result from lower possible costs in the private sector due to more flexibility in personnel practices and at times the ability to avoid using municipal unions (Ferris and Grady, 1987).

In a recent study, James Ferris and Elizabeth Grady (1987) used data available on the provision of local services to test a model of the decision to contract out for local hospital services. They found that the four most important variables in the decision to contract out were: population size, the relative supply of hospital beds, the number of occupied alternative beds per county, and whether the jurisdiction is a county. Smaller and larger jurisdictions are more likely to contract out than middle-sized ones. Cities are more likely than counties to contract out. The more externally supplied beds in an area, the more likely is the governmental unit to contract out. Overall, the most pivotal factor in the decision to contract out is the potential cost savings which a governmental unit might achieve. Within this area, the availability of external suppliers and, thus, the presence of local for-profit hospitals is a major factor. Even though the expansion of chains in the late 1970s and early 1980s led to more contracting out, their contraction in the late 1980s led to a slowdown, if not a decrease, in contracting out of hospital services to for-profit chains.

AMBULATORY CARE SECTOR

What is included in the ambulatory care sector, and which parts of this sector have been experiencing growth in for-profit care? As mentioned earlier in this chapter, in some ways most of ambulatory care has always been for-profit, because most physicians practice ambulatory care, are engaged in work for profit, and not infrequently incorporate to achieve financial stability and protection from liability on personal property. Most experts who discuss for-profit ambulatory care, however, are concerned about the trend of corporatization of ambulatory health care and the threats that brings to traditional professional dominance and autonomy (Montgomery, 1988; Relman, 1987; McKinlay and Stoeckle, 1988). This section deals with that aspect of the growth of larger for-profit entities in the provision of ambulatory care services and its impact on physicians. Much of the discussion about this trend concerns the increasing employment of physicians on a salaried basis, rather than as the independent entrepreneurs of old. This section also surveys the trends in several very specialized aspects of health care, especially the growth of for profit HMOs and managed care corporations, the trend toward ambulatory surgery centers, other for-profit ambulatory facilities such as freestanding primary care centers (sometimes called urgent care centers and other times with a more derogatory connotation, and special care ambulatory facilities such as kidney dialysis centers.

Managed Care and HMOs

Many of the large for-profit national chains prominent in the provision of hospital care expanded in the area of managed care and HMOs with very mixed results in the 1980s. Health maintenance organizations combine health services with an insurance function. Typically, such plans provide fairly comprehensive health care in return for payment of a set monthly premium. There have been two major models: (1) group HMOs (many of which are nonprofit) in which the plan hires or maintains a contractual relationship with a number of physicians to provide care at one or several central locations and which often include the operation of specialized hospitals, and (2) the individual practice model (often called the IPA for individual practice association) in which the plan contracts with many different physicians to provide care to members within a set boundary of rules. These physicians continue to operate out of their own offices; the linkages with the plan may be weaker or stronger depending on the percent of the physicians' patients who belong to the plan and the presence of profit sharing, bonuses, or other fiscal control mechanisms.

Even though HMOs have been around since the establishment of the Ross-Loos Health Plan in Los Angeles in 1929 and the early days of the Kaiser plan in the 1940s, growth was very slow in the 1950s and 1960s and most were nonprofit plans. In 1973 the Health Maintenance Organization Act passed by Congress required employers to offer local qualified HMOs as an insurance option and also provided grants and loans to encourage the development of new HMOs and to stimulate growth. Although these funds were terminated in 1981, HMO growth has continued.

For-profit HMOs are much more recent, however. Few existed before 1975. By 1985 there were 136 for-profit HMO plans with 3 million enrollees. At that point, 35 percent of all HMO plans and 26 percent of HMO enrollees were a part of for-profit plans. In 1983 the first HMO company to issue stock and be publicly traded was U.S. Health Care Systems, which converted from a not-for-profit corporation (Gray, 1986). Maxicare Health Plans was created in the same year as was Health America. These for-profit HMO corporations were well received by Wall Street; by 1984 seven HMO corporations were on the stock market.

While growth was occurring in this sector of the health care industry, profits and economic health were more illusive. Only half of the 650 HMOs in operation in 1987 were profitable. During that same year, fifty-six plans ceased operations, and thirty of these terminated all operations, with the rest involved in mergers (Kenkel, 1988). Start up of new plans also slowed in 1987, although enrollment continued to increase. Problems with profitability were occurring in the for-profit and not-for-profit sectors. Seven Travelers plans, part of the Travelers Insurance Corporation, shut down in 1987. Blue Cross-Blue Shield plans, typically not-for-profit groups, experienced large losses. The seventy-six plans in this category included ninety-seven HMOs and fifty-six PPOs. Collectively, the Blues lost $1.9 billion from all these operations (Kenkel, 1988).

Among the plans with large problems in 1987 were Maxicare, the nation's largest publicly held HMO. The company lost money in every quarter of 1987 and ended the year with a deficit over $60 million. This was after a year in which Maxicare embarked on great expansion, acquiring Healthcare, USA and Health America. In that same year, the CEO of Maxicare had been quoted as being bullish on the industry and confident of the role that Maxicare's computerized management information system could play in the company's ability to deliver cost-effective care (Maxicare's Wasserman, 1986). A competitor from United Health Care Corporation that same year described Maxicare's main strengths as size, staying power, and management ability (Traska, 1986). Yet by the next year the company lost money in every quarter and continued having such severe financial problems that they led to the resignation of Maxicare's top management in 1988 and questions about the management skills in the corporation (Is Maxicare on Shaky Ground or Its Last Legs?, 1988). Bankruptcy proceedings were started in the next year. Maxicare is currently trying to arrange a reorganization under the protection of the bankruptcy laws. Due to the failure of Maxicare, a number of states are considering rewriting their bankruptcy laws to bar HMO bankruptcies

(Mullen, 1989). Some states plan to license HMOs as insurance companies to protect consumers who arrange care under such plans in the future.

Not all plans have had HMO failures. After making large cuts in its HMO operations, Humana has begun to expand into certain limited markets and now has acquired several HMOs in Florida and is planning to purchase Maxicare Arizona. Humana appears to have streamlined aspects of its HMO operations and is beginning to be profitable. Kaiser, the largest not-for-profit staff model HMO, had enrollment increases of 24,000 in 1987 and now has an enrollment over 5 million. Its revenues also climbed 8.6 percent, although net profits declined 6 percent (still leaving a net profit however) due to start-up costs of several East Coast operations (Kenkel, 1988).

The preferred provider organization (PPO) form of managed care which usually involves preferential reimbursement arrangements with a limited set of providers, but less restriction or comprehensiveness of care than a traditional HMO, has experienced much growth in the last few years. Five million more people participated in PPOs in 1987 over 1986. Humana ranked first in the number of employees eligible to use their PPOs, although this was down from the year before due to its withdrawing from twenty-four markets.

The picture for HMOs is improving somewhat. While in 1988 only 36 percent of the nation's 607 HMOs were profitable, managers of health care stock funds estimated that 73 percent would be in 1989. Part of this increased profitability is due to HMOs raising their rates to adjust for rising costs. Plans that have their own physician staffs rather than contracting with independent physicians as is more typical in IPA type plans appear to be doing better financially. This includes Kaiser, the largest nonprofit plan as well as some for-profit plans.

Other Ambulatory Care Facilities

In addition to HMOs, the other major types of for-profit ambulatory care facilities are freestanding ambulatory care centers and freestanding primary care or urgent care centers. Both types of organizations had a period of rapid growth in the early 1980s, but are not doing as well now. These facilities were initially started by entrepreneurial physicians and later experimented with by some of the large for-profit hospital corporations as part of vertical expansion efforts.

The situation of freestanding ambulatory surgery centers is very mixed. The first one was built in 1967 and failed due to lack of support from physicians and problems with financial reimbursement (Gray, 1986). By 1980, 120 ambulatory surgery centers were available. Many of these are part of hospital efforts, however, and some of the major pushes by corporations to expand into this area have not been financial successes. Growth continues; in 1987 freestanding ambulatory surgery centers increased 46 percent to 865 centers (Henderson, 1988). It is estimated that these centers currently perform one of every six outpatient surgeries. Surgery that does not require an overnight hospitalization has been growing rapidly, due to revised reimbursement rates and growing acceptance of the safety and advantages of surgery in this setting by both patients and providers.

Ownership patterns of surgery centers have been changing; independently operated facilities now dominate the market. About three-quarters of all centers operate independently of hospitals or corporate chains (Henderson, 1988). In 1987 centers owned by corporate chains lost market share for the third straight year. The large chains of surgery centers are now generally not part of large for-profit hospital chains but instead concentrate on just this aspect of health care delivery. A major approach is the concentration by hospitals of expansion of their on-site outpatient surgery centers, rather than the growth of freestanding centers. The greatest concentration of surgeries are in the specialties of opthamology, ear, nose, and throat, and orthopedic areas.

Urgent care centers have also grown rapidly in the last decade. Typically, these centers now operate very much as private physicians' offices in terms of licensure, but with extended hours of operation. Appointments are not required, yet waiting times are often shorter than in a hospital emergency room and charges are lower. Typically, these centers are in suburban and high traffic areas (such as near malls) and are open every day from 8 A.M. to 8 or 9 P.M. In some very high traffic areas, they may be open until midnight. Although the early centers were often owned by physicians, typical ownership patterns have been changing; now more operations are run by larger for-profit corporations and also by nonprofit hospitals.

The first freestanding emergicenter opened in 1973 (Gray, 1986). Expansion was rapid, with 2,600 centers by mid–1985. Even though chains of such centers are now operating, most are small, locally oriented chains. Humana made a large push in this area in 1984 and 1985 and at that point was operating around 150 centers. They have withdrawn from most of this market, however.

Since 1986 growth patterns have slowed. From 1986 to 1987 ambulatory care centers increased minimally, and investor-owned chains continued to decrease their presence in this area, now operating only seventy-four such centers (Lutz, 1988). The not-for-profit portion of this market is continuing to grow, however, up 10 percent from 1986 to 1987. It appears that this service has found a niche in the American health care system but that the services are increasingly likely to be operated by not-for-profit groups or by small locally oriented chains. This area of operation has not been financially lucrative for the large for-profit hospital chains.

Special Care

Two of the largest special types of ambulatory health care centers are freestanding dialysis centers, long an important area of for-profit health services delivery, and birthing and infertility services. Dialysis services, although only a little over twenty years old, are an area in which the for-profit groups predominate. National Medical Care, the oldest of the for-profit providers, was started in 1969 but really grew after kidney dialysis became a covered service under the medicare program in 1972. Once medicare service was provided, the patients requesting this service grew rapidly from 18,000 in 1974 to more than 78,000 in 1984 (Gray, 1986). When these facilities were new in 1973, only 11 percent were freestanding versus 52 percent in 1984, of which 79 percent were for-profit (Gray, 1986). Physicians own many of these for-profit facilities at least partially.

There have been a number of criticisms of the role of for-profit corporations in this area of care. Critics have argued that dialysis rates are higher in states with a higher proportion of proprietary facilities and that there is more dialysis in the United States than in countries without for-profit care in this area (Schlesinger et al., 1989). They have also argued that in parts of the country in which for-profit centers are more common, there are lower rates of transplantation and of in-home dialysis because these are less profitable treatment regimens for the companies.

A recent study has tried to answer some of the criticisms of previous studies. These include that there is a high correlation between area of the country and style of practice and also between area of the country and the role of for-profit care, making some of the results and analyses of earlier studies unfair in that aggregate level data were used (Schlesinger et al., 1988). This study has used individual level data available from the Health Care Financing Administration datasets of people receiving medicare for dialysis services. Some important differences were found between the for-profit and not-for-profit sectors of care. Patients in nonprofit facilities are more likely to be transferred for transplantation or to receive in-home dialysis than are patients in for-profit centers. It does appear in this sector of care that ownership incentives have some impact on clinical decision making, leading to different choices in methods of dialysis particularly.

Birthing centers and centers for infertility treatment have been another recent area of growth in for-profit care. Birthing centers in some places are being developed as parts of joint ventures with obstetricians, again raising a possible issue of the impact of ownership incentives on clinical decisions. A new possibility for investor-owned facilities are clinics for in vitro fertilization (IVF)—more commonly known as test tube babies. Two groups of entrepreneurs, both including physicians as part of the investors, are opening for-profit clinics for this service. To be profitable, these clinics need a very large volume of patients to cover the fixed costs of the equipment. Some critics charge that many of the centers, whether at for-profit clinics or connected with universities, are not honest about their low success rates to keep the volume of patients high. As of 1989 only 45 of the 150 clinics had recorded any births and less than ten are responsible for two-thirds of the IVF births in the United States to this date (Blakeslee, 1989). The future of for-profit clinics in this area remains a question mark.

THE IMPACT OF FOR-PROFIT CORPORATIONS AND COMPETITION ON PHYSICIANS

The review of for-profit ambulatory care and especially the criticisms of IVF centers and dialysis centers help to raise many of the issues of the impact of for-profit care on physicians and on their patients. In both the area of dialysis and IVF care, there is a concern that ownership incentives impact on decisions about care modality and possibly the quality of care delivered. Fears about the growth of for-profit care have included that it changes the judgment of physicians, and that it inhibits the traditional concept of physicians as the predominant advocates for patients in treatment. Concerns raised by physicians also include a fear that the status of physicians is declining and that the loss of their role as independent practitioners could lead to a decline in their role as the advocates of their patients. In addition, a related debate is whether physicians could eventually become simply another employee group or whether their special professional orientation can be maintained.

This chapter has documented the growth of for-profit modes of delivery of services in inpatient and outpatient health care and, related to this, the growth of entrepreneurial and competitive forces in health care. It is important to review the traditional image of the physician and his or her role vis-à-vis the patient. Due to their superior knowledge and a code of professional ethics physicians were viewed as protectors of the interests of their patients. The relationship between patients and physicians had, in the classical Parsonian formulation, four major elements: It was (1) specific to technical concerns; (2) neutral in the sense that an emotional attachment should not develop between the patient and the physician; (3) universal in the sense that the practitioner is obligated to treat all patients fairly, regardless of social characteristics such as income or race; and (4) limited to specific functions, such that the physician should deal with medical and closely related matters, not with all aspects of life (Parsons, 1951, 1975; Wolinsky, 1980). A critical part of this formulation is that physicians fulfill a fiduciary role with their patients; they are the prime agents responsible for being sure that patients receive the best possible and most appropriate care. Each physician is to represent the patient's health and economic interests, even if these conflict with the physician's own economic self interest (Miller, 1983). The need for physicians to act as fiduciary agents relating to types of care was increased with the rise of health insurance which removed part or all of the direct costs of care from the patients' immediate interest and thus increased the willingness of patients to leave decisions about the amount and type of care consumed to the physicians.

This image of physicians as protectors of their patients has advantages for the profession. It contributes to society's willingness to allow the profession to be self-regulated (Freidson, 1970). It has traditionally enhanced the power of the profession regarding not only an individual patient but also the total society and the independence of the profession. Despite criticisms of aspects of this role that are overstated, most experts agree that typical physicians do adhere to strong ethical standards and have absorbed this image of their responsibility to patients as part of medical education and socialization, as well as part of general American culture. Obviously, some physicians violate this trust, and these cases make headlines as part of malpractice trials or licensure removal hearings. In reality, however, these are fairly rare events and make news because they diverge from the behavior of most physicians at most points in time.

Physicians have fiduciary interests over patients in two major respects in modern medicine. They apply professional expertise to decisions about health care treatment and modality of care, including decisions whether to hospitalize, to perform surgery, or to order tests. These decisions should be based on the best interests of patients, not what will make the most money for physicians. The second aspect of fiduciary responsibility is assuring patients that other professionals or organizations to which the physicians entrust the care of particular patients are indeed worthy of that trust (Gray, 1986). All systems of paying for services have the possibility of providing an incentive either to underserve or overserve. Traditional fee-for-service practice has an incentive to overserve patients because doctors derive income if they see patients or do things to patients. Certain HMO arrangements for care in which there is profit sharing if the patients of a particular physician use less care than a prearranged figure lead to an incentive to underserve. There has been an accepted notion within medicine that underservice is more dangerous than overservice within medicine, probably because most practitioners believe in the value of their services and that medicine generally does good. In reality, overservice itself can be harmful.

Of greater concern to many health care experts has been allowing physicians to derive secondary income from their patient care decisions through investments in organizations that provide services, such as laboratory and X-ray facilities owned by a physician. There is some evidence that if physicians own lab or X-ray facilities, they tend to use such services at a higher rate than physicians who do not (Gray, 1986). The IOM committee on for-profit care had three major recommendations about physicians' compensation systems and referral approaches. They recommended that it is best if physicians' compensation systems break the link between the treating of patients and the rate of return physicians earn on their time invested in medical practice. They also recommended that bonus incentive plans in which physicians received a share of surplus revenues are dangerous and, in the absence of being prohibited, at least in all cases should be revealed to patients. Their third recommendation was that it should be considered unethical for physicians to have ownership interests in health care facilities such as labs or X-ray facilities to which they make referral or to receive payments for such referrals. If this is not prohibited (as it is not currently), patients and third-party payors should be aware of the potential conflict of interest (Gray, 1986).

How have physicians responded to the increase in for-profit care and how has it affected practice patterns? Arnold Relman (1987) argues that the growth of commercialism in health care has caused some conflict between the altruistic ideals of medicine and corporate financial interests. Eli Ginzberg (1987) argues that one reason for rising costs in American health care is the attitudes of both physicians and consumers toward technology and the best possible care. Given growing concerns about costs, new forms of organization with potential to restrain growth in costs may be likely. Relman's (1987) recommendations for physicians are similar to the IOM report, including that physicians limit their practice incomes to fees or salaries earned from patient services personally provided or supervised. He also advises physicians in traditional office practice to avoid arrangements with corporate organizations that reward them for choosing a particular service or facility on referral. If employed as part of a for-profit hospital or HMO, the physicians, he believes, should be either self-employed or part of a self-managed and self-regulated medical group that contracts with the company. This is the arrangement that the nonprofit Kaiser HMO has maintained for years through the Permanente groups of affiliated physicians. Lastly, Relman (1987) argues that physicians should not enter an arrangement with any organization that directly rewards them for withholding services from patients.

What is the situation of physicians in salaried practice? Currently, between one-fourth and one-fifth of all nonfederal physicians are in salaried practice (Relman, 1988). These figures are much higher for physicians under 35 and are more common for young women (60 percent) than young men (40 percent). Two recent short articles by physicians in the *New England Journal of Medicine* raised the types of issues that physicians fear they may face if they become involved as employees in for profit corporate health care delivery. Each physician reported on his personal experience as a corporate employee.

In the first case, physician Randall Bock worked full time for four years in an ambulatory care center in a suburban area. In that center the current trend is to encourage physicians to become owner-operators, but most centers are still corporately owned. The nurses were actually corporate employees while the physicians were designated as independent subcontractors, the arrangement which Relman recommends. At this particular clinic, only a corporate employee could supervise the clinic; thus the nurses supervised the clinic and organized the patients to be seen. The corporation makes more money if the rate of patient flow is high and the charges per patient high, due perhaps to tests and X-rays being performed. Physicians were encouraged financially through incentives to order more tests. Their rates of reimbursement increased from $28 per hour to a commission of 22 percent of gross billing once their hourly rates exceeded $28. The corporation maintained a list ranking doctors by the additional charges they generated per hour. The three full-time doctors at the bottom of the charges generated list left the clinic in the next year; they included the author and one other doctor who was fired, the third resigned (Bork, 1988).

In the second article, physician Henry Scovern reported on his experiences as a physician in a for-profit HMO in 1985 and for the next two years (Scovern, 1988). He charges that the hospital trained their non-MD staff poorly, placed burdensome administrative tasks on the primary doctor if a referral visit or hospitalization to a nonparticipating hospital was required, did not provide time in the schedule for hospital rounds, and discouraged specialty visits and limited the number of visits to a specialist for a problem (Scovern, 1988). Scovern was concerned with pressure to undertreat, while Bock described pressure for overtreatment. Both articles reflect the fears of doctors as to their practice under corporate medicine, although it is hard to know how generalizable these specific cases are. They are examples of what John McKinlay and John Stoeckle (1988) describe as the proletarianization of doctoring. By proletarianization, they mean a process in which an occupational category is divested of control over certain prerogatives of the location, content, and tasks of the work; these are subordinated to the broader requirements of advanced capitalism. McKinlay and Stoeckle view this as the industrial revolution finally catching up with medicine.

Most of the writing in this area is anecdotal or prescriptive. Data are needed on the impact of these possible transformations on most physicians; few studies are available. One recent study did examine the implications of the move to corporatized medical care through a survey to 1,000 physicians who have left clinical work for administrative careers within medicine (Montgomery, 1988). Results are compared with similar data obtained from a random sample of physicians. The administrative physicians surveyed are members of the American Academy of Medical Directors, a specialty association for physicians in management. Physicians in this group are more likely to be white, male, and American born and educated than are all physicians. These physicians have a positive orientation toward management tasks and a major role in management, despite little formal training in that area. They viewed their peers more as other health care executives and less as other physicians.

These data provide some support for a contrasting argument to that of proletarianization, one of a divided profession with an emerging elite of administrative physicians. This administrative elite is still composed of physicians closely enough identified with the practice of medicine to help to maintain the professional status of physicians rather than to help create their transformation to employees. The implications of this debate are not yet clear, although health policy writers who are themselves physicians such as Arnold Relman and John Iglehart clearly believe that a strong, independent professional with clearer norms of practice is necessary both for physicians and for the protection of patients. Otherwise health care could become simply another commercial service transaction in which the old caveat of buyer beware will apply, yet the buyer (the patient) does not have adequate knowledge to know when to beware (Relman, 1988; Iglehart, 1989). Clearly this view by the medical profession itself is somewhat self-serving. Yet, it is difficult to easily imagine other mechanisms of social control, although a greatly increased role for government as a regulator and guarantor of quality would be one possibility. This appears to be an unlikely possibility in the United States at this point.

OVERALL ASSESSMENT AND CONCLUSIONS

This concluding section does not need to repeat the issues discussed earlier about the implications of the growth in for-profit care for the role of physicians or the care of patients, although that is one major aspect of an assessment of the for profit trend. In the case of physicians, and to a lesser extent in all ambulatory care, the for-profit sector is growing, but patterns of future growth may be more limited. In addition, ethical questions as to who looks out for the patient are an important and very real issue.

What about the provision of hospital and inpatient services by for-

profit providers and especially the growth of major for profit corporations and their increasing role in the delivery of health care service? Does
the growth of for-profit health care exacerbate current problems in the
health care delivery system and is there a difference in the types,
amounts, and quality of care delivered in for-profit versus nonprofit or
governmental sectors? Several important caveats need discussion. Most
importantly, at times it is hard to be sure what is actually being compared. In today's increasingly competitive health care delivery system,
all hospitals (and especially all nongovernment hospitals) worry about
the bottom line, whether that line is called a profit or additional revenues
available for future growth. Also, nonprofit hospitals are forming their
own chains to reap the advantages of purchasing and multi-institutional
arrangements. In addition, they are setting up for-profit subsidiaries.
These trends also tend to mute the importance of comparisons between
sectors, and emphasize instead the changing total environment in health
care delivery in which costs and competition between institutions are
much more important than twenty or thirty years ago.

What were the major conclusions of the IOM report, especially in the
critical areas of costs of care, quality, and access? The IOM report (Gray,
1986) concludes that the growth in for-profit health care has led to an
increase in costs of health care. Hospital charges per discharge are higher
for the average for profit hospital versus nonprofit hospitals. A few
studies find this less true in several states than in overall data. Perhaps
the most important conclusion from this area of costs is a clear dem-
onstration that for-profit hospitals do not have management secrets to
allow them to operate more efficiently. If the private sector has intro-
duced new and more efficient management techniques, those have so
quickly been adopted in all sectors of hospital care that few differences
can be demonstrated.

In quality of care, only limited indicators are available, because the
measurement of quality in health care represents a major problem for
researchers. The indicators available, including both structural factors
such as accreditation and board certification of staff and the very limited
data on outcomes as measures of quality of care, all show few consistent
differences that would indicate inferior or superior care in for-profit
versus not-for-profit hospitals.

Access is some ways is the most critical area in which to assess the
impact of for-profit care. Both the studies reviewed in this chapter and
the IOM report conclude that for-profit hospitals provide less uncompensated care than do not-for-profit hospitals, although there are wide
variations. Physicians who practice in both facilities also perceive a difference in access in for-profits, with those facilities being more likely to
restrict admissions of uninsured patients and sometimes of medicaid
patients. There is also some evidence of more patient dumping by for-

profit hospitals to public hospitals of the uninsured, although many nonprofits also engage in this practice at times.

In other areas of access, there are fewer differences. For-profit hospitals do not appear more likely to close and leave an area with no hospital, and the record on maintenance of specific services is also quite mixed. In addition, because for-profit hospitals do pay taxes while not-for-profit voluntary hospitals receive a tax break, nonprofits should provide more charity care than the for-profit sector.

One reason why access such a difficult, yet critical, area to address is the major access problems in the United States. The problems of access to health care services and care for the uninsured are broader in scope than those likely to be addressed by any one part of the hospital sector. Without government aid no hospital can solve its community's access problem and remain a fiscally viable institution. For-profit hospitals may exacerbate this problem slightly, but they did not create it. Even so, some analysts argue that privatization and reliance on market forces are more expensive than central control over costs, stronger governmental control, and a stronger governmental role in the delivery of health care services (Weller and Manga, 1983; Kronenfeld, 1990).

When one compares across the major areas of cost, quality, and access as well as more minor areas of education and research, the conclusion of the Institute of Medicine in 1986 still appears reasonable. They argued that available evidence on differences between for-profit and not-for-profit health care organization did not justify recommending either that for-profit ownership be supported or opposed as a public policy. All institutions in health care need to continue to exercise some social responsibility, however, and both government and researchers need to continue to be sure that quality and access concerns are met. All of us—and government is a reflection of the attitudes of the general public—need to address the issue of access to health care and the uninsured. No single provider of care or institution can meet this obligation alone.

REFERENCES

American Hospital Association, *Hospital Statistics: Data from the American Hospital Association, 1986 Annual Survey*. Chicago: American Hospital Association, 1987.

Becker, Edmund R., and Frank A. Sloan. "Hospital Ownership and Performance," *Economic Inquiry* 23 (January 1985): 21–36.

Berliner, Howard, and Carol Regan. "Multinational Operations of U.S. For-Profit Hospital Chains: Trends and Implications," *American Journal of Public Health* 77 (October 1987): 1280–84.

Bergthold, Linda A. "A General Hearing Testimony," in J. Warren Salmon and Jeffrey W. Todd, *The Corporatization of Health Care*. Springfield: Illinois Public Health Association, 1988.

"Billions in New Debt Challenges HCA Management," *Hospitals*, May 5, 1989: 18–19.

Blakeslee, Sandra. "Trying to Make Money Making Test Tube Babies," *New York Times*, May 17, 1989, business sec., p. 6.

Bock, Randall S. "The Pressure to Keep Prices High at a Walk-in Clinic," *New England Journal of Medicine* 319 (September 22, 1988): 785–87.

Coelen, Craig G. "Hospital Ownership and Comparative Hospital Costs," in Bradford Gray (ed.), *For-Profit Enterprise in Health Care*. Washington, D.C.: National Academy Press, 1986.

Cohodes, Donald R. and Brian M. Kinkead. *Hospital Capital Formation in the 1980s*. Baltimore, Md.: Johns Hopkins University Press, 1984.

Colman, Thomas W. "Private Capital Funds Public Hospitals," *Modern Healthcare*, December 18, 1986, p. 47.

Davis, L. J. "The M.D. Who Would Be a Tycoon," *The New York Times Magazine*, September 25, 1989, pp. 28–30, 45.

Donabedian, Avedis. *A Guide to Medical Care Administration: Vol. 2—Medical Care Appraisal-Quality and Utilization*. Washington, D.C.: American Public Health Association, 1969.

Ermann, Dan, and Jon Gabel. "Investor-owned Multihospital Systems: A Synthesis of Research Findings," in *For-Profit Enterprise in Health Care*. Washington, D.C.: National Academy Press, 1986.

Feder, J., J. Hadley, and R. Muller. "Falling through the Cracks: Poverty, Insurance Coverage, and Hospital Care for the Poor, 1980 and 1982," *Milbank Memorial Fund Quarterly/Health and Society* 62 (1984): 544–66.

Ferris, James S., and Elizabeth Graddy. "What Governs the Decision to Contract out for Local Hospital Services?" *Inquiry* 24 (Fall 1987): 285–94.

Freidson, Eliot. *The Profession of Medicine*. New York: Dodd and Mead, 1970.

Gaumer, Gary. "Medicare Patient Outcomes and Hospital Organizational Mission," in Bradford Gray (ed.), *For-Profit Enterprise in Health Care*. Washington, D.C.: National Academy Press, 1986.

Ginzberg, Eli. "For-Profit Medicine," *New England Journal of Medicine* 319 (September 22, 1988): 757–61.

———. "A Hard Look at Cost Containment," *New England Journal of Medicine* 316 (April 30, 1987): 1151–54.

Glazer, William A. *Paying the Hospital*. Boston: Jossey-Bass, 1987.

Gray, Bradford (ed.). *For-Profit Enterprise in Health Care*. Washington, D.C.: National Academy Press, 1986.

Hansmann, Henry B. "The Role of Nonprofit Enterprise," *Yale Law Journal* 89 (April 1980): 835–901.

Health Care Financing Administration. "National Health Expenditures, 1986–2000," *Health Care Financing Review* 8, No. 4 (1987): 1–36.

Henderson, John A. "Freestanding Centers Gaining on Surgery Suites," *Modern Healthcare*, June 3, 1988, pp. 84–87.

Herzlinger, Regina E., and William S. Krasker. "Who Profits from Nonprofits?" *Harvard Business Review* 65 (January-February, 1987): 93–106.

Hodgkinson, V. A., and M. S. Weitzman. *Dimensions of the Independent Sector*. Washington, D.C.: Independent Sector, 1986.

Hoy, Elizabeth, and Bradford H. Gray. "Trends in the Growth of the Major

Investor-Owned Hospital Companies," in Bradford Gray (ed.), *For-Profit Enterprise in Health Care*. Washington, D.C.: National Academy Press, 1986.

Iglehart, John K. "The Debate over Physician Ownership of Health Care Facilities," *New England Journal of Medicine* 321 (July 20, 1989): 198–204.

"Interview with David Jones," *Managed HealthCare* July 17, 1989: 10–13.

"Is Maxicare on Shaky Grounds or Its Last Legs?" *Hospitals*, April 20, 1988, p. 35.

Johnson, Donald E. "Investor Owned Chains Continue Expansion, 1985 Survey Shows," *Modern Healthcare*, June 7, 1985, pp. 75–90.

Kenkel, Paul. "Managed Care Growth Continued in 1987 Despite Companies' Poor Operating Results," *Modern Healthcare*, June 3, 1988, pp. 20–38.

Kronenfeld, Jennie Jacobs. "Access to Care under Prospective Payment and Competition," in Jennie Jacobs Kronenfeld, Roger L. Amidon, and Robert Toomey (eds.), *Competitive Strategies in the Health Care Market* Albany, N.Y.: Delmar Publishers, 1990.

Kronenfeld, Jennie Jacobs, and Marcia Lynn Whicker. *U.S. Health Policy: An Analysis of the Federal Role*. New York: Praeger, 1984.

Leberto, Tony. "Investment Group Snares AMI for $3.35 Billion," *Healthweek* 3 (July 17, 1989): 1, 33.

Lefton, Doug. "Will For-Profit Hospital Chains Swallow Up Nonprofit Sector?" *American Medical News* (June 18/July 5, 1985): 1, 35, 37.

Lewin, Lawrence S., Robert A. Derzon, and Rhea Marguiles. "Investor Owned and Nonprofits Differ in Economic Performance," *Hospitals*, July 1981, 1, pp. 52–58.

Light, Donald W. "Corporate Medicine for Profit," *Scientific Medicine* 255 (December 1986): 38–46.

———. "Social Control and the American Health Care System," in Howard E. Freeman and Sol Levine (eds.), *Handbook of Medical Sociology*, 4th ed., Englewood Cliffs, N.J.: Prentice-Hall, 1989.

Luft, H. "The Relationship between Surgical Volume and Mortality: An Exploration of Causal Factors and Alternative Models," *Medical Care* 18 (September 1980): 1987.

Lutz, Sandy. "For Profit Chains Retreat from Ambulatory Business," *Modern Healthcare*, June 3, 1988, pp. 74–80.

McKinlay, John, and John Stoeckle. "Corporatization and the Social Transformation of Doctoring," *International Journal of Health Services* 18 (1988): 191–205.

"Maxicare's Wasserman," *Hospitals*, November 20, 1988: pp. 84–86.

Metz, Maureen. "Trends in Source of Capital in the Hospital Industry, Appendix D," *Report of the Special Committee on Equity of Payment for Not-for-Profit and Investor-Owned Hospitals*. Chicago, Ill.: American Hospital Association, 1983.

Miller, Frances H. "Secondary Income from Recommended Treatment: Should Fiduciary Principles Restrain Physician Behavior?" in Bradford H. Gray (ed.), *The New Health Care for Profit*. Washington, D.C.: National Academy Press, 1983.

Montgomery, Kathleen. "The Threat of Corporatization and Its Recapture by the Medical Profession" (Paper presented at the American Sociological Association meeting, (Atlanta, Georgia) August 1988.

Mullen, Patricia. "States to Bar HMO Bankruptcies," *Managed Health Care*, July 17, 1989: 1, 25.

Mullner, Ross M., Calvin S. Byre, Paul Levy, and Joseph D. Kubal. "Closure among U.S. Community Hospitals, 1976–1980," *Medical Care* 20 (July 1982): 699–702.

"Multi-Unit Providers Survey, Volume I," *Modern HealthCare*, Special Issue, May 27, 1988.

Parson, Talcott. "The Sick Role and the Role of the Physician Reconsidered," *Milbank Memorial Fund Quarterly* 53 (1975): 257–78.

———. *The Social System*. New York: Free Press, 1951.

Pattison, Robert V., and Hallie M. Katz. "Investor-Owned and Not-for-Profit Hospitals," *New England Journal of Medicine*. 309 (1983): 347–53.

Pauley, Mark. *Doctors and their Workshops*. Chicago, Ill.: University of Chicago Press, 1980.

Reinhardt, Uwe. *Financing the Hospital: The Experience Abroad*. Washington, D.C.: Department of Health and Human Services, 1984.

———. "Flawed Methods Cripple Study on Not-for-Profits," *Hospitals*, April 20, 1987, p. 136.

———. "The Nature of Equity Financing: Appendix to Chapter 3," in Bradford Gray (ed.), *For-Profit Enterprise in Health Care*. Washington, D.C.: National Academy Press, 1986.

Relman, Arnold S. "The New Medical-Industrial Complex," *New England Journal of Medicine* 303 (October 23, 1980): 963–69.

———. "Practicing Medicine in the New Business Climate," *New England Journal of Medicine* 316 (April 30, 1987): 1150–51.

———. "Salaried Physicians and Economic Incentives," *New England Journal of Medicine* 319 (September 22, 1988): 784.

Rosenberg, Charles E. *The Care of Strangers: The Rose of America's Hospital System*. New York: Basic Books, 1987.

Schiff, Gordon. "Letter to the Editor," *New England Journal of Medicine* 312 (June 6, 1985): 1522.

Schlesinger, M., and R. Dorwart. "Ownership and Mental Health Services: A Reappraisal of the Shift Toward Privately Owned Facilities," *New England Journal of Medicine* 311 (1984): 959–65.

Schlesinger, Mark. "The Rise of Proprietary Health Care," *Business and Health* 2 (1985): 7–12.

Schlesinger, Mark, Paul Cleary, and David Blumenthal. "The Ownership of Health Facilities and Clinical Decisionmaking," *Medical Care* 27 (March 1988): 244–58.

Schlesinger, Mark, Judy Bentkkover, David Blumenthal, Robert Mustacchio, and Janet Willer. "The Privatization of Health Care and Physicians' Perceptions of Access to Hospital Services," *The Milbank Quarterly* 65 (1987): 25–58.

Schultz, Rockwell I., James R. Greenley, and Robert W. Peterson. "Differences in the Direct Costs of Public and Private Acute Inpatient Psychiatric Services," *Inquiry* 21 (Winter 1984): 380–93.

Scott, W. Richard, Anne Flood, and Wayne Ewy. "Organizational Determinants of Services, Quality, and Costs of Care in Hospitals," *Milbank Memorial Fund Quarterly* 57 (Spring 1979): 234–64.

Scovern, Henry. "A Physician's Experience in a For-Profit Staff-Model HMO," *New England Journal of Medicine* 319 (September 22, 1988): 787–90.

Sloan, F., J. Valvona, and R. Muller. "Identifying the Issues: A Statistical Profile," in F. Sloan, J. Blumstein, and J. Perrin (eds.), *Uncompensated Hospital Care: Rights and Responsibilities*. Baltimore, Md.: Johns Hopkins University Press, 1986.

Sloan, Frank A., and Robert A. Vraciu. "Investor Owned and Not-for-Profit Hospitals: Addressing Some Issues," *Health Affairs*, Spring 1983: 25–37.

Starr, Paul. *The Social Transformation of American Medicine: The Rise of a Sovereign Profession and the Making of a Vast Industry*. New York: Basic Books, 1982.

Steinwald, Bruce, and Duncan Neuhauser. "The Role of the Proprietary Hospital," *Law and Contemporary Problems* 35 (Autumn 1970): 817–38.

Traska, M. R. "HCA's Restructuring Solution: Employee Ownership," *Hospitals*, June 20, 1987, p. 20.

———. "Maxicare Seen as Feisty by Some of Its Competitors," *Hospitals*, November 20, 1986, pp. 70–72.

Wallace, Cynthia. "Difficult Times May Have Passed for Investor Owned Chains," *Modern HealthCare*, October 24, 1986, pp. 118–20.

Watt, J. Michael, Robert A. Derzon, Steven C. Renn, and Carl J. Schramm. "The Comparative Economic Performance of Investor-Owned Chains and Not-for-Profit Hospitals," *New England Journal of Medicine* 314 (January 9, 1986): 89–96.

Weller, Geoffrey R., and Pranlal Manga. "The Push for Reprivatization of Health Care Services in Canada, Great Britain, and the United States," *Journal of Health Politics, Policy and Law* 8 (Fall 1983): 495–518.

Wilson, Glenn, Cecil Sheps, and Thomas R. Oliver. "Effects of Hospital Revenue Bonds on Hospital Planning and Revenue," *New England Journal of Medicine* 307 (December 2, 1982): 1426–30.

Wolinsky, Frederic. *The Sociology of Health*. Boston: Little, Brown and Co., 1980.

5

The Elderly, Long-Term Care, and Home-Based Services

Two other population groups with a great need for specialized health care services are the elderly and younger people in need of long-term health-related services at a less intense level than that found in a hospital today. The types of care discussed in this chapter are nursing home care, home health care, and housing options for the elderly that may include some aspects of health care, such as retirement homes.

Before discussing specific types of care, however, it is important to understand how such care was initially provided and organized in the U.S. health care delivery system and how these services became differentiated from more traditional hospital care in twentieth-century America. Another important issue related to this population group and this care is general demographic trends, most especially the trend of an aging population.

BACKGROUND ON THE ELDERLY

Today, in contrast to the eighteenth and nineteenth centuries, we segment society into age groups and plan for their special service needs. We have already discussed the special service needs of the young due to their age. Similarly, some experts segment the elderly population as a group with special service needs due to their age. This is probably less true of the elderly as a total group than it is of the young because most of the special services considered as needs of the elderly vary depending on their health.

A person with no chronic health problems and no physical limitations on their activities uses services very similarly to other adults. It is true, however, that the proportion of people with any handicap or disability, including physical, mental, visual or hearing, increases as people get older. Arthritis, the leading cause of disability in the elderly, is found at an 8 percent higher rate in those sixty-five and older. Hypertension, the second most common cause of disability among the elderly, is 59 percent higher for the sixty-five-and-over age group. Among people forty-five to sixty-five years of age, about 72 percent have one or more chronic health problems and this increases to 86 percent among those sixty-five and older. Hearing and visual problems also become important limitations on health and the ability to live independently. In the seventy-five to seventy-nine age group, only fifteen people out of a hundred have vision that is correctable to 20/20. Three-quarters of the population over seventy-five have hearing impairment (Cox, 1988).

Thus we think of more custodial health-related services as particularly relevant to the elderly (ranging from meals delivered to the home and assistance in maintaining the home to assistance in nursing services delivered at home and twenty-four-hour care as provided in a nursing home). Actually, younger people with severe chronic illnesses also need these services. Still, these services are used at a much higher rate by the elderly, and it is the growth in the elderly population along with other demographic trends and changes in health-care financing that have led to the growth in the companies and other units providing these services. Before discussing these services and their own patterns of growth and development, it is useful to discuss the growth and changes in the elderly population in the United States.

Historically, this country has been formed by immigration with a relatively young population, typically younger than other countries such as in Western Europe. High rates of immigration traditionally make a population younger because it is the young who are most likely to migrate. In addition, death rates were higher at the turn of the century when fewer people lived to an old age; the major improvements in the average years of life have come from improvements at the beginning of life through reduced rates of infant and maternal mortality. Life expectancy refers to the average number of years a person has remaining in life at a certain age. Early data from Massachusetts indicate that its residents had life expectations of about thirty-five years at birth. By 1900 this had increased to forty-seven years. Fifty years later, this had increased to sixty-eight years, and in 1976 was almost seventy-three years (Harris and Cole, 1980).

At the turn of the century the lower life expectancy at birth combined with the higher probability of dying from certain infectious diseases in adulthood meant that a very small proportion of the population of the United States was elderly, using a typical definition of elderly as those sixty-five and over. Less than 5 percent of the U.S. population was sixty-five and over in 1900.

Now a much higher proportion of the population of the United States is sixty-five or older—about 12.5 percent in the early 1980s or 25.7 million people over the age of sixty-four in 1980. Estimates are that the proportion of the population over sixty-five will rise to 12.7 percent in 1990, 13.9 percent in 2010 and perhaps as high as 21.1 percent of the population in 2030. If these estimates hold, there will be almost 40 million elderly in the United States in 2010. The growth in the percentage of elderly is the result of high fertility across the developed world in the immediate post-World War II period and reduced fertility rates after the baby boom of the late 1940s and 1950s. A small proportion is due to improvements in mortality of the elderly. Over the past two decades, American life expectancy at age sixty-five has risen from 14.5 to 16.5 years (Hewitt and Howe, 1988). Actually, the biggest periods of growth in the proportion of elderly are yet to come as the baby boom itself ages, beginning in the second decade of the next century (Crystal, 1988). This increase in the proportion of elderly is not a unique phenomenon to America. All of the industrialized nations will experience an elderly boom in the first thirty years of the twenty-first century. Italy and Canada could have as much as 22 percent of their populations over the age of sixty-five by 2030, and the figure could even be 25 percent in West Germany (Crystal, 1988).

Not only will the percent of the population over sixty-five increase but also the older segment of the elderly (those over seventy-five) will increase even more rapidly. This seventy-five and over group is likely to fit the notion of a captive population group, with a substantial proportion of the people in that age group needing the custodial and health care services described in this chapter. The proportion of the population over seventy-five is expected to double by 2030, while the proportion over eighty-five will quadruple (Crystal, 1988).

The increasing proportion of elderly will have a major impact on health care costs in general, because the elderly utilize all types of health care services at a much higher rate than do the young. It will also have a major impact on the sources of revenue for the government, which is a very major source of the funds for health services used by this population group. The reasons for the major impact on sources of revenue for the government are that retired people usually draw benefits from government programs and are less likely to be current taxpayers. Economists talk about the dependency ratio, the proportion of children and elderly in a population to those who are working. This is an important aspect of governmental outlays for certain social services as contrasted with revenues coming in. In the case of the elderly, the ratio of current workers to retired persons is probably an even more critical fact to know. This is because so many of the programs the federal government runs for maintenance and health care services to the elderly are related to the social security program, which predominantly has separate trust funds supported by workers who are taxed a set percentage of their take-home pay to pay benefits to those who are retired.

At the start of the federal social security program in 1935, there had never been fewer than ten working-age adults for every American over the age of sixty-five (Hewitt and Howe, 1988). By World War II, there were nine workers to each person over sixty-five. Today, the figure is down to five, and estimates are that in fifty years there will only be two workers to every person over sixty-five (Hewitt and Howe, 1988).

The number of elderly is not the only factor in creating the ratio of current workers to retired persons over sixty-five. The average age at which people retire and the percentage of people over 65 who continue to work are also important. Despite much talk about how much healthier the average older person is and that older people may want to continue working, that trend is not yet evident. Laws have been changed removing mandatory retirement ages in many jobs, however; this would facilitate people working to older ages, if they so desire. In 1950 the proportion of people from sixty-five to sixty-nine who were in the labor force was 40 percent. It has currently fallen below 18 percent (Hewitt and Howe, 1988). The actual average age of retirement in the United States is now 62 (Ricardo-Campbell, 1988).

The last important factor in how special health and custodial care services are delivered to the elderly is to understand some basic facts about the economic picture for this group of people. At one point, the elderly definitely had the highest proportion of any age group in poverty; it was partially to deal with this problem and the problem of orphaned children and widows that the Social Security Act was passed. Numerous improvements to social security and expansions in the benefit levels have meant that the elderly are now much better off economically than they were thirty to fifty years ago. In 1959, 35 percent were below the federal poverty level for the elderly, while in 1986 only 12.4 percent were below the poverty level for this age group (Pollack, 1988).

Recently, given the great improvement in the proportion of the elderly below the poverty level, some people have begun to talk of the greening of the elderly and the unfair burden of taxation which growing numbers of elderly may place on a smaller number of working people. If this notion of the greening of the elderly is accurate, many of the elderly should have sufficient dollars on hand to pay for custodial care purchased in the private sector, either as part of for-profit corporations or special nonprofit service organizations. It would mean that the need for large governmental programs of special service delivery to the elderly poor would be small and that voucher or market-based systems might work well (Pascal, 1972).

Several experts argue convincingly, however, that even though extreme poverty in the elderly has been reduced, substantial numbers of the elderly remain at a fairly minimal income level (Pollack, 1988; Villers Foundation, 1987). They list seven major reasons why many elderly Americans continue to be in the lower sectors of society in real income, despite the reduction in poverty. First, the official poverty line for the elderly is lower than for other age groups. In 1986 the official poverty line for a single adult over sixty-five was $5,255 versus $5,701 for a younger adult living alone. The figure for the younger person living alone is 8.5 percent higher and the discrepancy is even greater for a couple, 11.2 percent (Pollack, 1988). If the same standard were used for all age groups, the proportion of elderly living in poverty would increase to 15 percent (Villers Foundation, 1987). Second, whichever standard is used, poverty is more widespread among the elderly than in any other age group except children. Third, poverty rates are not the same for all groups of the elderly. Older blacks and Hispanics and older women are more likely to live in poverty. Among elderly black women living alone, almost 60 percent were in poverty in 1986 (Pollack, 1988).

A fourth reason is that the elderly are less likely to have an opportunity to improve their economic circumstances. Their poverty tends to be long-term and to become worse over time as health care costs rise and other costs increase. The most important factor is the fifth: large numbers of elderly live just above the poverty level at any one point in time. One typical definition of the near poor is those who live above the poverty level but with incomes less than twice that level. Eight million of the elderly—over twice as many as are currently classified as poor—fall into this group making the two groups together comprise 42 percent of the total elderly population (United States Department of Commerce, 1986).

Six, out-of-pocket health care costs for the elderly have increased greatly in recent years. And seven, the elderly poor are not well protected by other safety-net programs. The elderly spend more out-of-pocket for health care than does any other age group, despite the presence of the federal medicare program. Without including long-term care costs, the average elderly spends three times as much for health care as other Americans (Pollack, 1988). The elderly today still spend 15 percent of their incomes on health care as they did when the medicare program was passed in 1965. This fact is discussed further in the next section. The main safety-net program for the elderly is Supplemental Security Income (SSI). Only 32 percent of the elderly with incomes below poverty participate, partially because of asset limitations as well as requirements on current income.

HISTORY OF CUSTODIAL SERVICES

Custodial and long-term care services today generally include a range of services: (1) nursing home care; (2) home health services that can range from a skilled, technologically oriented care to minimal nursing care; or from health care in the home by other groups such as physical therapists or occupational therapists to homemaker services or meals on wheels; and (3) retirement homes that may provide predominantly housing and very little in the way of health care, or homes in which congregate meals are served and nursing services are available in the home in an effort to keep people in a homelike setting and out of a nursing home.

How were these services provided in the past? Both our society and health care were very different several hundred years ago. Not only did people not live as long but also when they contracted a serious illness, they were much more likely to die of it quickly and not need custodial, long-term care. They were also more likely to live in an extended family household or close to relatives who could provide minimal nursing, food, and housekeeping services for sick, elderly relatives. Thus most people were far less likely to live to a point at which they needed such services, and if they did, care was more likely to be provided within the context of the family setting. Not everyone was fortunate enough to have family close by, however, with the economic means to provide such care. Early hospitals were, in many ways, custodial institutions. People stayed in them for weeks and months at a time, and the level of care was often what we would consider custodial services today—that is, minimal nursing care, beds, food, and some medical supervision (Rosenberg, 1987). From the colonial era up the turn of the century, public policy in the United States followed English poor law and left the care of the destitute to local government, usually through direct provision of care rather than income support as today (Vladeck, 1980).

As the level of medicine improved, doctors began to use hospitals differently and hospitals became places for the sick with some hope of being cured or a treatable problem (Rosenberg, 1987; Starr, 1982). With this trend, hospitals decreased in importance as custodial institutions and other places began to provide care for sick people who were not getting better or who had special problems. These people were few in number; most middle-class people with such problems still preferred and usually received care at home. For the poor sick elderly who had no relatives to help out, county poor homes and poor farms began to increase as social institutions to provide such care at the turn of the century. As the forerunners of modern day nursing homes, poor farms or poor homes tended to provide custodial care at governmental expense (usually the county or city government) for poor, sick, elderly. This care was viewed more as a social service by local government than a health service. There was also private support for the aged and ill; an equal number of people lived in charitable private homes run by religious and immigrant welfare societies as in county poor homes (Vladeck, 1980).

There were several other settings for chronic, long-term, and other custodial care by the turn of the century or shortly thereafter. People with mental health problems or evidencing a mental confusion linked to aging now identified as Alzheimer's disorders (and then possibly characterized as dementia or senile dementia), might end up in state mental hospitals. It is estimated that about as many aged individuals lived in mental hospitals as in poor farms and charitable homes (Vladeck, 1980). A widespread movement toward the creation of publicly owned, state-funded mental hospitals began in the middle of the 1800s; some of the later states adopted such reforms shortly after the end of the Civil War. These facilities provided very long-term care that was measured in years. Care was typically custodial, even in the best of such institutions in an era with limited understanding of mental problems and prior to any of the biochemical treatments that have been so successful in reducing the length of hospital stays for mental illness. Typically, the people in state mental health hospitals would be from poorer families, especially if they were aging and losing memory, but not dangerous. Wealthier families would maintain such a person with the family, frequently with the use of hired help.

Another system of state-run and financed long-term care institutions was the network of state tuberculosis (TB) hospitals created in the early twentieth century. As the accepted modality of treatment for TB became rest, healthy food, and improved air, most facilities were located away from crowded, urban areas. In general, these facilities were not a major source of care for the elderly, however. The advance of modern medications have led to the decline in this service as a provision of state government. Today, TB control programs are outpatient based and run by states with the assistance of the federal government (Starr, 1982; Kronenfeld and Whicker, 1984).

While conditions in mental hospitals were generally bad (and usually better in TB facilities), conditions in county poor farms and even some charitable homes for the aged were very poor. The poor conditions in these places partially led to the passage of the Social Security Act during the Great Depression.

Because of the very bad conditions in county-run facilities during the 1920s and early 1930s, in establishing a grant-in-aid program to the states for old age assistance (OAA), the Social Security Act prohibited the payment of any cash grant to any inmate of a public institution. This meant that OAA funds would not be used to support county almshouses and poorhouses and inadvertently built up a market for private services through voluntary and charitable homes and private board and care homes (Vladeck, 1980; Hawes and Phillips, 1986). The new flow of cash allowed some private homes to have more actual money around and to begin to provide some health services along with board and care. On the supply side, the poor economic conditions of the country encouraged some people with large homes and no viable jobs to begin nursing home care in their homes (Hawes and Phillips, 1986). From 1939 to 1950, nursing home facilities increased from 1,200 to 9,000 and the number of beds from 25,000 to 250,000 (Dunlop, 1979; Hawes and Phillips, 1986).

Although nursing home services (predominantly boarding and custodial care facilities), grew even through the Depression and World War II, there was not a large building of institutional facilities for the elderly who might need long-term care, partially because of a lack of funds for such people to pay for this care. After World War II, some chronic disease hospitals and some acute care hospitals added nursing home beds or included rehabilitative care. Nursing home care gradually shifted from being only board and room to include more medically oriented aspects. The passage of the Hill-Burton Act after World War II not only stimulated the growth of hospitals but also provided some governmental funds for nursing home construction. Two other trends of the 1950s also led to growth in nursing home care. Government loans through the Small Business Administration became more common and helped nonprofit nursing homes to grow. A vendor payment system was created by the 1950 and 1959 Social Security Act amendments that allowed federal matching funds to states for indirect payments to nursing homes.

At the same time these trends were occurring in health care, the broader social service trends previously mentioned as part of social security were developing. Related trends in early research on aging by the National Institutes of Health (NIH) in 1940 and a National Conference on Aging in 1950 were also important. Two key pieces of legislation passed in 1965 had a major impact on the elderly in general and on the delivery to them of health care services. The Older Americans Act was passed in 1965, as were the medicare and medicaid programs. Medicare was the major health program passed to deal with the health care needs of the elderly and organized as a supplement to social security. Not a means-tested program, its basic form (Part A) covered mostly hospital care and its supplemental form (Part B), which most elderly purchase as a deduction from their social security checks, covers physician and some outpatient services. Over the years, coverage has expanded somewhat; however, many long-term care services (especially nursing home costs and custodial care costs) are covered for only a brief time. Coverage for home health services if they are rehabilitative and not simply maintenance has expanded in recent years. Despite this coverage and some expansions in the medicare program, out-of-pocket costs as a proportion

of income for the elderly now exceed what they were prior to the implementation of medicare. Medicare now pays for less than half of the
expenditures of the elderly, predominantly because of the importance
of excluded items, such as coverage for long-term care, dental care,
eyeglasses, and preventive exams. The major expense of the medicare
program is hospital care (70 percent of all medicare expenditures). While
less than 5 percent of home health costs were covered in 1984, figures
should be somewhat better in future years due to expansion of coverage;
only 1 percent of nursing home costs in 1984 were covered by medicare
(Estes, 1988). Although catastrophic health care coverage for the elderly
was passed in 1988, pressure to change the program caused Congress
to repeal this coverage even before the legislation took effect. (Pauly and
Thomas, 1989).

NURSING HOMES

Medicaid, the federal program to provide health care services to the
poor in qualified federal categories, is the major payor of nursing home
services. If they require nursing home care, many elderly who were not
poor through most of their adult lives become eligible for this program
through the spend down provision. Under this provision, persons who
exhaust their own resources in paying for nursing home care can become
eligible for medicaid to pay for their nursing home care when they have
spent down all of their income and resources.

Role of Medicare/Medicaid

The enactment of the federal programs of medicare and medicaid,
along with the broader social and economic trends just discussed, led
to a growth in nursing home facilities in the United States. Between
1939 and 1969 the population of the United States increased about 50
percent while nursing home facilities jumped from 1,200 to 15,000—a
more than 1,000 percent increase. Much of this growth was in the for-
profit sector, so that by 1969 64.5 percent of United States nursing home
beds were for-profit or proprietary (Gray, 1986). Growth in the total
number of homes slowed down in the 1970s, although the for-profit
share increased so that for-profit facilities represented 81 percent of
homes and 69 percent of beds in 1980. One estimate is that the number
of beds in investor-owned chains and beds leased or managed by such
chains increased by 50 percent to more than 200,000 beds—17 percent
of all nursing home beds. Nursing home ownership includes a few very
large national chains and a much larger number of relatively small
chains, many of which are more regionally or even locally oriented. In

1984 the three largest systems together operated about 1,500 units, comprising 70 percent of the investor-owned nursing homes (Gray, 1986).

One very interesting difference between types of ownership in the nursing home industry and the hospital industry discussed in the previous chapter is that the nursing home sector has been dominated by proprietary ownership for decades. There have been large publicly held corporations involved in the area since the late 1960s, due to the growth in nursing home facilities related to the passage of the medicare and medicaid legislation. Thus, except for a few critics who have questioned the role of for-profits in the provision of this care (Vladeck, 1980), most experts do not question the dominance of for-profit institutions in this area.

Another interesting difference is how the care is actually paid for in this sector. Although most people pay for hospital costs through their private health care insurance which is paid for usually out of a mixture of employer fees and direct fees paid by the employee supplemented by personal funds for any copayment or deductible, government is the primary purchaser of nursing home care services through the medicaid program. Over half the dollars spent on nursing home care are federal or joint federal-state funds through medicaid. Few people have private health insurance in this area, although there have been recent suggestions of private long-term care insurance as a worksite option. The role of government in this sector then is quite different from the hospital area. Government is typically the payor of such care but rarely the direct provider. There are a few municipal facilities or state facilities left; many of the state-run facilities are long-term care facilities for mental health patients who are now elderly and also have physical health needs. The important role of government as a payor of nursing home care due to medicaid (and to a lesser extent medicare) gives government a role in determining quality of care and regulation of such facilities. The importance of government as a guarantor of quality is accentuated by the current estimate that 30 percent of patients living in nursing homes have no immediate family members and half have no family members living nearby (Brody, 1977). In many ways, our current long-term care system is a creature of government policy, yet issues relating to this sector of care have rarely been addressed as a public-policy issue of major importance.

Problems related to the provision of nursing home care and the need for such care were an issue at the time of the passage of the medicare and medicaid legislation and in the decade that followed. A dramatic increase in nursing home beds in the decade following the passage of those bills can be traced to four factors (Hawes and Phillips, 1986): (1) the availability of funding; (2) the method used to reimburse facilities; (3) increase in demand; and (4) federal health and safety regulations.

At the time of the passage of the medicare legislation, there were fears that the inclusion of long-term care services would bankrupt the program. On the other side, however, were concerns that hospital costs were experiencing substantial inflation during the 1950s and early 1960s, making it desirable to have less costly, alternative care available for persons convalescing from major illnesses (Vladeck, 1980). During the legislative process, coverage for convalescing patients in extended care facilities was added to the medicare program.

More important to the future development of long-term care services than this amendment, however, was Title 19 of medicaid. This amendment received relatively little debate at the time, and its coverage of long-term care services received even less attention. These services were covered because it was viewed as a modest extension of the vendor payment program to nursing homes for OAA recipients; this program had been started in 1950 and expanded in 1956. Later extended to include intermediate level care as well, this coverage was the basis for much of the expansion of the nursing home care industry. The availability of these funds led to a major increase in demand for nursing home care not only among the infirm aged residing in the community but also among elderly previously supervised in other settings, such as mental health institutions. One estimate is that 25 percent of the increase in nursing home utilization between 1960 and 1970 was due to deinstitutionalization or diversion of individuals from mental health facilities into nursing homes, using medicaid as the payment source (Hawes and Phillips, 1986). The percentage of elderly persons in nursing homes rose 107 percent between 1960 and 1970.

Even though availability of some funding was one factor in this increased growth, the actual level of reimbursement and the way in which it was calculated was very important, as was the regulatory policy about the building and setup of such facilities. Initially, the goal of medicare/medicaid policy was to encourage service providers to participate in the program. The payment system adopted for nursing homes was cost-based reimbursement with no ceiling on reimbursement costs. In addition, for-profit nursing homes received a profit based on their net invested equity in the facility, reimbursement of mortgage interest, and depreciation of capital equipment, including the facility. Initially this made it very hard to lose money in a nursing home because mortgage payments were covered and depreciation would provide a positive cash flow (Vladeck, 1980; Hawes and Phillips, 1986). While each state had passed its own regulations on the medicaid financing of nursing home care, most states paid in a similar manner to medicare (often at a somewhat lower rate) although some states did pay a fixed rate to all facilities. The open-ended nature of the medicaid program made it a major source of financing for nursing home care, however, because it initially paid for the care of all eligible program beneficiaries. Only later did states begin to limit the dollars spent on nursing home care.

The pattern adopted by the government for facility regulation was also premised on the need to encourage participation and new facilities. Because of a fear that few homes would meet the minimum health and safety regulations initially adopted for medicare, facilities were allowed to participate in the program if they were in substantial rather than full compliance with the regulations. Homes could present to the appropriate certification agency a plan to correct violations. These patterns encouraged new facilities, with an increase in beds from 460,000 in 1965 to 1.1 million beds in 1973, or an increase of 139 percent in less than a decade (Hawes and Phillips, 1986).

Growth Patterns

The medicare and medicaid programs accelerated the trend in nursing home care away from government and nonprofit facilities and into proprietary facilities. Although for-profits have always been a factor in the nursing home area, there have been government-run nursing homes and voluntary (private, nonprofit) nursing homes. The private homes can be split into those run by religious or other special voluntary associations (Episcopal home, Jewish home, or Elks facility) or those open to the general public, but run on a nonprofit rather than a for-profit basis. Proprietary facilities are becoming the dominant deliverer of nursing home care in the United States, up from 64.5 percent in 1969 to more than 80 percent by 1980. Moreover, many nursing home owners are now corporate chains that are large, investor-owned businesses. In 1966 only a few nursing home chains were listed on the stock exchange; 58 were by 1969 and almost 90 by 1970 indicating the rapid shift to corporate chains after the implementation of medicare and medicaid.

The nursing home industry had undergone several different patterns of growth. One rapid period of expansion from 1965 to 1970 was fueled by the enactment of medicare and medicaid. At one point in the late 1960s, nursing home stocks were considered one of the hottest items on Wall Street, and the companies were averaging expected returns on investment of 20 to 25 percent each year. Price/earnings ratios were as much as 40 times higher than traditional blue-chip stocks (Elliot, 1969; Hawes and Phillips, 1986). This period of euphoria was not to last, however, and by 1971–72 stock prices in this sector fell below the high marks of 1969. The first major corporation in nursing home care to be listed on a major stock exchange, Four Seasons Nursing Centers, was bankrupt at the end of this period and had officers indicted for securities violations (Hawes and Phillips, 1986). Stock fraud such as this along with scandals about the quality of care in many of these nursing homes led to a slowdown in growth, especially growth of corporate chains (Mendelson, 1974). Other factors were problems discovered in the sale and resale of nursing homes and inflated lease and rental charges all of which artificially raised the costs of care.

The period from 1970 to 1975 was one of very slow growth. Some parts of the county had an oversupply of nursing home beds; many homes were not filled to capacity and had a very hard time breaking even. By the late 1970s, however, another period of increasing growth combined with concentration of ownership and corporatization had begun. Between 1982 and 1983, the twenty-five largest corporations increased their control of total beds by 15 percent (Hawes and Phillips, 1986). The three largest chains providing mainly nursing home care in 1980 were Beverly Enterprises, ARA Living Centers, and Hillhaven. The first two still had the most units and beds by 1986 and 1987 (Multi-Unit Providers Survey, 1988).

What were some of the reactions of the government as the major payor of nursing home services to the scandals of the late 1960s and how has that related to trends in growth? Stricter building codes and fire and safety code regulations were put into place, forcing some of the smaller mom-and-pop facilities out of business. This increased consolidation of chains and other corporate owners.

A number of cost reforms were put into place. All of these are too detailed to go into for this chapter; however, major changes included requirements in 1972 that homes report their costs to the state medicaid agency and that reimbursement would be based on those reported costs considered reasonable. There are still advantages related to capital reimbursement and depreciation and payment of mortgage interest. Even though most of these changes do not favor for-profit chains, they are not at any disadvantage.

A related aspect to cost reforms has been the introduction of health planning and certificate of need (CON) legislation. Up to 1973 the supply of nursing home beds had increased about 8 percent annually since 1963. The introduction of health planning led to a decline in new nursing home units. The rate of growth was slightly less than 3 percent from 1976 to 1980 and declined even further to less than 2 percent from 1981 to 1983. These national figures mask large amounts of variability from state to state; some states have actually lost units since 1981 (Hawes and Phillips, 1986). Other states have had multiple year periods of no growth to be followed by some new building. While part of the limitation on growth was to slow the increase in public expenditures for nursing home care through the medicaid program, these cost containment policies also allowed higher revenues to be generated for private nursing homes, especially through higher charges to private pay patients and discrimination against patients with medicaid funding when patients with any other type of payment were available. Nationwide, these slowed patterns of growth have meant that nursing homes average a 95 percent occupancy rate and are typically profitable. Combined with the better access to capital that is available to chains and the favorable aspects of the tax codes, the nursing home industry has been particularly attractive and financially lucrative to for-profit corporations, leading to greater concentration in chains.

Several factors have contributed to the greater concentration of nursing home ownership. New and stricter licensing and certification standards have given an edge to larger, more sophisticated operators, as has the increasing complexity of public reimbursement systems. Demand is still strong in many areas, however, and occupancy rates are very high in a number of states, raising the potential for large profits for a corporation that keeps up with trends on a state-by-state basis. The attempt by states to control the number of new beds and, thus, their total medicaid costs have encouraged acquisitions by companies that wish to grow. Such companies may not be able to acquire permits for new construction, thus furthering concentration of facilities. Tax policies and the laxity toward antitrust proceedings in the Reagan years have also encouraged concentration (Hawes and Phillips, 1986).

It would be unfair to characterize the nursing home industry as dominated by only a few chains, however, since the picture is much more complex. Although a few such as Beverly and ARA are very large, as are a few of the hospital chains with a large investment in nursing home care (such as National Medical Enterprises), there are still many individual owners and a large number of local and regional five-to-twenty-units chains. Much of the growth of the largest companies has not come from building new facilities but from mergers and takeovers. The *Modern Healthcare* annual survey of multifacility systems in 1988 listed fifty-eight different investor-owned systems, with the units owned per company ranging from more than a thousand to three. They also listed twenty not-for-profit nursing home systems ranging in size from 159 units to 2 units and about seventy for-profit, not-for-profit, and governmental hospital systems ranging in size from NME at 384 units to about twenty-five with only 2 units (Multi-Unit Providers Survey, 1988).

Beverly Enterprises is currently the largest for-profit nursing home chain and has been for some while. Beverly Enterprises operated as many as 950 homes in 1984 and with more than a thousand units, but since 1986 has been withdrawing its nursing homes from certain markets. In 1987 Beverly owned 1,073 units with over 116,000 beds and managed 53 units. They cut back some in 1987, to 1,005 units with 110,703 beds plus 48 managed units. The second largest for-profit nursing home chain, ARA, has also downsized slightly from 1986 to 1987, going from 250 units to 237 units. The dropoff in size from Beverly to the next largest points out just how much Beverly towers above the other companies in size. The third largest firm, National Heritage, does not own homes as such but operates 231. Manor Care was the fourth largest in 1987 and mostly owned units. Of the hospital systems, NME operates 384 units, with a rapid dropoff to 87 units by Adventist Health Systems and 25 or fewer in the other hospital systems. There are also a very few large providers in the not-for-profit systems, most of which are religious. The largest is Good Samaritan Society of Sioux Falls, South Dakota, with 159 units, after which it drops to systems with 30 or fewer units, most centered in a regional or local area (Multi-Unit Providers Survey, 1988).

Beverly has not been a corporation without problems recently; the following discussion of their difficulties illustrates well the current issues and quagmires in the nursing home field, especially in the for-profit sector. Although the largest of the for-profit chains, Beverly has been burdened with a reputation for poor-quality care and acquired over $1 billion in debt over the past seven years due to a large number of acquisitions. In 1987 Beverly lost $30.5 million despite having revenues of more than $2 billion. Estimates in late 1988 were that losses in that year would be around $10 million. Some of those losses were related to a forced sale of assets to pay creditors and avert bankruptcy (Feder, 1988).

Why has Beverly been running deficits of this size? Its occupancy rate has fallen, partly due to its reputation for lower quality. Its beds are heavily occupied by medicaid recipients; in recent years, some states' rates have risen very slowly, making the nursing home business less profitable than in the 1970s and early 1980s. In some cases, competition for new properties has driven prices to very high levels, and medicaid in many states has limited reimbursement for acquirers' financing costs. Lower rates of unemployment in many parts of the country have also raised labor costs, as the industry has been forced to hire more of its low-skill workers at rates above the minimum wage. For example, the average daily payment in a home with skilled staff was $52 per patient in 1985, the last year in which data are available from the Health Care Financing Administration, the federal agency responsible for the medicare and medicaid programs. Since then, it is estimated that payments have risen only 4 percent but labor costs have risen 11 percent.

In the case of Beverly, management may have allowed it to get too big and not paid enough attention to administrative details and local rules. For example, it owns forty-two nursing homes in Minnesota accounting for 9 percent of the beds in that state. This state has very stringent quality assurance standards. To save administrative costs, the homes were administered from a regional office in Fort Smith, Arkansas. When two homes did not meet quality assurance standards, it appears management did not realize that under Minnesota law the failure of any of the chain's homes to meet quality standards could lead the state to deny licensure renewal to all the homes (Feder, 1988).

One serious blow to the reputation for quality at Beverly homes oc-curred in California. The state argued that poor care at several homes resulted in nine deaths. Inspections found fifty life-threatening citations in a fifteen-month period. As a settlement of this problem, in October 1986 Beverly paid $724,000 in fines without admitting to any specific charges of wrongdoing (Feder, 1988).

Not all homes have experienced the same level of problems. Manor Care, another large for-profit chain, has tried to locate its homes in wealthier areas. As a result, many of its homes have 60 percent of the patients as private pay patients and overall the corporation has main-tained healthy profits. The future for growth in the nursing home in-dustry may be downsizing of the largest chains with more attention to placement of homes, adherence to regulations (most of which are state specific), and greater attention to management and a reputation for quality.

Quality, Costs, and Access

As the recent experience of Beverly, the industry leader in total size, makes partially clear, critical issues for the future of nursing home chains and for our assessment of the large role that for-profit institutions play in this sector of care for the elderly are those of quality of care, costs in delivering the care, and access to care. Quality of care is clearly a critical issue, both for the patients in the home and perhaps for the economic health of the company or nursing home in the long run as well. One critical issue in all nursing homes is that the economic incentives in support of quality of care are less apparent than in hospitals. While hospitals compete for the loyalty of physicians on the basis partially of quality and good facilities and have the frequent presence of physicians in the institutions and their commitment to patient care as constraints to keep quality up, this is not true in nursing homes. Physicians rarely come to nursing homes, and because of the patients' physical and mental disabilities and social isolation, many are not strong advocates for quality of care. Most incentives in favor of quality are based on either ethics and community or religious commitment or avoidance of regulatory problems. In the past, most nursing home regulations had focused on building and fire safety standards, rather than health and patient care standards (Vladeck, 1980).

Only a few studies have compared the quality of care between the for-profit and nonprofit sectors of the nursing home industry. Despite limitations on the use of resource measures rather than outcome meas-ures and the confusion of adding in mom-and-pop proprietary nursing homes along with the larger for-profit chains as part of for-profit nursing homes, most studies on quality have similar conclusions of higher quality in the nonprofit sector, although a few report no quality differences between nonprofits and for-profits (Lee, 1984; Hawes and Phillips, 1986; Fottler et al., 1981; Levey et al., 1984). The not-for-profit mode of operation appears to have higher quality, especially in the areas of number of patient care staff, expenditure of food, complaints to state regulatory agencies, and nonconformity with regulatory requirements among others (Gray, 1986; O'Brien and Saxburg, 1987). Church-related nonprofits appear to have the highest quality. In most cases, not-for-profits have a higher level of nonmedicaid patients.

Related to an assessment of quality is determining how much it costs to produce a certain service. Most studies have found nonprofit homes to have higher costs than for-profit ones, although there is concern that the measure of case mix is inadequate. This is very important because there is some evidence that for-profit homes may have a more intense case mix of patients, that is, sicker patients on average (Hawes and Phillips, 1986). Non-profits appear to spend more on average on patient care. This was clearly demonstrated in one study using data from Ohio (Hawes and Phillips, 1986). Few differences of note appear between for-profit and nonprofit nursing homes with respect to management behavior (Hawes and Phillips, 1986).

There are clear access issues in nursing home care because many states report a shortage of beds. It appears however, that for-profits are likely to have a higher proportion of medicaid than other nursing homes. Thus, the for-profits do admit all types of patients, although all types of nursing homes prefer patients who either are self-paying or have private insurance. It also appears that medicaid patients are more likely to be in nursing homes with deficits in quality of care, because on average there are more problems in quality with some of the larger chains than with the nonprofits, especially religious ones. Private pay patients are much more lucrative for nursing home owners because of medicare and medicaid payment limits. Discrimination in access to nursing home care is found in all sectors of the nursing home industry and operates against patients with heavy care needs and medicaid patients. In the nursing home sector, quality, cost, and access are very intermingled, and the discrimination against medicaid patients appears to raise quality issues. It also reflects major issues about the public's role in the financing of such care and conflicts between pressures on the government to contain rising costs and yet heed the implications of such moves for access and quality.

HOME HEALTH CARE

Home health care is a growing sector of services provision for both the elderly and those recovering from hospitalization for acute or chronic illnesses, whether elderly or younger. Home care services include a broad range: skilled nursing care, occupational therapy, physical therapy, speech therapy, respiratory therapy, and custodial and housekeeping services. The providers of such services include nurses, home health aides, homemakers, and many specialized therapists. The groups that provide these types of care also range greatly, including local health departments that run a home health services agency as part of their array of services, private nonprofit voluntary groups (often called visiting nurses associations in the past), for-profit facilities that are part of large national chains, and home health services run by hospitals, or, in some cases, nursing homes that are part of major medical supply companies.

Although these services have been a part of the health care picture for a long time, they were generally small, provided by government or private, nonprofit locally organized groups, and a stable part of the health care system. There was some impetus for growth after the passage of the medicare and medicaid legislation, because these programs made some public funds available to pay for this service. The 1972 amendments to the social security legislation greatly increased the use of home health services by removing certain copayment requirements and expanding both the conditions for which care would be reimbursed and the services that could be provided.

Medicare does certify home health agencies, although in any given area more agencies are probably operating than are certified. To the extent national data are available, however, they focus on certified agencies. In 1966 there were 1,275 medicare-certified home health agencies in the United States. By 1982 this had increased to 3,639, and within two more years, had grown by 50 percent to 5,427. Rates of growth tapered off, but absolute numbers have still increased slightly up to 5,783 medicare-certified agencies in 1987 (Bergthold, 1988).

Several other important trends are part of this growth. Most experts agree that the medicare prospective payment reimbursement system of DRGs has increased the need for home health services, because it has provided a financial incentive for hospitals to release patients earlier with some needs for additional care at home. The for-profit sector has experienced particularly rapid growth, going from only 20 in 1969 to 145 certified agencies in 1978 and to 1,569 in 1984 (Gray, 1986; Bergthold, 1988). Growth was due to a specific change in the medicare reimbursement legislation. The Omnibus Reconciliation Act of 1980 removed one restriction, the growth of for-profit home health agencies. Prior to that legislation, for-profits could not be certified in states not having a home health agency licensure law. Other changes in the law in 1980 facilitated the growth of home health services in general, including the elimination of a requirement that such services could only follow a three-day hospitalization period and a removal of a limitation on the total number of visits which could be covered.

Perhaps due to the remnants of the pre–1980 restrictions, as well as to other differences in the population and service mix in other categories in different parts of the country, both the numbers and types of certified agencies are unevenly distributed throughout the country, ranging from as few as 8 in Arkansas to a high of 154 agencies in Texas (Bergthold, 1988). A number of states lost agencies in 1987, particularly in the south central region. Texas lost thirty and Oklahoma lost fifty-six. In contrast, some states such as New York and Florida experienced growth, with nine new agencies each. The picture on who drops out is very mixed. Over half of those who quit this area of service recently had been in business for over five years, and one-quarter had been certified for twenty years or more (Bergthold, 1988). There appears to have been more turnover in the for-profit agencies.

The major providers of such services today are varied. Although public home health agencies and voluntary nursing associations continue to provide services, they are decreasing. There were thirty-five different independent home health care companies listed in an industry survey in 1988, although this included private duty home health care agencies not certified by medicare (Wagner, 1988). Among the largest were Up-john, with 255 facilities in forty-two states; Glasrock Home Health Care Corporation of Atlanta with 300 units in forty-six states; Foster Medical Care Corporation with 290 units in thirty-seven states; and Lifetime Corporation of New York with 313 units in forty-four states. This sector of the industry also included agencies that specialize in rental of durable medical equipment and home infusion therapies, although some companies specialize in only one service. Upjohn, for example, offers all services but durable medical equipment; by contrast, Foster offers only durable medical equipment (Wagner, 1988).

Medicare expenditures for home health have been on the increase. In 1971 less than 1 percent of total medicare expenditures went to home health services. From 1979 to 1984, such expenses tripled and represented about 2.6 percent of medicare expenditures. In actual dollars, such expenses were more than $2 billion in 1988 (Bergthold, 1988).

One recent study has assessed the changes in home health services since 1984 through a survey of 175 randomly selected home health agencies in nine metropolitan areas in California, Florida, Washington, Texas, and Pennsylvania. Data were gathered through telephone surveys, key informant interviews, and secondary data sources (Bergthold, 1988). The survey found that more for-profit agencies are entering and leaving the market than not-for-profits. Most of the changes in organizational structure are leading to greater complexity and affiliation with larger systems.

Only a few changes in tax status are occurring. In this study's data base, from 1984 to 1986 eight agencies switched from nonprofit to for-profit, while in 1987 two agencies switched from for-profit to nonprofit as part of a selling off of facilities to a nonprofit hospital system. In addition, most agencies were trying to reduce their reliance on medicare funds that nationally averages around 80 percent (Bergthold, 1988). There were no differences between ownership of home health facilities in their intentions to try to attract private funding in the future (Bergthold, 1987). For-profit agencies do report a higher proportion of contract and part-time employees. Larger for-profits were somewhat less likely to serve higher proportions of low-income populations, but there were no differences by ownership in the proportion of minorities served. For-profits were more likely than nonprofits to refuse services to someone because they could not afford the copayment (Bergthold, 1987).

Overall, home health care services have been growing rapidly, especially since 1980. Growth has been even more rapid in the for-profit sector. The trends in growth have been linked to changes in federal reimbursement policies for medicare. Most home health agencies wish to become less dependent on government funding as their source of income. Home health services presents the interesting situation of a growing for-profit industry largely dependent on federal funding of services for its existence. The dangers in this area are not only that the needs of the captive population itself—the sick and elderly—will become lost in policy debates over the amount of public funds that should be spent on such care but also that the agencies will want to become more profitable and expand their services to a broader population, one with more means to pay for such care with private funds.

RETIREMENT HOMES

The last type of health care services focused primarily on the elderly are retirement homes with some health care options and life-care communities. Modern retirement communities tend to be places in which housing is purchased by the elderly who have close and convenient access to health care facilities. Life-care or continuing care communities are one example of retirement homes in which persons typically purchase into the facility while younger; in exchange the facility agrees to provide certain services. These services can range from as little as some housecleaning and transportation to the doctor up to more complete housekeeping, food, and laundry services, social activities, and health services ranging from in home care to skilled nursing care.

The financial strength of a life-care community is greatly related to the age of its members (Hartzler, 1985). The number of retirement centers owned, leased, or operated by firms or hospital systems in the United

States has been increasing (Dine, 1988). Multi-unit hospital systems owned or operated more than 100 such centers in 1987. Other major owners or operators were nursing home chains that operated 216 in 1987. Not-for-profit providers are currently dominating this market, whether in the sector owned or managed by hospitals or by nursing home chains (Dine, 1988).

CONCLUSIONS

This chapter has reviewed three major types of care focused primarily on the elderly—nursing home services, home health services, and retirement home services. Nursing home care is dominated by the for-profit sector but paid for mostly with public funds. Home health care traditionally was dominated by the public or voluntary sector but is increasingly dominated by for-profits and is also largely dependent on public funds, while the retirement home sector is dominated by nonprofit facilities and private funding.

In the United States in nonhealth and social service sectors, there has often been a bias that the private market is a superior mechanism for the allocation of most resources and that private provision increases efficiency and consumer choice (Bergthold, 1987). But in the case of the services discussed in this chapter, the private market is partly an illusion. Services may be provided through private market, for-profit approaches, but most funding of services comes from government programs and thus tax revenues. The one sector with the least public funding (retirement homes) is the sector with dominance by nonprofit groups.

To some extent, this country has been experiencing a privatization policy in health and social services for the elderly in the past several years. It has resulted in an expansion of reimbursement for medical services but a contraction of some other social services for the elderly; a targeting of benefits to the frail and poor elderly but away from the less ill elderly; and some shift of resources away from the public to the private sector, along with a policy formulation process that is itself corporatized as corporations intervene in the policy process on behalf of their consumers of care (Bergthold, 1987; Taylor, 1987).

What are the implications of these shifts for those who require care? The increased emphasis on privatization has been linked with concerns about cost containment and efficiency. A government seeking economic efficiency does not necessarily place a high value on equity or access to care. If cost and efficiency are the main criteria, social priorities are often undervalued. Those in the weakest position (the most captive populations such as the poor or minority elderly) may experience the greatest problems. This may become an ever more serious problem as we move into the twenty-first century and the proportions of the population sixty-five and over increase. In addition, quality concerns are an issue, and it appears that an overemphasis on profit from the institution's perspective and perhaps on total costs from the government's perspective can come at the expense of quality of care. Again, watching this in the future will be particularly important because the costs of services discussed in this chapter will increase as the numbers of elderly increase. All these issues bear watching in the future especially if the role of for-profit providers continues to expand.

REFERENCES

Berliner, Howard, and Carol Regan. "Multinational Operations of United States For-Profit Hospital Chains: Trends and Implications," *American Journal of Public Health* 77 (October 1977): 1280–84.

Bergthold, Linda A. "General Hearing Testimony," J. Warren Salmon and Jeffrey W. Todd (eds.), in *The Corporatization of Health Care*. Springfield: Illinois Public Health Association, 1988.

———. "The Privatization of Home Health Services for the Elderly" (Paper presented at the American Public Health Association meeting, New Orleans, Louisiana, October 1987).

Bergthold, Linda, James H. Swan, Pamela Hanes Spohn, and Carrol L. Estes. "Running as Fast as They Can: Organizational Changes in Home Health Care" (Paper presented at the American Sociological Association meeting, Atlanta, Georgia, August 1988).

Brody, E. M. "Environmental Factors in Dependency," in A. N. Exton-Smith and J. G. Evans, (eds.), *Care of the Elderly: Meeting the Challenge of Dependency*. New York: Grune and Stratton, 1977.

Cox, Harold. *Later Life: The Realities of Aging*. Englewood Cliffs, N.J.: Prentice-Hall, 1988.

Crystal, Stephen. "Work and Retirement in the Twenty-First Century," *Generations* 12 (Spring 1988): 60–64.

Dine, Deborah D. "Demand for Retirement Housing Accommodates Industry Growth," *Modern Healthcare*, June 3, 1988, pp. 56–62.

Dunlop, Bruce. *The Growth of Nursing Home Care*. Lexington, Mass: Lexington Books, 1979.

Elliot, J. R., Jr. "No Tired Blood: Nursing Home Operators Are Long on Enthusiasm, Short on Experience," *Barron's*, March 24, 1969, p. 9.

Estes, Carrol. "Healthcare Policy in the Later Twentieth Century," *Generations* 12 (Spring 1988): 44–47.

Feder, Barnaby J. "What Ails a Nursing Home Empire?" *New York Times*, December 11, 1988, sec. 3, pp. 1, 8.

Fottler, M. D., H. L. Smith, and W. L. James. "Profits and Patient Care in Nursing Homes: Are They Compatible?" *The Gerontologist* 21 (1981): 432–38.

Ginzberg, Eli. "For-Profit Medicine," *New England Journal of Medicine* 319 (September 22, 1988): 757–61.

————. "A Hard Look at Cost Containment," *New England Journal of Medicine* 316 (April 30, 1987): 1151–54.

Glazer, William A. *Paying the Hospital*. Boston: Jossey-Bass, 1987.

Gray, Bradford (ed.). *For-Profit Enterprise in Health Care*. Washington, D.C.. National Academy Press, 1986.

Harris, Diana K., and William E. Cole. *Sociology of Aging*. Boston: Houghton Mifflin Co., 1980.

Hartzler, J. Emerson. "Life Care: An Industry with Unique Financial Characteristics," *Healthcare Financial Management*, January 1985: 76–80.

Hawes, Catherine, and Charles D. Phillips. "The Changing Structure of the Nursing Home Industry and the Impact of Ownership on Quality, Cost, and Access," in Bradford H. Gray (ed.), *For-Profit Enterprise in Health Care*. Washington, D.C.: National Academy Press, 1986.

Health Care Financing Administration. "National Health Expenditures, 1986–2000," *Health Care Financing Review* 8, No. 4 (1987): 1–36.

Hewitt, Paul S., and Neil Howe. "Future of Generational Politics," *Generations* 12 (Spring 1988): 10–13.

Hudson, Robert B. "Renewing the Federal Role," *Generations* 12 (Spring 1988): 23–26.

Iglehart, John K. "The Debate over Physician Ownership of Health Care Facilities," *New England Journal of Medicine* 321 (July 20, 1989): 198–204.

Kronenfeld, Jennie Jacobs, and Marcia Lynn Whicker. *U.S. Health Policy: An Analysis of the Federal Role*. New York: Praeger, 1984.

Lee, Y. S. "Nursing Homes and Quality of Health Care: The First Year of Results of an Outcome-Oriented Survey," *Journal of Health and Human Resource Administration* 7 (1984): 32–60.

Levey, S., H. S. Rucklin, B. A. Stotsky, D. R. Kinloch, and W. Oppenheim. "An Appraisal of Nursing Home Care," *Journal of Gerontology* 28 (1984): 222–28.

Light, Donald W. "Corporate Medicine for Profit," *Scientific Medicine* 255 (December 1986): 38–46.

Mendelson, M. A. *Tender Loving Greed*. New York: Alfred A. Knopf, 1974.

"Multi-Unit Providers Survey: Nursing Homes," *Modern Healthcare*, June 3, 1988, 40–55.

O'Brien, Jack, and Borje O. Saxburg. "A Study of For-Profit and Nonprofit Nursing Homes" (Paper presented at the American Public Health Association meeting, New Orleans, Louisiana, October 1987).

Pascal, Anthony, *Clients, Consumers, and Citizens: Using Market Mechanisms for the Delivery of Public Services*. P–4803. Santa Monica, Calif.: Rand Corporation 1972.

Pauly, David, and Rich Thomas. "The Elderly Duke It Out," *Newsweek*, September 11, 1989, pp. 42–44.

Pollack, Ronald F. "Serving Intergenerational Needs, Not Intergenerational Conflict," *Generations* 12 (Spring 1988): 14–18.

Relman, Arnold S. "The New Medical-Industrial Complex," *New England Journal of Medicine* 303 (October 23, 1980): 963–69.

————. "Practicing Medicine in the New Business Climate," *New England Journal of Medicine* 316 (April 30, 1987): 1150–51.

————. "Salaried Physicians and Economic Incentives," *New England Journal of Medicine* 319 (September 22, 1988): 784.

Ricardo-Campbell, Rita. "Aging and the Private Sector," *Generations* 12 (Spring 1988): 19–22.

Rosenberg, Charles E. *The Care of Strangers: The Rise of America's Hospital System.* New York: Basic Books, 1987.

Starr, Paul. *The Social Transformation of American Medicine: The Rise of a Sovereign Profession and the Making of a Vast Industry.* New York: Basic Books, 1982.

Taylor, M. "Contradictions in Federal Policies Put Elderly at Risk of Health Care Neglect," *Home Health Care Services Quarterly* 7 (Summer 1987): 5–12.

U.S. Department of Commerce, Bureau of the Census. *Money, Income, and Poverty Status of Families and Persons in the United States: 1986.* Washington, D.C.: U.S. Government Printing Office, 1987.

Villers Foundation. *On the Other Side of Easy Street: Myths and Facts about the Economics of Old Age.* Washington, D.C.: Villars Foundation, 1987.

Vladeck, Bruce. *Unloving Care: The Nursing Home Tragedy.* New York: Basic Books, 1980.

Wagner, Mary. "Providers of Home Health Care Expand and Consolidate to Meet Rising Demand," *Modern Healthcare,* June 3, 1988: 80–83.

6

Summary and Conclusions

After surveying the four human and social service areas of education, prison care, health care, and care for the elderly, what are the similarities and differences across the four service and captive population areas? What have been the traditional modes of provision and how are they changing? What is the current role of for-profit care or service delivery as contrasted with nonprofits or governmental provision in each of the areas and what is the impact of the differences in sectors of service delivery on quality of care in each of those areas? Lastly, can we arrive at any recommendations about the role of for-profit care in all sectors or in some of the sectors?

One factor that has been clear throughout this book focusing on captive population groups (although it is least true of prisons and prisoners) is the similarities in basic operating characteristics between for-profit, nonprofit, and public agencies in each area. Similarly, all service areas share a general feeling, part of what Robert Reich (1987) described as an American mythology. It holds that individuals should be able to fend for themselves and protect themselves and that government is corruptible if not corrupted, thus making it better for society if government is small rather than large and less rather than more intrusive in the affairs of individuals. There has often been in American society a general cultural bias against greater governmental involvement, whether through more funding into a service area or the direct provision of services. Education may have escaped this more than other areas, although the mythology was partially transformed into opposition to a federal role in education and a belief that only the local unit of government—the unit closest to the people—could be trusted.

SIMILARITIES AND DIFFERENCES ACROSS THE FOUR
SERVICE AND CAPTIVE POPULATION AREAS

Traditionally we in the United States have considered the provision of certain needs—especially education—to be a function of a unit of government, usually the local government, and more recently the state and federal government as well. In the past this has been a unique aspect of the United States, although now most developed and many other countries also consider education to be a function of government. Our nation was among the first societies to so designate it. This early designation related to elementary and secondary schools (what we think of as public education) not day-care or nursery services or college education. Most of the chapter on education addressed that level of educational services, although some attention was also paid to day care. College was not covered, partially because college students, being adults with full societal privileges are not a captive population in the same way that these other groups are.

Provision of prison services has also been a function of government, with the unit of government varying depending on the nature and severity of the crime. Thus, there have been and continue to be federal, state, and local prisons in the United States.

In health care, provision of hospital services to any except the poor is of more recent origin than the other two service areas discussed. The early provision of hospital services was viewed as a mixed function, primarily one for private, nonprofit charitable services, but a need to be met by local government if no other alternative was found. As the perceived value of hospital services increased and they became a commodity desired by the middle and upper classes, nonprofit voluntary facilities continued to dominate and grew to become the typical method of service provision, although governmental and for-profit units were always in existence. The other major aspect of care for the sick, physician care, was always dominated by for-profit provision but in a mode the public considered as being different from a large corporation trying to earn a profit. The dominant mode of provision traditionally was an individual physician or group of physicians practicing in a community and earning a living from that practice as for-profit entrepreneurs but with strong norms of professionalism to constrain commercial impulses and images within the service sector.

For the elderly, the traditional method of service provision was available by family members or with the money to purchase surrogate family members. For those with no other alternatives, local government was the provider of the service, as in health care because it has been the traditional provider of services in the United States. In the last twenty-five years, however, the provision of services to the elderly has shifted from being viewed ultimately as a responsibility of the family or the local government to being a responsibility of the state and federal government. Unlike these other service areas, however, the dominant provider of services (as contrasted with the payor of the services) is a nongovernment unit, with for-profits dominating somewhat over nonprofit service providers.

MODES OF PROVISION IN EACH SERVICE AREA AND CHANGES

In education, the dominant deliverer of services is the public sector, and it is also the dominant provider of care. One change in the last thirty years is that while local governments are still the major providers of care, the federal government has become more important as a funder of care, although only 8 percent of all public school funds originate with the federal government. Even though private schools continue to exist, they are not increasing as a proportion of the services delivered. Within the private sector of elementary and secondary education, there has been some increase in the nonreligiously oriented private schools, and an associated decline in the parochial or religious schools. Most of this decline is due to a decline in Catholic schools. Eighty-nine percent of school students still attend public elementary and secondary schools, and this is true in all parts of the country and in richer areas as well as poorer areas, although there are some large and medium-sized cities with a very high rate of enrollment in private schools. For students who attend private schools, 89 percent attend nonprofit schools; very few for-profit elementary or secondary schools exist.

Schools have always been a major expenditure for local units of government. In many areas, the majority of the local property tax goes to support public schools. One concern for the future is that the amount of commitment to public schools may be declining as a smaller proportion of the population at any given time has children in school. In addition, in the past, many people rarely questioned the necessity of maintaining strong local schools, perhaps because of the more limited geographical range of peoples' lives and the assumption that if they themselves did not have children in the school other relatives would or their own grandchildren would be in such schools soon. These assumptions are less true as the population shifts, mobility rates increase, and the very small basis of school districts means that even if people have children or relatives living in the same metropolitan area, they may not have anyone they care about with school age children living within their own school district. As the introductory chapter pointed out, because it is difficult to measure program output in these service areas and because of concerns about rising costs and inflation in society, support for publicly funded schools may be declining.

In day-care services, there has never been much of a role for public provision of services except during very specialized periods. During the Depression, some day care was provided to children of mothers employed under the Work Projects Administration. During World War II, the federal government provided daycare through the Lanham Act to encourage women to go to work to replace the lost male workforce. As soon as the war was over, these programs disappeared. The Head Start program has created day-care programs for the children of the poor as an educational and poverty reduction strategy beginning in the 1960s. Since 1954 some support for child care was provided through a child-care tax deduction that was shifted to a tax credit in 1976.

We are now in a period of increased public discussion of the need for governmental support or provision of day care. Despite some suggestions for public provision of such services, the major approach appears to be the subsidization of day care. Through the dependent care provision of the tax code, workplaces could provide dependent care accounts which partially shelter earnings to pay for day care, most of which is actually provided through for-profit companies or small, for-profit businesses in local areas. The other major method of providing day-care services is through nonprofit, mostly religiously oriented day-care centers. To some extent, public provision of these services is increasing. Almost all states now provide public kindergarten whereas before World War II most of those services were private. Some states now also provide care for four-year-old children but typically only for special needs children.

In prisons, care has traditionally been provided by and paid for by government. Having said this, there are some examples in U.S. history of contracting prisoners out to provide labor to local industries. In these cases, care (such as it was) was not provided by the government even though supervision of the care ultimately did rest with the government. The money for the service was typically still partially supported by the state, although there were cases in which the labor was supposed to equal the costs of caring for the prisoners, and thus few governmental dollars were spent on the care of the prisoners.

Recently, there has been an increased attempt to provide prison services through contracting with private, for-profit groups. In most cases, the prison grounds themselves are still owned by the government and the money for the care comes from the government, but the actual provision of all services or certain services such as food or laundry may be contracted to a private group on the assumption that this is cheaper for the government unit in the long run.

Traditionally, hospital care was voluntary nonprofit. However, government hospitals were started fairly early to provide services for the poor and some for-profit hospitals were also started by the turn of the century. In fact, in total hospital beds for-profits have only recently exceeded their total in the 1930s; however, the type of for profit hospital is now very different. Such hospitals today tend to be part of large corporate chains, rather than being owned by one or a small group of physicians as in the past.

The dominant type of hospital today is still a voluntary, nonprofit hospital. However, that hospital is more likely to be part of some partner group, either for shared buying of certain goods or as part of a nonprofit chain. The landscape in the hospital care industry is rapidly shifting, with growth of nonprofit chains and mergers and selling off of parts of corporate chains so that the major for-profit chain today is not likely the same as it was twenty years ago and may not be the same ten years from today. Most importantly in today's increasingly competitive health care system, all hospitals (and perhaps especially nongovernment hospitals) worry about the bottom line and profits, whether that line is actually called a profit or additional revenues available for future growth.

In other areas of health care, change continues to be a very important word. The health maintenance organization industry has seen enormous changes in numbers of companies and their profitability; one of the most rapidly growing and most profitable HMOs is a nonprofit, Kaiser. In the last five years, operation of ambulatory surgery centers has shifted from large corporate chains to independently operated facilities. In contrast to urgent care centers, a shift has occurred from individual physicians' ownership to ownership by for-profit chains and nonprofit hospitals. In terms of physicians, between one-quarter and one-fifth of all nonfederal physicians are now in salaried practices, which means that most patients still obtain their care from doctors in a traditional fashion.

Nursing home care and other services for the elderly have undergone a very different pattern of growth than more general health care or education. Originally, much of nursing home care was provided by the government in the form of county poor farms, along with some gradual growth in nonprofit facilities (especially religious ones). Since the passage of the medicare and medicaid programs in 1965, the trend in nursing home care has been toward a greater role for proprietary (for-profit) facilities. They now provide over 80 percent of nursing home care in the United States. In contrast to health care in which five or six large corporations dominate the for-profit sector, however, a large number of different corporations are involved in nursing home care. This includes fifty-eight different investor-owned systems and twenty nonprofit systems. In education, by contrast, there are not only very few for-profit schools but also much less connection between either the few for-profits or the larger number (although still small in percentage terms) of non-profit, mostly religiously oriented private schools. Most Catholic schools, for example, are run by local dioceses, rather than a strong national organization that dictates policy and curriculum for all Catholic schools.

Some aspects of services for the elderly share similarities and differences with nursing homes. The typical method of delivery of home health care before the passage of medicare and medicaid was either a private nonprofit voluntary nurses association in many states or public facilities through visiting public health nurses in some states. For-profit corporations are now growing in importance as care providers in home health. In retirement communities, by contrast, nonprofit providers are currently dominating the provision of services.

IMPACT OF SERVICE DELIVERY MODE, ESPECIALLY ON QUALITY

In each area, one very important question concerns the impact of different modes of service delivery on quality of care. This is a very difficult question to answer, partially because the assessment of quality in these aspects of human services delivery is so difficult. Despite that, some studies in each area have tried to assess quality of care. In education, there is some evidence that the private sector provides a higher quality of care, especially the Catholic school system (Coleman et al., 1981, 1982). A major cautionary note on these findings, however, is that the studies of quality in education have not generally controlled for the advantages of private schools having students of a higher socioeconomic status at the beginning and also having greater resources to use in the educational process in the non-Catholic private school sector.

In prisons all services in some way are part of governmental systems. In the past, the system of turning over responsibility for care and actual provision of care to private businesses through the contracting out of prison labor—the old prison chain gang—created major abuses and mistreatment. Given the abuses in the past in prison care, such systems have been discontinued in the United States, leading to the conclusion that quality of care is better under tighter governmental supervision and under governmental provision of services.

Regarding in-hospital care, while there are important caveats as to the measurement of quality, most studies do not show consistent differences indicating inferior or superior care in either for-profit or not-for-profit hospitals (Gaumer, 1986). Access—a very critical issue in health care—again is one in which the problems are larger than that of any single institution although there is slightly more evidence that for-profit hospitals may exacerbate the problem, which they clearly did not create (Schlesinger, 1985; Sloan et al., 1986).

In nursing home care and other areas of services to the elderly, more studies report higher quality in the nonprofit sector, although some studies report no quality differences between nonprofits and for-profits (O'Brien and Saxburg, 1987). A major caution in this area is that nonprofit nursing homes appear to have higher costs than for-profits, perhaps helping to explain their higher quality. In addition, there is some evidence that for-profit homes have sicker patients on average and also have more medicaid versus private pay patients (Hawes and Phillips, 1986). There may be conflicting pressures between goals for the government of containing cost and quality of care.

RECOMMENDATIONS

In the United States especially in sectors other than health and social services, there has often been a bias that the private market is a superior mechanism for the allocation of most resources and that private provision of care increases efficiency and consumer choice. These chapters demonstrate that, in general, this does not appear to be true in the four populations and groups of services under discussion. Certainly, there is little evidence that for-profit hospitals have major secrets about how to run hospitals better or at a lower cost. In fact, in hospital and health care what may be most important is how little difference there is between the operation of hospitals regardless of ownership. Perhaps this is because there is not really a private market, as is even clearer in nursing home and prison care. In care for the elderly, a private market is mostly an illusion because most funding for the elderly comes from the government wherever the care is provided. This is even truer in prisons in which all funding is from the government; here the reason for turning to for-profit concerns is to cut costs to the government of running the prison system. In education, the private sector has led to more choices, and perhaps, better quality. Especially with the public sector, the issue of greater choice in education has become a recent area for policy experimentation.

Another future issue in the provision of services to captive populations is the notion of competition. Competition was a popular term during the Reagan administration; its goal of increasing competition and the role of the for-profit private sector in the delivery of services formerly identified with public or nonprofit sectors was a major impetus for many of the studies reviewed in this book. The continued presence of a Republican administration and its associated emphasis on private enterprise and business-oriented solutions to social problems continues to guarantee some emphasis on competition in service delivery areas. A major part of the debate over the spread of for-profit service delivery modalities into the areas of service provision as discussed in this book has been an assumption that more competition produces better services in some way—whether better means more care for the same dollars, care being produced more efficiently, more access to care, or higher quality care.

Based on the studies reviewed, it appears that competition may work better in areas where the client has not only the possibility of a choice as to deliverer of services (the goal for pro-competition approaches) but also the financial means and physical ability to choose among places and types of care. In hospital care, competition has probably not been harmful to quality and while clearly not helpful to access is not the major issue in problems of access to hospital care. Perhaps in elderly services, more equal choice would be helpful. Recipients currently can choose a place of care, at least technically, and there are many different providers available, but in many states high levels of occupancy combined with low medicaid rates make such a choice an illusion rather than a reality. In addition, frequent movement of individuals, even to better nursing homes, is not a possibility for most disabled elderly and would not lead to quality care due to disruption of social patterns and the physical and emotional strain.

Public schools have traditionally been an area in which people have few choices, and while individuals are free to choose a private school, local public schools are so strongly identified with the local property tax that many people want a choice among the public schools, schools for which they have already paid. Also, especially as concerns about quality have raised the specter that some public schools provide much better quality care than others, the ability to pick and choose among different public schools may be more valued by taxpayers and raise commitment to public schools in general. A recent policy expression for this concern has been the discussion of voucher plans in public education. Minnesota is currently experimenting with such a system. Advantages in the education arena are that such choice of provider (as is really currently available in many aspects of health care, both general and elderly) may restore a sense of commitment to public schools to the general population—especially among parents who tend to be very negative about increasing taxes for public school expenses if they are sending their own children to private schools.

With the exception of education, in the service areas discussed in this book, the increased emphasis on privatization, competition, and a role for for-profit care has been linked with concerns about cost containment and efficiency. There are dangers in a preoccupation with such concerns, however. A government seeking economic efficiency does not necessarily place a high value on equity of services or access to services. Social priorities are frequently undervalued in times when costs are dominant. Leaving aside some aspects of health care with large amounts of payment for the services from nongovernmental funds, most of the captive populations received services due to the role of government as a payor of care if not a direct provider of care. Even in hospital care, major innovations in how services are paid for have come due to the role of the federal government as a purchaser (but generally not direct provider) of services for the elderly. Thus, costs appear to drive the system in all areas, especially the concerns of the past decade to hold down costs and government spending. A fear is that such cost concerns could overwhelm concerns about access in health care, care for the elderly, and education and quality in all four areas (if one counts a concern with rehabilitation and return to regular life rather than just warehousing of persons as a measure of quality of prison systems).

It appears that the ability of the client to make effective demands— or just how captive the population really is—may be a major factor in quality of care. If clients are more dependent, there is more need for public control to maintain adequate quality, either through regulation in nursing home care and services to the elderly or through direct provision of the service in prisons. Also, the more that the recipients of care are not viewed as part of the general population about which people care because they may need those services or are closely connected to people with such need for care, the more we need to watch out for quality. Again, the relevant contrast is to compare nursing home care with hospital care. In hospital care, quality concerns are not generally a major issue and there is less evidence of differences in quality depending on whether care is given by a for-profit or not-for-profit provider. In nursing home care, quality remains a major concern and there is some evidence that for-profit nursing homes have lower quality care and that publicly funded patients (through medicaid) are more likely to reside in nursing homes in which the quality of care is lower.

Quality of care has long been suspect in prisons, because prisons provide care to a segment of society about which few people care greatly and a captive population with whom the general public feels little sense of identification. In contrast, in the past most people felt a sense of identification with school age children. In addition to having been in schools themselves as children, they had expectations of having their own children or children of close relatives in the schools. Thus, high-quality schools and hospital care have long been a source of civic pride in the community, in contrast to prison care and nursing home care, which are typically more invisible and with which the community as a collective group does not have a sense of identification.

The large declines in quality in some public schools, especially inner-city schools in major metropolitan areas, have led experts to fear that the school population is increasingly not being viewed as part of the general population in which everyone shares an interest. Other evidences of this concern are the increasing failure of school bond issues to provide new capital resources and more acrimonious debates over increases in local property taxes due to an increase in the school budget.

In modern American society, everyone is concerned about pocketbook issues and costs of services. Services to captive populations, and to some more than others, are particularly at risk because of desires to hold down spending and maximize individual welfare rather than focusing on the collective good. We hope to have made a contribution to the public debate about services and the provision of health and social services in our society. All of us need to be concerned about the provision of services to these groups in the population. All need to share a concern that the services be delivered appropriately and funded adequately. Despite some variability across service areas, overall adequate funding of services and regulations to assure access and quality may be more important in guaranteeing that everyone receives services and receives services worth having than extended debates about which sector of the economy (government, nonprofit, or for-profit) is most able to deliver a reasonably priced, high-quality service.

REFERENCES

Coleman, James S., Thomas Hoffer, and S. Kilgore. *Public and Private High Schools*. Washington, D.C.: National Center for Education Statistics, 1981.
————. *High School Achievement*. New York: Basic Books, 1982.
Gaumer, Gary. "Medicare Patient Outcomes and Hospital Organizational Mission," in Bradford Gray (ed.), *For-Profit Enterprise in Health Care*. Washington, D.C.: National Academy Press, 1986.
Hawes, Catherine, and Charles D. Phillips. "The Changing Structure of the Nursing Home Industry and the Impact of Ownership on Quality, Cost, and Access," in Bradford H. Gray (ed.), *For-Profit Enterprise in Health Care*. Washington, D.C.: National Academy Press, 1986.
O'Brien, Jack, and Borje O. Saxburg. "A Study of For-Profit and Nonprofit Nursing Homes" (Paper presented at the American Public Health Association meeting, New Orleans, Louisiana, October 1987).
Reich, Robert B. *Tales of a New America*. New York: Vintage Books/Random House, 1987.
Schlesinger, Mark. "The Rise of Proprietary Health Care," *Business and Health* 2 (1985): 7–12.
Sloan, F., J. Valvona, and R. Muller. "Identifying the Issues: A Statistical Profile," in F. Sloan, J. Blumstein, and J. Perrin (eds.), *Uncompensated Hospital Care: Rights and Responsibilities*. Baltimore, Md.: Johns Hopkins University Press, 1986.

Bibliography

Borna, Shaheen. "Free Enterprise Goes to Prison." *The British Journal of Criminology* 26, No. 4 (1986): 321–33.

Bozeman, Barry. "Exploring the Limits of Public and Private Sectors: Sector Boundaries as Maginot Line." *Public Administration Review* 48, No. 2 (1988): 672–74.

Coleman, James S., Thomas Hoffer, and S. Kilgore. *Public and Private High Schools*. Washington, D.C.: National Center for Education Statistics, 1981.

————. *High School Achievement*. New York: Basic Books, 1982.

Estes, Carrol. "Healthcare Policy in the Later Twentieth Century." *Generations* 12 (Spring 1988): 44–47.

Fottler, M. D., H. L. Smith, and W. L. James. "Profits and Patient Care in Nursing Homes: Are They Compatible?" *The Gerontologist* 21 (1981): 532–38.

Gaumer, Gary. "Medicare Patient Outcomes and Hospital Organizational Mission," in Bradford Gray (ed.), *For-Profit Enterprise in Health Care*. Washington, D.C.: National Academy Press, 1986.

Gray, Bradford (ed.). *For-Profit Enterprise in Health Care*. Washington, D.C.: National Academy Press, 1986.

Hawes, Catherine, and Charles D. Phillips. "The Changing Structure of the Nursing Home Industry and the Impact of Ownership on Quality, Cost, and Access," in Bradford H. Gray (ed.), *For-Profit Enterprise in Health Care*. Washington, D.C.: National Academy Press, 1986.

Herzlinger, Regina E., and William S. Krasker. "Who Profits from Nonprofits?" *Harvard Business Review* 65 (January-February 1987): 93–106.

Hirschoff, Mary-Michelle Upson. "Public Policy toward Private Schools: A Focus on Parental Choice." In Daniel C. Levy (ed.) *Private Education: Studies in Choice and Public Policy*, pp. 33–56. New York: Oxford University Press, 1986.

Iglehart, John K. "The Debate over Physician Ownership of Health Care Facil-
    ities." *New England Journal of Medicine* 321 (July 20, 1989): 198–204.
Kamerman, Sheila B. "Child-Care Services: A National Picture." In Carol H.
    Thomas (ed.), *Current Issues in Day Care: Readings and Resources.* Phoenix,
    Ariz.: Oryx Press, 1986.
Kolderie, Ted. "The Two Different Concepts of Privatization." *Public Adminis-
    tration Review* 46, No. 4 (1986): 285–91.
Kronenfeld, Jennie Jacobs, and Marcia Lynn Whicker. *U.S. National Health Policy:
    An Analysis of the Federal Role.* New York: Praeger Publishers, 1984.
Kronenfeld, Jennie Jacobs. "Access to Care under Prospective Payment and
    Competition," in Jennie Jacobs Kronenfeld, Roger L. Amidon, and Robert
    Toomey (eds.), *Competitive Strategies in the Health Care Market.* Albany,
    N.Y.: Delmar Publishers, 1990.
Light, Donald W. "Corporate Medicine for Profit." *Scientific Medicine* 255 (De-
    cember 1986): 38–46.
Logan, Charles H., and Sharla P. Rausch. "Punish and Profit: The Emergence
    of Private Enterprise in Prisons." *Justice Quarterly* 2, No. 3 (1985): 303–18.
McKinlay, John, and John Stoeckle. "Corporatization and the Social Transfor-
    mation of Doctoring." *International Journal of Health Services* 18 (1988): 191–
    205.
Morgan, D. R., and R. E. England. "The Two Faces of Privatization." *Public
    Administration Review* 48, No. 6 (1988): 979–87.
Nelson, John R., Jr. "The Politics of Federal Day Care Regulation," in Edward
    F. Zigler and Edmund W. Gordon (eds.), *Day Care: Scientific and Social
    Policy Issues,* pp. 267–306. Boston: Auburn House Publishing Co., 1982.
O'Brien, Jack, and Borje O. Saxburg. "A Study of For-Profit and Nonprofit
    Nursing Homes" (Paper presented at the American Public Health As-
    sociation meeting, New Orleans, Louisiana, October 1987).
Reich, Robert B. *Tales of a New America.* New York: Vintage Books/Random
    House, 1987.
Relman, Arnold S. "The New Medical-Industrial Complex." *New England Journal
    of Medicine* 303 (October 23, 1980): 963–69.
———. "Salaried Physicians and Economic Incentives." *New England Journal of
    Medicine* 319 (September 22, 1988): 784.
Robbins, Ira P. "Privatization of Corrections: Defining the Issues." *Judicature* 69
    (1986): 324–31.
Schlesinger, Mark. "The Rise of Proprietary Health Care." *Business and Health* 2
    (1985): 7–12.
Sloan, F., J. Valvona, and R. Muller. "Identifying the Issues: A Statistical Profile,"
    in F. Sloan, J. Blumstein, and J. Perrin (eds.), *Uncompensated Hospital Care:
    Rights and Responsibilities.* Baltimore, Md.: Johns Hopkins University Press,
    1986.
Vladeck, Bruce. *Unloving Care: The Nursing Home Tragedy.* New York: Basic Books,
    1980.
Whicker, Marcia Lynn, and Raymond A. Moore. *Making America Competitive:
    Policies for a Global Future.* New York: Praeger Publishers, 1988.

Subject Index

Author Index

ABOUT THE AUTHORS

JENNIE JACOBS KRONENFELD is a professor in the School of Health Administration and Policy, College of Business, Arizona State University, Tempe. Kronenfeld holds a doctorate (1976) and a masters (1973) in sociology from Brown University and a B.A. (1971) in sociology and history from the University of North Carolina, Chapel Hill. Prior to coming to Arizona, she held a faculty position at the University of Alabama in Birmingham and the University of South Carolina.

She has published about seventy articles in public health, medicine, and sociology. She has coauthored four books, one in 1981 on the social and economic aspects of coronary artery bypass surgery, one in 1984 (Praeger) with Dr. Whicker on the federal role in health policy, a third in 1986 (Praeger), also with Dr. Whicker, on the impact of technology on sex roles and social change, and 1990 a book on competitive strategies in health care. Kronenfeld has held numerous national offices in various professional sociological and health associations. She currently teaches courses on health care policy and social, economic, and political factors in health care.

MARCIA LYNN WHICKER is a professor in the Department of Public Administration at Virginia Commonwealth University in Richmond. She holds six degrees: a Ph.D. (1976) and a M.A. (1974) in political science and a M.S. (1974) in economics from the University of Kentucky; a M.P.A. (1971) in public administration from the University of Tennessee; a B.A. (1970) in political science and economics from the University of North Carolina; and an A.E.T. (1986) in electronic engineering technology from Midlands Technical College in Columbia, S.C. Prior to coming to Virginia in 1986, she held faculty positions at Wayne State University in Detroit, Temple University in Philadelphia, and the University of South Carolina in Columbia.

Whicker has worked for a variety of government agencies, including the U.S. Comptroller of the Currency; the U.S. Department of Health, Education, and Welfare; the Tennessee Valley Authority; the U.S. Congress, the North Carolina Department of Public Instruction; and the Pennsylvania and South Carolina legislatures. She has coauthored six books and has published over forty scholarly and journal articles spanning the fields of political science, history, sociology, public policy, and public administration.